AN EPIC PILGRIMAGE

History and Antiquity of Pehowa: Ancient Pṛithūdaka

AN EPIC PILGRIMAGE
History and Antiquity of Pehowa: Ancient Pṛithūdaka

(A Mahābhārata Site on the Sarasvatī)

DEVENDRA HANDA

ARYAN BOOKS INTERNATIONAL
NEW DELHI

AN EPIC PILGRIMAGE
History and Antiquity of Pehowa: Ancient Pṛithūdaka

ISBN-81-7305-272-2

Published in **2004** by
ARYAN BOOKS INTERNATIONAL
Pooja Apartments, 4B, Ansari Road, Darya Ganj, New Delhi - 110 002 (India)
Tel. : 23287589, 23255799; Fax : 91-11-23270385
E-mail : aryanbooks@vsnl.com

Computer Typeset at ABI Prints & Publishing Co., New Delhi
Printed in India at B.B.N. Printers, New Delhi

To

my wife

PREFACE

Pehowa, the ancient Pṛithūdaka, is one of the most sacred places of India. It is said that Kurukshetra is holy, that the Sarasvatī is holier than Kurukshetra, that all the tīrthas are holier than the Sarasvatī, but Pṛithūdaka is the holiest—

Puṇyamāhuḥ Kurukshetraṃ Kurukshetrāt Sarasvatīm /
Sarasvatyāścha tīrthāni tīrthebhyaścha Pṛithūdakam //

Respect for the old has been a characteristic feature of the Indian culture. The sanctity of Pehowa may have rested on the fact that it was one of the very old *tīrthas*. According to myth recorded in the *Mahābhārata* and the *Vāyu Purāṇa*, it was here on the bank of the Sarasvatī at Pṛithūdaka that Brahmā contemplated the creation of the fourfold world. After the Mahābhārata war, Yudhishṭhira performed the obsequies of all who died in the war, at Pehowa. Since then it is the pious pilgrimage to perform the funerary rites in the region. Tradition connects Pehowa with King Pṛithu, son of Vena, who is considered to be the first king after whom the earth became known as Pṛithvī. The Paurāṇic description that the hilly tracts were levelled and different kinds of villages, cities, and towns were organized for the first time during his reign indicates that he introduced agriculture and sedentary life in the region. The myth assumes greater significance when considered against the geological fact that Pehowa is located on the clayey loam of the Sarasvatī in the flat alluvial flood plain of the Satluj-Yamunā divide which consists of the siltation of the different streams flowing through the region and belongs to the Pleistocene period.

The early Aryans were settled in this region where their princes and sages lit the sacrificial fires on the banks of the Sarasvatī, Dṛishadvatī, and the Āpayā rivers. The Sarasvatī was considered as the river par excellence then. Pṛithūdaka, situated on the Sarasvatī, must have been one of the very important places of the early Aryans. Its importance probably continued to grow with the passage of time. The association and visits here of various kings, heroes, sages, etc., seem to have led to the growth of numerous pilgrimages around this place. Various myths may have been created later to show their antiquity and importance.

Fertility of the soil and the availability of abundant water may have resulted in surplus production of food and growth of population. Its religious importance attracted hosts of pilgrims, which perhaps necessitated the development of roads and transport. Such a development contributed to its growth as a trade centre. The Garibnath Temple inscription reveals that people even from far off countries used to come here for trade purposes during the Pratihāra period. Prosperity and patronage resulted in the establishment of temples and shrines dedicated to different deities in this holy city. It also seems to have developed into an important centre of art. It was but natural for the alien invaders to attack such a place. After Mahmud Ghaznavi's sack, Pehowa, could not recover its lost glory. An effort was made in this direction during the Maratha occupancy in the eighteenth century when many *ghats* and temples were renovated and rebuilt. The defeat of the Marathas at Panipat in 1761, however, snatched all possible chances of development of Pehowa and it was reduced thereafter to an insignificant village. The British rule also did not help. The pace of development has now fortunately accelerated during the past few decades, more so after the formation of Haryana on 1 November 1966.

Though a large number of scholars from the days of Alexander Cunningham have been attracted to its religious significance and archaeological wealth, yet no comprehensive and in-depth account of one of the oldest and holiest pilgrim centre of India is available.

My interest in Pehowa goes back to 1964, when I first visited it and acquired from the site two fragments of a Vishṇu image showing *gadā* (mace) and *chakra* (discus) with attached stelae carrying the representations of Brahmā-Sarasvatī and Śiva-Parvatī respectively. These relics were deposited with Dr. Buddha Prakash, the then Director of the Institute of Indic Studies, Kurukshetra University. Since then I have sustained my interest in the history and archaeology of Pehowa and have also been bringing to light some of its important relics. The richness of the archaeological wealth of Pehowa has attracted many other scholars also whose writings I have used. I am indebted to all those scholars. In the preparation of this monograph, I made many visits to Pehowa during which my friends and colleagues, Prof. Ashvini Agrawal, Dr. Vipnesh Bharadwaj, Dr. Lalman, and Shri Dasharath Malik, Shri Madhav Acharya and Shri Vinod Gupta, to mention only a few, have been of great help. Prof. O.P. Bharadwaj and Shri R.N. Parasher were very kind to extend help and facilities of studying and photographing the objects in the collection of the Department of Archaeology and Museums, Haryana, of which they were the Directors at different periods. Prof. Kuldip Gupta and Sanjay Sharma of Pehowa, too, helped me during my visits. I received important information and help from

Shri Upendra Sharma Chakrapani, Mahanta Banshi Puri, Mahanta Ravi Giri, and others, to whom all I extend my thankfulness. Prof. Suraj Bhan and Dr. Mohinder Singh helped me by providing some negatives and books used in the preparation of this work. Prof. H.A. Phadke, the then Head of the Department of Ancient Indian History, Culture and Archaeology of the Kurukshetra University, provided me the photograph of the terracotta discovered by him from Pehowa, now in the Departmental Museum. Dr. Manmohan Kumar of the Department of History, M.D. University, Rohtak, provided the photograph of the fragmentary inscription in the Garibnath Temple at Pehowa. The photograph of Mahendrapāla's *praśasti* was obtained from the Director, Government Museum, Lahore. The line drawing of the terracotta originally published by Cunningham has been copied from Shri R.C. Agrawala's article published in the *Artibus Asiae.* Dr. O.C. Handa, too, has been very kind and helpful in various ways. I am indebted to all of them. It will be mere formality if I thank my son Tushar who has prepared the map and has also helped in the final selection of the illustrations.

Shri Vikas Arya of the Aryan Books International, and of course his entire team, have spared no efforts to bring out the work in its present form.

I crave the indulgence of the readers for the errors of omission and commission and printing which might have occured in spite of my best efforts.

Devendra Handa

CONTENTS

LIST OF PLATES

1

GEOGRAPHICAL AND ARCHAEOLOGICAL BACKGROUND

LOCATION AND TOPOGRAPHY

Pehowa[1] is situated in 29° 59' North Latitude and 76° 35' East Longitude in district Kurukshetra on the southern bank of the Sarasvatī, about 25 km west of Kurukshetra-Thanesar with which it is connected by a metalled road (Pl. 1). It is also connected with Ambala, Patiala, Gulha, Kaithal, [2] Pundri, Nilokheri and Karnal by metalled roads. Its railway station, Pehowa Road by name, is situated about 9 km south of it on Kurukshetra-Narwana section of the Northern Railway and is also connected with the town by a link road.

Pehowa is located in the flat alluvial flood-plain of the Satluj-Yamunā divide which though seemingly monotonously level, descends gradually towards the south-west to which direction most of its rivers and runnels flow. The town is actually situated in the low-lying area of the Markanda *bet* and the Nailli-Chhachhra track consisting of clayey loam along the Sarasvatī. Geologically this plain consists of the siltation of the different streams flowing through it and belongs to the Pleistocene period.[3]

The *Vāmana Purāṇa*[4] refers to the Vaitarṇī, Āpagā, Mandākinī Gaṅgā, Madhusravā, Vāsunadī, Kauśikī, Dṛishadvatī and Hiraṇvatī as the ephemeral and rain-fed rivers of the Kurukshetra region, besides of course the Sarasvatī. Of these the Āpagā and the Dṛishadvatī have been mentioned in the *Ṛigveda*[5] and subsequent literature also. Das has expressed the possibility of the former being the Markanda or the Chitang.[6] The Markanda, which emanates from the lower Siwalik hills near Nahan and is joined by the Sadadeni (ancient Śaradaṇḍā)[7] and Begna in its upper course, flows east-west at a distance of about 8 km north of Pehowa. The Tangri falls into it and then it joins the Ghaggar about 20 km north-west of Pehowa near Dhandhaota village and nearly 8 km east-north-east of Gulha.[8] The Ghaggar must have been a mighty river in ancient times.[9] It joined the Sarasvatī in Rajasthan. Das has wrongly identified the ancient Dṛishadvatī with the Ghaggar[10] as the former lay south of the Sarasvatī.[11] According to Bhargava, the present West Jumna Canal with its Hansi-Hissar branch represents the ancient Dṛishadvatī.[12] The region lying between the Sarasvatī and the Dṛishadvatī was known as Brahmāvarta in ancient times—

> सरस्वतीदृषद्वत्योर्देवनद्योर्यदन्तरम् ।
> तं देवनिर्मितं देशं ब्रह्मावर्त्तं प्रचक्षते ।।[13]

CLIMATE

The climate of the area around Pehowa is hot in summer and cold in winter, with temperature varying between 32°F in December-January and 116°F in May-June. The monsoon rains start in the first week of July and continue up to September. The winter months of January-February also witness some rain. The average annual rainfall of the district has been varying quite often. When normal, it is about 75 cm.

FLORA

The commonest trees and plants grown around Pehowa are mango (*Mangifora indica*), mulberry (*Morus abla*), jamun (*Syzygium jambolina),* pipal (*Ficus religiosa*), shisham (*Dalberga sisoo),* kikar (*Acacia arabica* and *nelotica*), siras (*Abbizia labbek*), dhak (*Melia azadorech*), lasura *(Cordia obliqua*), simbal *(Salmalia malbaricum*) and palm *(Phoenix sylverstris,* only in Nailli circles). The deciduous trees like dhak *(Butea monosperma*), hingot (*Balanites aegyptiaca),* jal (*Salvadora cleoides*), jand (*Prospis cineraria*) and jhar (*Zizyphus mummlaria*) may also be seen in the open lands. Kair (*Capparis decidur*), amaltas (*Cassia fistula*), bodh (*Ficus benghalensis)* and ber (*Ziziphus mauntaiana* and *zuzuba*), too, are met with here and there.

The different varieties of grasses found in the district are sarkara (*Sacharum spontaneum*), munj (*Erianthus munja*) and dab (*Dastanostachya bipinunate*). *Nara* is found in the waterlogged areas. *Koma* and *bhabar* which are extensively used in paper industry, are also met with in the region.[14]

FAUNA

Pigs, jackals, hares, foxes and deer are the animals found in the Pehowa region. The birds of the area include blue pigeons, doves, crows, mynas, jungle fowls, pelicans, cranes, saras, kunjas, teals, comb-ducks, kingfishers, etc. Nosed crocodiles, tortoises and porpoises may be seen in the rivers. Rohru, sewal, backwa, mahser and chilwa varieties of fish are also available. Amongst the reptiles and venomous beings mention may be made of gohs, karaits, cobras and scorpions. Lizard is the ubiquitous reptile.[15]

NAME

The modern name Pehowa is a corruption of the Sanskrit word Pṛithūdaka which was the original name of the town as we learn from the Garibnath Temple inscription of this place.[16] Rājaśekhara (tenth century A.D.)[17] has also mentioned Pṛithūdaka as an outpost of *Uttarāpatha*. The *Mahābhārata* and the Purāṇas[19] also refer to Pṛithūdaka as a holy place. Traditionally, it derives its name from Pṛithu,[20] son of king Vena who was a scion of Hiraṇyakaśipu and wicked like him, and was cured of his leprosy by bathing in the Sarasvatī. He was killed by the churning of his right hand. Pṛithu thought it his filial duty to do something for the good of his father. So after cremating his father's body, he performed the usual funeral rites and sat on the bank of the Sarasvatī river for twelve days offering water (*Udaka*) to all comers.[21] The spot, therefore, came to be known as Pṛithūdaka (Pṛithu + *udaka*), i.e. Pṛithu's water or pool, and the city which he built on or near the spot was also named similarly.[22] Pt. Gajanana Sharma, an honourable local scholar, besides having accepted the aforesaid explanation of the nomenclature of the place,[23] has given the following derivations also[24]—

(a) पृथोर्महाराजस्य उद्गतानि नष्टानि अकानि दुःखानि यस्मिन् सः पृथूदकः ।

i.e., where the troubles of king Pṛithu were destroyed.

(b) सकलदेवमहर्षियोगात् पृथु अतिशयितं पुण्यतममुदकं यस्मिन् सः पृथूदकः ।

i.e., where the water is the most meritorious because of its association with all the gods and great sages.

(c) पृथु प्रख्याने धातोः पृथुशब्दो निष्पद्यते । पृथुशब्दः प्रथनवाचको
वर्तुलवाचकश्च तथा सति पृथूनि वर्तुलाकारेण स्थितानि वर्षाकाले उदकानि यस्मिनिति पृथुदकः ।

i.e., the word *Pṛithu* is derived from the root *pṛith* and means great, extensive, round. So Pṛithūdaka means a place 'where there are extensive rainy waters'.

(d) पृथुशब्देन परममहत् वस्तु उच्यते । उच्छब्देन उत्कृष्टता क
शब्देन सुखमुच्यते, न विद्यते परं कं यस्मात् सुखात् तत्
अकम् परमसुखम् साक्षात्कृतब्रह्मात्मैक्यरूपमित्यर्थः ।
तथा च (समुदायार्थः) पृथु परममहत् उत् उत्कृष्टमकं यस्मिन्
श्राद्धदानस्नानजपहोमादिकर्तृणां मृतानां च भवति इति पृथूदकः ।

i.e. the word *Pṛithu* stands for the biggest, greatest, best, most excellent, etc.; *udaka* = *Brahmasukha* (*Ut* = best + *a* = greatest + *ka* = happiness). Pṛithūdaka thus means 'where the pilgrims performing *śrāddha* (funeral rites), *dāna* (giving donations), *snāna* (taking bath, ablution), *japa* (muttering prayers) and *homa* (offering oblations), etc. obtain the most excellent happiness.

All the derivations, however, seem to be only the modern efforts to explain the name linguistically, of course, in the perspective of local history and tradition. Rodgers recorded that "The people say that Prithvi Raja built a temple and called it by the name *Prithveswar*. It stood in front of the place now occupied by Garibnath's establishment. Much sculpture has been found there. The word Prithveswar contracts more easily into Pehoa or as some call it Pehowa than does Pṛithūdaka".[25] Sound analogy seems to have led some people and Rodgers to recall the name of Pṛithvīrāja who probably had nothing to do with this temple and place. The sculptures found in the temple, as we shall see subsequently, belong to a period anterior to that of Pṛithvīrāja Chauhan. There is a local tradition that the temple was founded by King Pṛithu. Being dedicated to Śiva (Īśvara) it may have been and is still known as Pṛithvīśvara Mahādeva Temple.[26] There are numerous instances in history where the *liṅga* was known after the person who founded the temple and suffixed by the word *Īśvara*.[27] Taking into consideration the etymology and the actual remains of the Pṛithvīśvara Mahādeva Temple, its association with Pṛithu seems to be more appealing than with Pṛithvīrāja Chauhan.

Some scholars give another explanation for the name of the town. They believe that because of geo-tectonic changes and aeolian winds advancing from the west, the bed of the river Sarasvatī got choked resulting in the formation of a reservoir of fresh and deep water in its present bed. The place where abundant (*Pṛithu* means abundant also) water (*udaka*) was available was thus called Pṛithūdaka.[28]

That there existed *udaka* ending place names in the ancient period in this region and elsewhere is evidenced by Agrodaka (*Agroha*),[29] Āmrodaka (Amroha), Bahūdaka,[30] etc. Myths and traditions connect Pehowa with king Pṛithu. Till the discovery of more definite evidence and a more reasonable explanation, we may rely upon the derivation of the name Pṛithūdaka from Pṛithu, son of king Vena, whose association with the place is vouched by literary references also. Pṛithu is considered the ninth incarnation of Vishṇu and the first king who introduced agriculture.[31] It is after him that the earth became known as Pṛithvī.[32] The Pauranic description that the hilly tracts were levelled and different kinds of villages, cities and towns were organised for the first time during his reign[33] indicates that Pṛithu was a pioneer king to introduce agriculture and sedentary life in the region. He is said to have performed one hundred *aśvamedhas* (horse-sacrifices) on the Sarasvatī.[34]

BOUNDARY

Pṛithūdaka as founded by king Pṛithu is said to have extended to eight *krośas*—

पृथूदकस्थं राजानं पृथुराजं महाबलम् ।
अष्टक्रोशात्मकं येन पृथूदकमधिष्ठितम् ।।[35]

The various *tīrthas* of Pṛithūdaka are located not only in the present town but in some of the surrounding villages also. The boundaries of the Pṛithūdaka region are described to have extended from the village Aruṇāya, located about 6 km east-north-east of Pehowa, to the hermitage of the sage Maṅakaṇaka which is believed to have existed in the Mangana village, nearly 10 km west-south-west of Pehowa:

अरुणाया पश्चिमे भागे यावन् मंकणको मुनिः ।
तावत् पृथूदकं क्षेत्रं सर्वदेवैरलंकृतम् ।।[36]

Obviously, Pṛithūdaka extended from Aruṇāya to Mangana for about 16 km along the Sarasvatī river on the banks of which were located various pilgrimages and hermitages.

IMPORTANCE AND SANCTITY

Pṛithūdaka has been regarded as one of the most important *tīrthas* of India. Located in the Kurukshetra region[37] which is comparable to heaven, [38] it is one of the most sacred places. It is situated on the bank of the Sarasvatī river which has been held as the most divine and the best of the rivers in the *Ṛigveda*[39] and has been eulogised much in the later literature.[40] It was created by Brahmā himself along with all the beings and the five elements and Pṛithūdaka stood gloriously on its bank —

पूर्वं प्रजेयं प्रपितामहेन सृष्टा समं भूतगणैः समस्तै :।
मही जलं वह्निस्समीरमेव खं त्वेवमादौ विबभौ पृथूदकम् ।।[41]

Famous in all the three worlds (त्रैलोक्यविश्रुतम्)[42] it has been regarded as possessing many merits, remover of sins and auspicious —

बहुपुण्ययुक्तं पृथूदकः पापहरं पापहरः शिवं च ।[43]

There is no other holy place more meritorious, sacred and sanctifying than Pṛithūdaka—

पृथूदकात्पुण्यतमं नान्यत्तीर्थं नरोत्तम ।
एतन्मेध्यं पवित्रं च पावनं च न संशयः ।।[44]

Any wrong committed by man or woman, knowingly or unknowingly, is obliterated by taking a bath in Pṛithūdaka and he or she gets the merit of a horse-sacrifice and goes to heaven—

अज्ञानाज्ज्ञानतो वापि स्त्रिया वा पुरुषेण वा ।
यत्किंचिदशुभं कर्म कृतं मानुषबुद्धिना ।।
तत्सर्वं नश्यते तस्य स्नातमात्रस्य भारत ।
अश्वमेधफलं चापि स्वर्गलोकं च गच्छति ।।[45]

Even those who have committed sins also go to heaven merely by taking a dip here.[46] It is said that a sin committed at another place is destroyed at Prayāga, the sin committed at Prayāga is destroyed in the Gaṅgā region, a sin committed therein is undone at Kāśī, a sin committed at Kāśī is destroyed at Kurukshetra and a sin committed at Kurukshetra is destroyed at Pṛithūdaka, but a sin committed at Pṛithūdaka becomes infallible—

अन्यक्षेत्रं कृतं पापं प्रयागे तु विनश्यति ।
प्रयागे हि कृतं पापं गंगाक्षेत्रे विनश्यति ।।
गंगाक्षेत्रे कृतं पापं काशीं प्राप्य विनश्यति ।
काशीक्षेत्रे कृतं पापं कुरुक्षेत्रे विनश्यति ।।
कुरुक्षेत्रे कृतं पापं पृथूक्षेत्रे विनश्यति ।
पृथूक्षेत्रे कृतं पापं वज्रलेपो भविष्यति ।।[47]

The sins of a person who recalls the name of Pṛithūdaka even thoughtlessly disappear instantaneously.[48] The forefathers declare those descendents as useless who have not seen, heard or remembered Pṛithūdaka.[49]

Those who die at Pṛithūdaka even without obsequial rice-ball, lamp and funeral rites go to heaven.[50] It is said that heaven is one *yojana* from Gayā, half from Prayāga, one *krośa* from Haradvāra but only a cubit from Pṛithūdaka.[51] The merit of visiting Pṛithūdaka for one day is equal to visiting the Kuru-jāṅgala during the four months of the rainy season.[52] Kuru-jāṅgala was the north-eastern part of Kurukshetra.[53]

The very name of Pṛithūdaka relieves one of his sins and it is the only place in the Kurukshetra region where Śiva resides permanently—

पृथूदकसमं तीर्थं नाम्ना पापप्रमोचनम् ।
कुरुक्षेत्रगतं नान्यद्यत्र शंभोः सदास्थितिः ।।[54]

Kārttikeya is also said to reside here day and night along with his numerous *gaṇas*-

अहर्निशं कार्तिकेयो यत्र सेनापतिः प्रभुः ।
विराजते सदेवोऽत्र गणकोटिभिरावृतः ।।[55]

The sages have said that even the sinners go to heaven by taking a bath at Prithūdaka—

तत्र स्नात्वा दिवं यान्ति येऽपि पापकृतो जनाः ।
पृथूदके नरश्रेष्ठ प्राहुरेवं मनीषिणः ।।[56]

A person who dies on the bank of the Sarasvatī while uttering prayers at Prithūdaka is relieved of the pangs of birth again —

सरस्वत्यास्तु तीरे यः संत्यजेदात्मनस्तनुम् ।
पृथूदके जप्यपरो गर्भवासं न पश्यति ।।[57]

It is said that one gets emancipation in the waters of the Gaṅgā, and on the land and in the water at Vārāṇasī but one is released at Prithūdaka (by dying) in water, on land or in space (i.e., on bed)—

गंगायां जले मुक्तिर्वाराणस्यां जले स्थले।
जलेस्थले चान्तरिक्षे त्रिधामुक्तिः पृथूदके ।।[58]

It is a great *tīrtha* (महातीर्थ), the best of the pilgrimages (तीर्थवर) and the remover of the fear of sins (पापभयापहम्).[59] Its importance has been sung by Sanat Kumāra and Vyāsa.[60] It was visited by Balarāma[61] and all the gods including Indra.[62] Yudhishṭhira performed the funeral rites here of all who died in the great war at Kurukshetra[63] and is thus a great *tīrtha* for the propitiation of the manes.[64]

People say that Kurukshetra is holy, that the Sarasvatī is more sacred than Kurukshetra, that all the united *tīrthas* more virtuous than the Sarasvatī, but Prithūdaka is more meritorious than all the *tīrthas*—

पुण्यमाहुः कुरुक्षेत्रं कुरुक्षेत्रात् सरस्वतीम् ।
सरस्वत्याश्च तीर्थानि तीर्थेभ्यश्च पृथूदकम् ।।[65]

There are numerous holy spots at Pehowa which are associated with various gods and sages.

ANTIQUITY

The town of Pehowa is built partly upon the low ground and partly on an old mound as lofty as that of Thanesar, or from 30 to 40 feet high.[66] We have already referred to an inscription in the Garibnath Temple belonging to king Bhoja (Pratihāra) and dated year 276 of the Harsha era (i.e., 276 + 606 = A.D. 882).[67] Another inscription from this place is now preserved in the Lahore Museum. It belongs to Bhoja's successor Mahendrapāla.[68] These inscriptions reveal that Pehowa was a flourishing town in the ninth-tenth centuries A.D. The fact of its being a famous town in the ninth century can be guessed from the fact that a certain scholar Pṛithūdakasvāmi by name wrote a commentary at Kurukshetra on Brahmagupta's *Brahmasphuṭa-siddhānta* (seventh century A.D.) shortly before A.D. 864 under the Pratihāra monarch Bhoja.

Cunningham had found large sized bricks, 18 x 12 x 2½-3 inches, from Pehowa.[70] Rodgers has also recorded bricks of 13½ x 9 x 2½ inches and fragments of sculptures and temple remains at Pehowa[71] but it is difficult to date them precisely in the absence of illustrations.[72] A terracotta figure obtained by Cunningham from Pehowa, amongst other remains, was illustrated by him and may be dated to the Gupta period.[73] Another brick-panel containing the figure of a *dvārapāla* datable to *circa* fourth-fifth century A.D. has also come to light from Pehowa.[74] Kushāṇa and Kuṇinda coins recovered from the site by Rodgers push back its antiquity to about the beginning of the Christian era.[75] Since a great part of the ancient mound is now under habitation, the early history of the town seems to be sealed under it. The earliest remains known so far, however, are in the form of potsherds which were collected from the southern and south-eastern part of the mound now under habitation.[76] These potsherds are known to the archaeologists by the name of Painted Grey Ware which belong to the first-half of the first millennium B.C.[77] Similar pottery has also been obtained from Hastināpura, Indraprastha (Inderpat = Purana Qila, New Delhi), Tilpat, Sonipat, Panipat, Asandh (ancient Āsandīvat), Baghpat, Kurukshetra and many other sites mentioned in the *Mahābhārata*.[78] Pehowa, too, has been described as a holy pilgrimage in the great epic and is thus as old as the above-mentioned places.

Pṛithūdaka had a very large number of *tīrthas* as we shall see subsequently. Such a large number of holy places could not have been established on the banks of a desiccated river. The sanctity of the Sarasvatī river and of the *tīrthas* on its banks eulogised so often in religious works indicates that they were established on the sacred, mighty, perennial river as depicted in the *Ṛigveda*. Some of the *tīrthas*, too, are reminiscent of the facts and events recorded in the Vedic literature.

Pṛithūdaka owes its origin to king Pṛithu, son of Vena, who is mentioned not only in the *Ṛigveda* and the *Atharvaveda* but also in many other Vedic works like the *Kāṭhaka Saṁhitā* and *Pañchaviṁśa, Śatapatha, Taittirīya* and *Jaiminīya Upanishad Brāhmaṇas*.[79] He composed a hymn also[80] and is described in the *Ṛigveda* as one of the richest persons.[81] The allegorical description in the *Atharvaveda* that he was the milker of the Cow-Earth which yielded the milk of agriculture and crops[82] indicates that he was inventor of agriculture. Surplus crops must have made him affluent and powerful. He is referred to as the first consecrated king of the world. His son Pṛithu, too, composed Vedic *mantras* and was an eminent ruler. The town founded by him may thus be as old as the *Ṛigveda*.[83] The definite life-history of the town may, however, be known only when the old mound of Pehowa is excavated systematically.

NOTES AND REFERENCES

1. Also spelt as Pehoa, Peheva and Pehowa. See *Imperial Gazetteer of India, (IGI)*, XX, New Series, Oxford, 1908, p. 100; *Karnal District Gazetteer*, 1890, pp. 31 ff; C.J. Rodgers, *Revised List of Objects of Archaeological Interest in the Punjab*, Lahore, 1891, pp. 56-57, etc.
2. Ancient Kapishṭhala. For details see V.S. Agrawala, *India as Known to Pāṇini*, 2nd ed., Varanasi, 1963, p. 67; N.L. Dey, *Geographical Dictionary of Ancient and Medieval India*, 3rd ed., Delhi, 1977, p. 92; Rodgers, *Revised List*, pp. 19-20.
3. D.N. Wadia, *Geology of India*, London, 1957, p. 61; M.S. Krishnan, *Geology of India and Burma*, Madras, 1956, pp. 528ff.
4. *The Vāmana Purāṇa* (edited by A.S. Gupta, Varanasi, 1957), *Saromahātmya (SM)*, XIII, 6-8 (Unless otherwise indicated, all subsequent references are to this edition). Also see M.L. Bhargava, *The Geography of Ṛgvedic India*, Lucknow, 1964, p. 100.
5. *Ṛigveda (RV)* III. 23, 4. The Āpagā has been mentioned in the *RV* as Āpayā.
6. A.C. Das, *Ṛgvedic India*, 3rd ed., Delhi, 1971, pp. 68ff.
7. *Rāmāyaṇa* (Lahore ed.), II. 74.12. A people known as Śaradaṇḍās are mentioned in the *Kāśikā* (IV-1.73), Vaijayantīkośa (I-3, 1, 38-39) and the *Chandravṛitti* on Chāndravyākarāṇa (II.2, 103) as a part of the Sālvas. For the identification of the Śaradaṇḍā with Sadadeni, see O.P. Bharadwaj, *Studies in the Historical Geography of Ancient India*, Delhi, 1986, pp. 92, 114 ff., etc.
8. This description is based on the Survey of India topo-sheets and a recent map of the Haryana Irrigation Department seen by us through the courtesy of our friend Sh. Ashok Gulati, an engineer in the said department.
9. O.H.K. Spate, *India, Pakistan and Ceylon: The Regions*, 3rd ed., London, 1972, pp. 536ff. It is identified with the Sarasvatī by some scholars. See Dey, *op. cit.*, p. 233.
10. Das, *op. cit.*, p. 71. Cf. O.P. Bharadwaj, *Ancient Kurukṣetra: Studies in Historical & Cultural Geography*, New Delhi, 1991, pp. 45-59.
11. Kurukshetra is described as located to the south of the Sarasvatī and north of the Dṛishadvatī—
    दक्षिणेन सरस्वत्या उत्तेरण दृषद्वतीम्।
    ये वसन्ति कुरुक्षेत्रे ते वसन्ति त्रिविष्टपे ।।
    (*Mahābhārata*, Cr. ed. III.81, 175).
12. Bhargava, *op. cit.*, pp. 53-54.
13. *Vāmana Purāṇa* (henceforth *VP*) *Saromahātmya*, XII, 9; *Manu Smṛiti* II.17.

14. *Panjab District Gazetteers,* Vol. III, Part A: *Ambala District 1923-24,* Lahore, 1925, p. 18.
15. *Ibid.,* pp. 15 ff.
16. *Epigraphia Indica,* Vol. I, p. 187, l. 3
17. *Kāvyamīmāṁsā* of Rājaśekhara, edited by C.D. Dalal and R.A. Sastry, GOS, Baroda, 1934, p. 94:
    पृथूदकात्परत उत्तरापथः यत्र शककेकयवोक्काणहूणवाणायुज-कम्बोजवाह्लीकवह्लवलिम्पाककुलूत-कीरतङ्गणतुषार-तुरुष्कबर्बरहरहूरवहूहुक सहुडहंसमार्गरमठकरकण्ठ-प्रभृतयो जनपदाः।
18. *Mahābhārata* (Critical ed.) III.81, 122 ff.
19. *VP* XXII.20 & 23; XXIII 43; XXIV.1; XXV.73; *SM* XVIII.20ff, etc.; *Bṛihannāradīya Purāṇa,* 65.107; *Padma Purāṇa* I.27, 31, etc.
20. For the story of Pṛithu, see *Mbh.* I.2; II.53; VI.9; VII.55-71; XIX.29; 59; 166; 227; XIII.115; 151; 166; *Harivaṁśa* (Gita Press ed.) I.13, 39; *Vāyu P.,* 62. 126 ff.; *Brahma P.,* Ch. 4; *Bhāgavata P.* IV.14-24; *Matsya P.* 4.44; 8.2-12; *Padma P.* I.127; *Vishṇu Purāṇa* I. 13, 39.
21. Alexander Cunningham, *The Ancient Geography of India* (rpt., Varanasi, 1963), p. 283; *Archaeological Survey Report,* XIV, p. 101; *IGI,* XX, p. 100.
22. *Ibid.* It is, however, notable that neither the *Mahābhārata* nor any Purāṇa confirms this version.
23. Gajanana Sarma, *Pṛithūdaka (Pihovā) Mahātmyam* (*PM*), Pehowa, V.S. 1980, p. 65:
    पृथुना विष्ण्ववतारभूतेन पित्रादिभ्यो दत्तमुदकं यस्मिन् सः पृथूदकः।
24. *Ibid.,* pp. 65-67.
25. C.J. Rodgers, *Report of the Punjab Circle of the Archaeological Survey for 1888-89,* p. 17.
26. Mahanta Banśī Purī (ed. & pub.), *Saṁkshipta Śrī Pṛithūdaka Tīrtha: Pihovā: Mahātmya evaṁ Kurukshetra Parichaya,* Pehova, 1989.
27. E.g. Kapileśvara, Upamiteśvara (after Kapilāchārya and Upamitāchārya, Mathura Pillar Inscription of Chandragupta II's reign, Gupta era 61; B.Ch. Chhabra and G.S. Gai, *Corpus Inscriptionum Indicarum,* Vol. III, pp. 203 ff), Pṛithvīśvara (*ibid.,* pp. 280 ff.), Mihireśvara (J.F. Fleet, *CII,* III, pp. 286 ff.), etc.
28. S.P. Shukla, "Relics of Ancient Art from Pehowa", *Panjab University Research Bulletin (Arts),* Chandigarh, Vol. XI (1980), p. 69.
29. J. Przyluski, *Ancient Peoples of the Punjab: The Udmnbaras & Salvas* (Rpt., Calcutta, 1960), pp. 10-11.
30. *Brahmāṇḍa Purāṇa* (Baṅgavāsī Office, Calcutta), I.2.16, 67 ff.
31. *Brahmāṇḍa Purāṇa* I.3, 14; II.7, 9; III.1, 22; IV.13, 20; *Mbh.,* Vana Parva, 185.8 ff; Sānti Parva, 59, 98 ff., etc.; *Matsya P.* IV. 44; VIII, 2.12; *Vishṇu P.* I.13, etc.
32. *Harivaṁśa* I.6, 46; *Bṛ P.* II 36, 83.
33. *Harivaṁśa* I.6, 47; *Bhāg.P.* IV.17-18; *Vishṇu P.* I.13.
34. *Bhāg. P.* IV 19-20. When 99 horse-sacrifices were over, the jealous Indra ran away with the sacrificial horse. Pṛithu's son, however, recovered the animal and came to be known as Vijitāśva. On Vishṇu's instance, Pṛithu cast off his enmity towards Indra and became friendly to him.

35. *PM*, p. 2.
36. *Ibid.*, p. 16.
37. *VP* XXII, 23a:
कोऽयं कुरुक्षेत्र इति यत्र पुण्यं पृथूदकम् ।
Kurukshetra has been mentioned in the *Mbh.* and the Purāṇas as the region lying between the Sarasvatī and Dṛishadvatī rivers which was ploughed by King Kuru and hence got its name (literally meaning 'field of Kuru'). Known as Uttaravedi and Samanta-Pañchaka earlier, it extended five *yojanas* on all sides and lay between Tarantuka, Arantuka, Rāma-Hrada and Machakruka:
तरन्तुकारन्तुकयोर्यदन्तरं रामह्रदानां च मचक्रुकस्य च ।
एतत् कुरुक्षेत्रं समन्तपञ्चकं प्रजापतेरुत्तरवेदिरुच्यते ।।
Mbh., Śalya Parva, ch. 52. 20; *VP (SM)* I.14.
For details see R.C. Agrawala, "Kurukshetra in Early Sanskrit Literature", *Journal of Indian History*, XXXIII (i), No. 97 (April 1955), pp. 85-90; O.P. Bharadwaj, *Ancient Kurukṣetra*, pp. 1-21.
38. दक्षिणेन सरस्वत्या उत्तरेण दृषद्वतीम् ।
ये वसन्ति कुरुक्षेत्रे ते वसन्ति त्रिविष्टपे ।।
— *Mbh.* III.81, 175.
39. *RV* II.41, 16; III.54, 13; V.42, 13; VI.50, 12; VIII.54, 4; X.30, 12; 75.5; 131.5 etc.
40. *AV* IV.4, 6; V.3, 2; VII.68. 1; XIV.2, 15; XVI.4, 4; XIX. 32, 9; *Taitt. Saṁ.* VIII.2.1, 4; *Pañch.Br.* I.4.1, 14; *Ait.Br.* II.19, 12. *Kāt. Śr.S.* XII.3, 20; XXIV.6, 22; *Lāṭ.Śr.S.* X.15, *Āśv.Śr.S.* XII.6.2, 3; *Śāṅk.Śr.S.* XIII.29; *Mbh.* I.16, 19-21; III.12, 14; 36, 41; 84, 66; 90, 3; 100, 13; IX.35-54, etc.; *Bhāg. P.* I.4, 15; IV.19; *Bṛ. P.* II.12, 16; *Vāyu P.* 45, 95; 55, 43; *Matsya P.* 7.5, 121, 64-65; *Vasishṭha* I.8; *Baudh.* I.12, 9; *Bṛih. Up.* VI.3, 8, etc. Also see Svāmi Kūṭasthānanda, *Śrī-Sarasvatī-Mahānadī-Nirṇayaḥ* (Hindi), Hoshiarpur, V.S. 2024; Mohd. Israel Khan, *Sarasvati in Sanskrit Literature*, Ghaziabad, 1978; Raghunath Airi, *Concept of Sarasvati*, Rohtak, 1977, etc.
41. *VP* XXIII.44.
42. *Mbh.* (Cr. ed.) III.81, 122.
43. *VP* XXIII.43.
44. *Mbh.* (Cr. ed.)III 81, 128; *PP.* I.27, 36-37.
45. *Ibid.*, III.81, 123-24; *PP.* I.27, 32-33.
46. तत्र स्नात्वा दिवं यान्ति अपि पापकृतो जनाः ।
Mbh. (Cr. ed.) III.81, 129.
47. *Bṛihajjābālopanishad* as quoted in *PM*, p. ग.
48. *PM*, p. 43:
पृथूदकेति नाम्नि संस्मृते तथाऽविवेकतः ।
दुरंहसो विलीनतां प्रयान्ति त्राहि तत्क्षणात् ।।
49. *Ibid.*
पृथूदकं यैर्न दृष्टं न श्रुतं न स्मृतं तथा ।
इति नस्ते वृथाः पुत्राः पितरः प्रवदन्ति हि ।।

50. *Ibid.*, pp. 62.63:
पृथूदके मृता ये च न पिण्डं न च दीपकम् ।
न प्रेतस्यैव संस्कारः स्वर्गलोके महीयते ।।
51. *Ibid.*
गयायां योजने स्वर्गः प्रयागे चार्द्धयोजने ।
क्रोशमेकं हरद्वारे हस्तमात्रं पृथूदके ।।
52. *Ibid.*
श्रावणादि चतुर्मासे सेवनं कुरुजाङ्गले ।
भ्रमते सर्वतीर्थानि एकरात्रिभिः पृथूदके ।।
53. O.P. Bharadwaj, *Ancient Kurukṣetra,* pp. 10-11.
54. *PM*, p. 69.
55. *Ibid.*, p. 45.
56. *Mbh.* (Cr. ed.) III.81.129; *PP* I.27 37-38.
57. *PM*, p. 68. Cf. *VP (SM)* XVIII.20:
सरस्वत्युत्तरे तीर्थे यस्त्यजेदात्मनस्तनुम्
पृथूदके जप्यपरो नूनं चामरतां व्रजेत् ।।
Also cf. *Mbh.* (Cr. ed.) III.81, 126 and *PP* I.27, 34-35; *Bṛ. P.*, Uttarakhaṇḍa, 65.107.
58. Śaṅkaropādhyāya as quoted in *PM*, p. 68.
59. *VP XXIV* 1-2.
60. *Mbh.*(Cr. ed.) III.81, 127.
61. *Ibid.* IX.38.
62. *VP* XXIV.4.
63. Upendra Sarma Chakrapani, *Pṛithūdaka (Pihovā) Tīrtha: Mahātmya*, Pehowa, n.d, p. 45.
64. Cf. *VP* XXIV.1-9; *Bṛ. P.*, Uttarakhaṇḍa, 65.120.
65. *Mbh.* (Cr. ed.) III.81, 125; *PP* I.27, 33-34.
66. *CASR, II*, p. 224.
67. *EI*, I, pp. 184-90.
68. *Ibid.*, pp. 242-50.
69. David Pingree, 'Brahmagupta, Balabhadra, Pṛthūdaka and Al-Bīrūnī', *Proceedings of the First International Sanskrit Conference*, Vol. II, Pt. II (Ed. V. Raghavan), New Delhi, pp. 166 and 175, fn 4.
70. *CASR*, II, p. 224.
71. Rodgers, *Report*, pp. 15-17.
72. Rodgers has referred to the plates in his *Report*, but these plates do not seem to have been published anywhere, nor are they traceable anywhere now.
73. *CASR*, XIV, Pl. XXVII. A. See also *Artibus Asiae*, XX (2-3), pp. 163-64.
74. Shukla (1980), *op. cit.*, pp. 71-72, Fig. 2.
75. Rodgers, *Report*, List of Coins, p. 3.
76. *Ancient India*, No. 10-11, p. 141.
77. *Ibid.*, pp. 21 ff. Also see *Purātattva*, No. 9 (1977-78), pp. 64-80.
78. *Ibid.*, pp. 138-40 and 150.

79. *Vedic Index,* Vol. II, p. 16.
80. *Ṛigveda* X.148.
81. X, 93, 14.
82. *Atharvaveda* III, 10, 24.
83. See also Bharadwaj (1986), *op. cit.,* p. 198.

2

HISTORICAL SURVEY

ANCIENT PERIOD

Lithic evidence from over small cuspate flattish terraces and their stratified deposits formed by ephemeral runnels which get dissipated just below the piedmont where they debouch on the plains indicates human activity in the sub-mountainous region of Haryana from late Pleistocene to Holocene periods.[1] Late Soan type tools[2] found from the Pinjore-Nalagarh *dun* reveal that a spurt occurred and the habitat was expanded towards the close of the Pleistocene, probably during one of the quiescent interludes in the tectonic history of the region.[3] Moginand and Nagal on the Nadlan *choe,* Nada Sahib on the Nada *choe,* Chauki on Chauki *khadd* and Mansa Devi, Dera-Kharauni, Surajpur, Nepli, Mahadeo on the Ghaggar and Saketri on the Sukhna *choe,* however, seem to have remained the popular resorts of early man in the Chandigarh-Naraingarh region of the Siwalik Frontal Range[4] and Pinjore, Kalka, Ratpur, Barhgodam, Marhanwala, Barotiwala, etc. in the Pinjore-Nalagarh range.[5]

Some Middle Stone Age tools have been recovered from the Dhosi hills near Narnaul and Firozpur-Jhirka in southern Haryana.[6] Late Stone Age tools, microliths (small stone artefacts), which represent the Mesolithic Culture, have also come to light recently from the vicinity of Gurgaon[7] and neolithic specimens, though very rare, are also said to have been found from the Chandigarh-Pinjore area.[8] The Neolithic phase in Haryana is not well enunciated and if the Neolithic Culture of the Kashmir valley[9] provides any clue, it may be assumed to have been very late, probably coeval with the proto-historic culture of the state.

Though there is some evidence that the people in the Indo-Pak subcontinent lived with their indigenously developing cultures from about the eighth millennium B.C.,[10] yet it seems to have been in the third millennium B.C. only that the early habitations flourished in Haryana at Mitathal and Tigrana (Dist. Bhiwani), Siswal (26 km west of Hissar), Rakhigarhi and Balu (Dist. Jind), Rukhi (near Rohtak), Bananwali, Bani and Kunal (Dist. Sirsa) and various other places in Kurukshetra, Karnal, Sonipat, Mahendragarh and Gurgaon districts.[11] These sites have yielded the so-called pre-Harappan relics comparable to those of Rehman Dheri and Kot Diji in Pakistan and Sothi and Kalibangan I in Rajasthan in India. Though Pehowa has not yielded any pre-Harappan, Harappan or late-Harappan remains, yet the pre-Harappan sites of Barsana (29° 07' N & 76° 35' E) and Ratta Khera (30° 07' N & 76° 27'E), the latter site yielding Harappan relics also, and the late-Harappan sites of Baraut, Bibipur, Bodha, Chandlana, Cheeka, Garhi Rodan, Garhi Sardaran, Kheri Raiwali, Malakpur, Nandukhera, etc. all in district Kurukshetra, indicate that sedentary life began in the Pehowa region along with other parts of the state.[12] The pre-Harappan, Harappan and late-Harappan cultures of this region may not have been different from those of other regions but for certain local innovations and features. Daulatpur near Kurukshetra has yielded charred lump of rice seeds and husks, both of wild and cultivated varieties, belonging to the late-Harappan period.[13] It is interesting to note that even at present, Kurukshetra district is known as the rice-bowl of Haryana.

Excavations at Bhagwanpura near Kurukshetra have brought to light an overlap between the late-Harappan culture and the Painted Grey Ware (PGW) culture[14] which is generally associated with the Aryans and the Mahābhārata people.[15] B.B. Lal has placed the PGW in the date-bracket of 1100-800 B.C.[16] Pehowa, as noted above, has yielded PGW sherds from the southern and south-eastern part of the old mound much of which is now under habitation. We do not know if any earlier remains lie buried under the inhabited parts of the mound. The probability, however, cannot be ruled out altogether.

Though PGW was the main ceramic industry, black-slipped, ordinary red and red-slipped wares were also used by the people. They knew the technique of preparing burnt-bricks but mostly used mud or mud-bricks for construction. Reed-walls and mud-plaster have also been witnessed. Their cultural equipment included copper arrow-heads, nail-parers, antimony rods; weights of chert and jasper; bangles of glass; terracotta animal figurines, discs, feeding cups; bone styli or knitting needles, etc. They knew iron also and rice continued to be an important item of food.[17] Straight-sided bowls, cups and dishes with incurved sides and saggar or convex base remained the popular types throughout.[18] It will not be irrelevant here to quote R.S. Sharma who observes that "The stage of material equipment of the PGW phase, called so because of the distinctive character of this pottery, is comparable on many counts to the material culture of the later Vedic texts. We notice beginnings of territorial state formation, advent of social stratification, and the emergence of administrative machinery, in the later Vedic texts; all these presuppose a full-fledged agrarian society, not typical of the RV phase".[19]

The discovery of the PGW from Pehowa and its mention in the great epic as a holy place visited by Balarāma in his *tīrtha-yātrā* and by Yudhishṭhira for the obsequies of all those killed in the Great War indicate that the place had gained prominence in the first quarter of the first millennium B.C.[20] and was also looked upon as a holy place. Being close to Kurukshetra, it must have been visited by a host of the heroes and important personages of the *Mahābhārata* but there is no account available to us which could give us the details. The non-mention of Kṛishṇa's visit to the place and the non-existence of any *tīrtha* connected with him at Pehowa, however, indicate that it was not visited by Kṛishṇa. Though it has been suggested that the Sarasvatī had lost moṣt of its flow by the PGW period[21] yet the sanctity attached to the Sarasvatī and this place, however, may have continued to attract many prominent persons and sages not only to visit it but also set up their abodes and *āśramas* here which subsequently developed into various *tīrthas* at and around Pehowa.[22]

The desendants of the Purus whose kings Durgaha, Girikshit, Purukutsa, Trasadasyu, Hiraṇyin, Trikshī, Tryaruṇa and Kuruśravaṇa have been referred to in the Vedic literature[23] may be supposed to have been living on the banks of the Sarasvatī during the first half of the first millennium B.C. They had, however, merged with the Bharatas, another powerful Aryan tribe, because of certain socio-political compulsions and came to be known as the Kurus. Settled between the Sarasvatī and the Dṛishadvaṭī, a region known as Kurukshetra, Kurudeśa and Kururāshṭra after them, they laid the foundations of one of the most grandiose civilisations of the ancient world. They excelled not only in military skill but had the best and purest speech.[24] From the Kurukshetra region, they spread south and eastward taking with them the message of material prosperity and spiritual elevation.[25] The Kurus ruled from Hastināpura[26] till a flood in the Gaṅgā forced king Nichakshu, fifth in descent from Abhimanyu, to shift his capital to Kauśāmbī.[27] Janaka, the philosopher king of Videha, was contemporary of Ushasta or Ushasti Chākrāyaṇa (during whose time disaster befell the Kurus) or probably of Nichakshu.[28] Kuru was one of the ten important states at that time.[29] It continued to be one of the sixteen *Mahājanapadas* in the time of Buddha (*c.* sixth century B.C.)[30] when it was ruled over by a king called Koravya who lived in the well-known city of Thullakoṭṭhita[31] which has been identified with Dhankot near Gurgaon by Silak Ram[32] and with Thol Kurri near Pehowa by Bharadwaj.[33] Aśvaghosha gives us the Sanskrit version of the name as Sthūlakoshṭhaka and explained that it was so named as the town was a prosperous market-place surrounded by fertile and affluent country, plentiful in grains which kept the stores of the inhabitants always full.[34] This description and philological plausibility indicate that Bharadwaj's identification may be nearer to the truth. If this be so Pehowa too must have been a prosperous town then. Though Buddha is said to have visited various places in the Kuru country,[35] yet Buddhism could not gain popularity at Pehowa. It has not been mentioned in the Buddhist literature. The *Somanassa Jātaka*[36] refers to king Reṇu of Kurukshetra who may have ruled over Pehowa also but it is difficult to determine his exact date.

In Pāṇini's time (*c.* fifth century B.C.) Pehowa was not as developed and well-known as Kapishṭhala (Kaithal), Śoṇaprastha (Sonipat), Taushāyana (Tohana), Śairīshaka (Sirsa), Yugandhara (Jagadhari), Srughna (Sugh), etc. which have been mentioned by the grammarian.[37] He, however, refers to the Kauravyas as one of the independent warrior communities.[38] Pāṇini has mentioned some republican tribes which we find inhabiting Haryana later.

In the fourth century B.C., the kingdom of Magadha passed into the hands of Mahāpadma of the Nanda dynasty from the Śaiśunāga dynasty. He is said to have overthrown, besides the Śaiśunāgas, the Ikshvākus, Kurus, Pañchālas, Śūrasenas and all the Kshatriyas (*Sarva-Kshatrāntaka*) to become the sole monarch (*ekarāṭ*).[39] It is, however, not certain whether Pehowa too came under his sway or was occupied by some republican people who were occupying the territories beyond Nanda's dominions. When Alexander invaded India, his forces revolted to march further beyond the Beas. At that time, we are told by the Greek historian Arrian, "The country beyond the Hyphases (Beas) was exceedingly fertile, and that the inhabitants were good agriculturists, brave in war, and lived under an excellent system of government, for the multitude was governed by the aristocracy who exercised their authority with justice and moderation".[40] Jayaswal has rightly pointed out that this description of Arrian tallies with Kauṭilya's account of some *gaṇas* as *'vārtāśastropajīvinaḥ'* and was inclined to identify the great republican territory beyond the river Beas with the Yaudheya state.[41] Smith also regarded the Beas as the boundary between the Yaudheyas on its east and the Madrakas on its west.[42] Altekar also endorsed the suggestion of Jayaswal.[43]

Soon after Alexander's invasion, the whole of northern India was conquered by Chandragupta Maurya who also seems to have subjugated the tribes of the present day Haryana, Punjab and parts of Pakistan. Though no Mauryan relics have come to light from Pehowa yet there cannot be any doubt to its having been under the Mauryan hegemony till the last. It must have also formed part of the dominions of Pushyamitra Śuṅga who had usurped the Mauryan empire by assassinating Bṛihdratha in *circa* 185 B.C. According to the *Divyāvadāna* and Tāranātha, Pushyamitra's dominions included Jālandhara and Śākala (Sialkot now in Pakistan) in the north.[44] Repeated attacks by the Bactrian Greeks weakened the Śuṅgas and northern region seems to have slipped out of their hands after Pushyamitra's death in about the middle of the second century B.C. From this date we start getting the coins of independent rulers from Mathurā and of the Yaudheyas from Bahudhānyaka region around Rohtak.[45] We do not know for certain whether the Yaudheyas wielded any influance over Pehowa at that time or not. The whole region, however, may have come under the sway of the Indo-Greeks whose coins have been found from Ambala, Naraingarh, Sadhaura, Kapāla-mochan, Sugh, Kaithal, Theh Polar, Rājā Karṇa kā Qilā (Kurukshetra), Karnal, Naurangabad, Rohtak, Sonipat, etc. in Haryana.[46] The Indo-Greeks could not stay in the region for long as we find the Yaudheyas issuing their coins again, probably from another mint at Naurangabad, which town they seem to have made their capital now.[47] Almost contemporaneously or a little later, we find the Kuṇindas and Agras also issuing their coins. Kuṇinda coins have been found from Pehowa, Karnal, Sugh, Jagadhari, Sadhaura, Buria, Bari Krori, Naraingarh, etc. in Haryana besides various other places in Himachal Pradesh, Punjab and Uttar Pradesh.[48] Agra coins were localised in Agroha[49] but stray pieces have been obtained from Mathurā,[50] Pandusar (in Rajasthan), [51] Naurangabad and Rājā Karṇa kā Qilā.[52] We cannot be sure as to which tribe wielded more influence at Pehowa. Only a few kilometres north at Ghuram have been dug out a large number of Mitra coins[53] whose state stretched from south of the Beas in Hoshiarpur district to Ghuram, 37 km from Patiala towards Pehowa.[54] All these tribal and monarchical powers of the first century B.C. were eclipsed by the Śakas in the later part of the first century B.C. Maues, generally identified with Moga of the Taxila plate, had established himself firmly over the Kāpiśa-Gandhāra region and his satraps probably conquered the country up to Mathurā. Some scholars think that it was Azes II or Rañjubula[57] who conquered the whole territory from Jammu to Mathurā during the last few decades of the first century B.C. The discovery of the coins of Azes from Amritsar and Kaithal, [58] however, indicates that he may have been the first to take Scythian arms to the Punjab-Haryana region. Rañjubula, whose coins too have been recovered from Nurmahal, [59] Sultanpur Lodhi, [60] Sunet, [61] Sanghol[62] and Ambala City[63] may have reconquered the territory to establish a firm hold. Soon, however, the region seems to have gone into the hands of the Parthian king Gondophares whose coins have been reported, in some cases in very large numbers, from Ambala, Naraingarh, Chhoti Krori, Bari Krori, Thanesar, Rājā Karṇa kā Qilā and Pehowa.[64] The nameless ruler Soter Mega's coins from Ropar, Bondal and Sanghol (Ludhiana district), Kaithal and Naraungabad indicate that he wrested the region from Parthian clutches to bring it under the Kushāṇa rule. Kushāṇa coins from Wima Kadphises onwards are so numerous from the entire region, including Pehowa, that it is not possible to enlist them. Explorations and excavations of the sites where Kushāṇa levels have been exposed indicate that Kushāṇa rule was characterised by unprecedented progress and development.[65]

The Scythian, Parthian and Kushāṇa ascendancy forced the Yaudheyas to find shelter in the hilly tracts of Garhwal-Kumaon. It is not improbable that they may have descended into the plains at the death of Huvishka to wrest their original homeland from the alien yoke. Huvishka's successor Vāsudeva I may have sent his forces and also instructed his allies, the Western Kshatrapas, to fight against the Yaudheyas. The battle must have been a fierce one and the alien forces, though able to defeat the Yaudheyas, must have tasted their valour. This is reflected in Rudradāman's brag that he defeated the warlike Yaudheyas 'who were rendered proud by having manifested their title of heroes among all kshatriyas'.[66] The Yaudheyas, too, seem to have learnt something from the military organisation of the Western Kshatrapas as is betrayed by the adoption of the title *svāmi'*[67] on their coin-legends (of Class 3)[68] and *Mahākshatrapa* on their seals.[69] When the position of the Kushāṇas towards the end of Vāsudeva II's reign (*c*. A.D. 210-30) became very critical, [70] the Yaudheyas declared their independence and asserted their authority on their original territory as also the adjoining areas wherever they could.[71] Pehowa must have formed part of their dominions then.

The Yaudheyas were subjugated by Samudragupta along with many other tribes and made to accept his overlordship and agree to pay taxes and tributes.[72] It seems that Pehowa was a flourishing town during the Yaudheya-Gupta period and some temples adorned with large-sized terracottas were built here. Being located in the Punjab-Haryana region, the Yaudheyas seem to have suffered another blow at the hands of the Hūṇas in the fifth century A.D.[73] The Hūṇas wielded their authority till the Pushpabhūtis gained ascendancy in this region during the second half of the sixth century A.D.[74]

The Kurukshetra region was known as Śrīkaṇṭha *Janapada* during the Gupta-Pushpabhūti period as can be gathered from *Āryamañjuśrīmūlakalpa*[75] and Bāṇa's *Harshacharita*.[76] The latter work gives a vivid description of the *janapada*. Ādityavardhana, the third ruler of the known genealogy, was married to Mahāsenaguptā, probably the sister of Mahāsenagupta, a later Gupta monarch of Magadha. This matrimony seems to have boosted the Vardhana power. His son Prabhākaravardhana probably extended the dynastic dominions and became independent with Sthāṇvīśvara (Thanesar) as his capital. Śrīkaṇṭha-*janapada* known after Śrīkaṇṭha *nāga* killed by his semi-legendary ancestor king Pushpabhūti, was naturally to gain importance with the emergence of this new political power at Thanesar. The popularity of Śaivism in Śrīkaṇṭha *janapada* is well attested by Bāṇa's *Harshacharita,*[75] the account of the Chinese pilgrim Hiuen Tsang who visited India during the reign of Harshavardhana in the first half of the seventh century A.D.[76] and the *Vāmana Purāṇa,* a work of about A.D. 700.[77] Some of the Śaiva temples at Pehowa, too, may have been built during the Vardhana period, but there is no literary or epigraphic evidence to prove it. Nor is there any evidence that any of the Pushpabhūti rulers ever visited Pehowa though it is quite possible and likely.[78] With the shifting of the capital to Kanauj by Harsha, the political importance of the region may have waned, but it continued to maintain its religious importance. It is, however, difficult to reconstruct the history of the Pehowa region after the death of Harsha in A.D. 647. It has been suggested that Harsha's cousin (maternal uncle's son) Bhaṇḍi established himself over this region and his family continued to rule here till the ascendancy of the Pratihāras.[79] The Bhaṇḍis may have remained subservient to the Kanauj throne. Vākpatirāja refers to the march of Yaśovarman's army through Marudeśa, Śrīkaṇṭha, Kurukshetra, etc. to check the Pārasīka invasion in the northern region.[80] Yaśovarman (*c.* A.D. 690-740) was accompanied by his Pratihāra feudatory Nāgabhaṭṭa I (*c.* A.D. 725-56) in this march.[81] Kalhaṇa tells us that Yaśovarman was defeated at the hands of the Kashmirian ruler Lalitāditya Muktāpīḍa (*c.* A.D. 695-732).[82] The Kurukshetra-Pehowa region, however, seems to have remained under the rule of Bhaṇḍikula from which it was wrested by Vatsarāja Pratihāra (A.D. 775-95), the grandson of Nāgabhaṭṭa I.[83] Vatsarāja is also credited with victories against the rulers of Karṇāṭa and Lāṭa, Jayāpīḍa of Kashmir, the lord of Gauḍa (Dharmapāla), the Mlechchha (Muslim) and Kīra (Kangra) rulers.[84] Soon, however, Dharmapāla (A.D. 770-810) seems to have avenged his defeat and having defeated Vatsarāja and his nominal overlord Indrāyudha, installed Chakrāyudha on the imperial throne of Kanauj. A grand assembly was called at Kanauj on this occasion in which the Kuru king was also present.[85] Nāgabhaṭṭa II (*c.* A.D. 796?-833), who succeeded Vatsarāja, vanquished Chakrāyudha as well as Dharmapāla, and established himself on the throne of Kanauj.[86] His vast dominions included Pehowa and extended even to the Punjab.[87] The importance of Pehowa as a socio-cultural and commercial centre during the subsequent Pratihāra regimes is well illustrated by two inscriptions from the place, one belonging to Nāgabhaṭṭa II's grandson and successor Mihira Bhoja (*c.* A.D. 836-90)[88] and the other of the time of his successor Mahendrapāla (*c.* A.D. 890-910).[89] The former, dated Saṁvat 276 (of Harsha era, i.e. A.D. 882-83), recorded "the fact that certain pious horse-dealers who met at the horse fair held at Pehoa-Prithūdaka on the fourteenth day of the half-month preceding the bright half of Vaiśākha, agreed to impose upon themselves and upon their customers certain taxes or tithes, the proceeds of which were to be distributed among some temples, priests and sanctuaries, in proportions specified".[90] The 'worthies' belonged to 'various countries' and the donees included, among others, the temple of Vishṇu in his Yajñavarāha form built by Bhūvaka in Pehowa, the *pūjaka* or temple priest of Yajñavarāha and the *sthāna* or sanctuary of Prithūdaka, who received respectively (1) 1/24 of the tax paid by the merchants and 6/12 of the tax paid by the customers, (2) 1/24 and 2/12 and (3) 1/24 and 4/12 parts of the taxes respectively which were:

(i) two *dharmas*, to be deducted from the sum received by the dealer for each animal and
(ii) one *dharma* to be paid by the buyer of each animal in addition to the price stipulated.[91]

The inscription is thus an important document bearing on the socio-cultural and economic conditions of northern India, Pehowa in particular. It is fixed in the wall of the temple of Garibnath at Pehowa.

The second inscription, an undated *praśasti* of the reign of Mahendrapāla, was found fixed in the wall of a house, Siddhagīr kī Havelī,[92] and used as a seat. It was later removed to the Lahore Museum where it is preserved now. "The object of the inscription is to record the building, it would seem, of a triple temple of Vishṇu, and it contains a so-called *Praśasti* or eulogy, as is expressly stated in verse 26. It opens with a *maṅgala* of four verses, verses 1-2 being addressed to Vishṇu, verse 3 to Kurukshetra, and verse 4 to the sacred stream Sarasvatī, which flows near Prithūdaka-Pehoa. Verse 5 praises the ruling king of the country, Mahendrapāla".[93]

The next fourteen verses give us the pedigree of the ruling Tomara family as follows—

Jāula (vv 6-8)
|
Vajraṭa, married to Maṅgaladevī (vv 9-10)
|
Jajjuka, married to Chandrā and Nāyikā (vv 11-13)

Gogga (v.14)	Pūrṇarāja (vv.15-16)	Devarāja (vv. 17-19)

Jāula is mentioned as *rājā* indicating his feudatory status. Gogga, too, is mentioned as *bhūnātha*, 'protector of earth', betraying the continuity of the same position. Gogga and his two brothers Pūrṇarāja and Devarāja built the triple Vishṇu temple at Pehowa (vv. 20-21). The reference to this temple (*idam=āyatanaṁ*) in the next verse reveals that it was a triple shrine 'containing three statues and three adyta, united under one roof.' The architect of this temple was Achyuta, son of Rāma, who hailed from Kamboja (v. 23). Three villages, Yakshapālaka, Gejjara, and Pāṭala[94] were assigned for the *bhoga* of the deity (v. 24). In the next verse future princes are exhorted to respect this donation. Verse 26 reveals that the name of the poet began with Mu- and that his father was Bhaṭṭa Rāma. The last verse (v. 27) gives the latter part of the engraver's name as - ālāditya, son of Durlabhāditya.[95]

To the genealogy of Tomaras, another name may now be supplied from Vatsarāja's Sirsa inscription dated Śaka 717 (= A.D. 795) which refers to a Tomara chieftain Vyāghra who was vanquished by Vatsarāja's subordinate Śrīvarmaka.[96] According to the Rajasthan bardic tradition, Delhi was founded in A.D. 736 by the Tomaras.[97] The association of the Tomaras of Delhi with Haryana is hinted at by the Delhi Museum inscription of A.D. 1328.[98] Tomara ruler Vyāghra being a contemporary of Vatsarāja Pratihāra may have, therefore, been the grandfather or the great-grandfather of Vajraṭa of the Pehowa inscription. The Tomaras of Pehowa continued to owe allegiance to the Pratihāras till their decline, and may have become independent thereafter. Harsha inscription of V.S. 1030 tells us that a Tomara chief Rudra was killed by Chāhamāna Chandrarāja.[99] Fragmentary Ajmer Museum *praśasti* refers to an expedition of Chāhamāna Arṇorāja, son of Ajayarāja and Somaladevī, into the Haritānaka country and carrying arms up to the Sindhu and the Sarasvatī.[100] Hemachandra,[101] a contemporary writer, tells us that he was helped by the rulers of eastern Madra[102] and the towns of Vāhīkadeśa[103] in his northern expedition and mentions him as *Udīchyapati*. This literary evidence and the discovery of Somaladevī's coins from Sunam (Dist. Sangrur) and Samana (Dist. Patiala) to the north-west of Pehowa implies that Arṇorāja had vanquished the Tomaras of Pehowa.[104] The final blow to the Tomaras seems to have been dealt by Vigraharāja IV in V.S. 1208.[105] The evidence of the *Kharataragachchhabṛihadgurvāvalī* of Jinapāla (V.S. 1393)[106] and Ṭhakkura Pheru's *Dravyaparīkshā*[107] indicates that the Tomaras continued to rule thereafter as the feudatories of the Chauhans of Śākambharī. With the death of Pṛithvīrāja Chauhan in A.D. 1192, history took a decisive turn and the region passed into the hands of the Turks with which began an era of oppression.

MEDIEVAL PERIOD

Muslim invasions on India had started in A.D. 712 when Muhammad bin Qasim attacked Sind. Thereafter, we find Yaśovarman, Nāgabhaṭṭa I, Vatsarāja and others stemming their tide. In the second decade of the eleventh century, Mahmud Ghaznavi raided Thanesar, [108] ravished it and took away the life-size idol of Chakrasvāmi[109] and placed it in the hippodrome of Ghazna to be desecrated further by the people there. His aim of extirpating idolatory[110] may have taken him to Pehowa also where he ransacked the temples and broke images. The paucity of post A.D. 1000 images and temple-remains indicates in this direction. The region was raided by him[111] and his successor Masud[112] repeatedly subsequently also. Masud's son, Majdud, governed the whole region from Hansi to the Indus but when his brother Maudud ascended the throne of Ghazni, he refused allegiance to him. Maudud wanted to punish him but died at Lahore under mysterious circumstances, perhaps due to poisoning, in A.D. 1040. Maudud occupied the whole territory held by Majdud and appointed his own confidents to govern Thanesar, Hansi and other places in Haryana.[113] The internal dissensions of the Ghaznavids, however, provided an opportunity to the confederacy of Chauhan, Paramāra and Kalachuri potentates to recapture Hansi, Thanesar and Punjab up to Lahore.[114] Obviously, Pehowa too must have been liberated. After a brief respite the Muslim aggression started again and in A.D. 1075 Masud's grandson Mahmud (son of Ibrahim), who was then the governor of Punjab, led an expedition to Ujjain.[115] Taking advantage of the disturbed conditions, the Lahore kings of Kashmir, Ananta and his son Kalaśa, invaded Haryana and probably reached Kanauj also.[116] Their sway over the Haryana region was cut short by the Tomaras who reasserted their authority.[117] The Tomaras served as the feudatories of the Chauhans. With the defeat of Pṛithvīrāja Chauhan in the second battle of Tarain in A.D. 1192, the whole northern region came under the Muslim sway.

After Muizz-ud-Din's death in A.D. 1206, Qutb-ud-Din Aibak became the *malik* and *waliahd* of the Indian territory. When the former's son Yalduz rose against him he was checked immediately and adequately to retreat to Kohistan. Aibak shifted his capital to Lahore and set up military posts at Thanesar, Sirsa, Sonipat, Rohtak, Rewari, Hansi, etc.[118] Pehowa does not find any mention in contemporary literature as probably after its sack during the time of Mahmud Ghaznavi, it had lost all political importance. When, during the reign of Iltutmish, the kingdom was divided into various *iqtas*. (divisions) from administrative viewpoint, Pehowa fell in the Pipli *iqta*. When Balban increased the number of *iqtas* to facilitate civil administration, it is not clear whether it remained under Pipli or went to the Kaithal *iqta*.[119]

We know almost next to nothing about the history of Pehowa during the Khilji and Tughlaq regimes. It may, however, be surmised that the people of this town, too, like those of Samana, Sunam, Kuhram and Kaithal, may have refused to pay the oppressive taxes during the rule of Muhammad-bin-Tughlaq.[120] Pehowa has not been mentioned in Ibn-Batuta's travels[121] nor does it figure even in Timur's march from Samana to Kaithal en route Delhi.[122] Its continuous existence may, however, be vouched by the local tradition that it was visited by Guru Nanak (A.D. 1469-1539) in memory of which a gurudwara was built in the town. If we believe the local tradition, the temples of Pehowa, including the Pṛithvīśvara Mahādeva Temple, had been destroyed earlier by Nadir Shah Abdali in A.D. 1739 during his raid of Thanesar and other places.[123] Nadir Shah's invasion weakened the central Mughal authority and brought in various depredating and plundering forces in the region and the whole country between Karnal and Ludhiana was reduced to a jungle.[124] In the middle of the eighteenth century, Haryana was parcelled out among the local chiefs and Pehowa seems to have come under Nazbat Khan Ruhela who held parts of Karnal and Kurukshetra.[125] Soon, however, Ahmad Shah Durrani invaded the area and captured the entire country up to the neighbourhood of Panipat from the Mughal emperor and Nazbat Khan was made to pay a sum of rupees twenty lakh.[126]

The Mughal emperor was obliged to seek Maratha help which came forth immediately. The emperor showed his gratitude by issuing a royal *firman* on 25 October, 1754 according to which Kurukshetra and Gaya, the two sacred Hindu pilgrimages, were given to the Peshwa and put under his agents, Hingne brothers.[127] The fourth Durrani invasion in 1756 brought the Marathas in Delhi and Haryana, Ahmad Shah's plenipotentiary Najib was ousted from Delhi in September with an indemnity of rupees five lakh to the Marathas. During the Maratha ascendancy, many new temples were built at Pehowa and the old ones renovated. Probably the *pucca ghats* were also provided on the banks of the Sarasvatī at Pehowa under their patronage. Some Malhar women who came to Kurukshetra (and perhaps Pehowa also) to have a holy dip on a Somavatī Amāvasyā on 9 January, 1758 were attacked by a contingent of Abdus Samad Khan, Abdali's governor at Sirhind, at Shahabad. The incident gave the Maratha leader Raghunath Rao an opportunity to attack the Muslims. He advanced as far north as Attock and Peshawar.[128] At this, Ahmad Shah got infuriated and invaded India again in 1759. The Marathas were ultimately defeated in the third battle of Panipat in 1761 which was rather a national disaster. Falling under the Sirhind *sarkar*, Pehowa came to be governed by *Faujdar* Zain Khan.[129] With the rise of the Sikhs to power, Pehowa came into the possession of the Bhais of Kaithal. In 1763, Desu Singh and his brother Buddha Singh, defeated Zain Khan and seized from him Pundri, Thanesar and Pehowa, besides Kaithal of course.[130] The independent chiefs of Thanesar, Ladwa, Kaithal, Jind, etc. were taken under British protection in 1809[131] and when the rulers of these estates died heirless, they were confiscated by the British: Kaithal in 1843, Ladwa in 1845, Thanesar in 1850 to name only a few.[132] The British used the palace built by the Bhais of Kaithal at Pehowa as a rest house.[133]

MODERN PERIOD

By 1805, the East India Company had established itself on sound footings in Haryana, after having reduced the Marathas under Daulat Rao Sindhia, who was the main prop of the Mughal emperor Shah Alam, in the Anglo-Maratha war of 1803.[134] Following the policy of expansion, they had been annexing state after state on some pretext or the other. It was, therefore, not surprising that they took possession of the Pehowa estate also in 1834 when Jamait Singh died without an heir, as noted above. The administration of the upper parts of Haryana, i.e., the present districts of Karnal, Kurukshetra and Ambala, was conducted through the Superintendent of the Political Affairs and agent to the Governor at Ambala until 1849 when they were placed under the charge of the Punjab Government.[135]

Pehowa continued to retain its religions importance and people used to visit it. On 27 April, 1844, Sardar Atar Singh Sandhanwalia, who was regarded as the strongest Sikh chief after Hari Singh Nalwa and was conferred with various titles, like Ujjal Didar, Sardar Waqar, Ali Tabar, Shamsher Jang Bahadur, etc. by Ranjit Singh, passed through Pehowa.[136] The ashes of Raja Suchet Singh were immersed in the Sarasvatī on 30 April, 1844.[137] Evidently, Pehowa has remained sacred to both, the Hindus and the Sikhs, for centuries and continues to be so even now. Very recently, a part of the *asthis* of Rajiv Gandhi, the former Prime Minister of India, were immersed in the Sarasvatī at Pehowa on 28 May, 1991.

The importance of Pehowa waned further with its lapse to the British Government as is indicated by its population decreasing from 3,408 in 1881 to 2,048 in 1901.[138] The history of this town up to 1947 is not different from the history of the region under the British. Kamar Lal, son of Ram Chand Saraf, and Giani Veer Singh, son of Lakha Singh of Pehowa, took part in the freedom struggle. As a part of the country it became independent in 1947 and formed part of Punjab. When this state was bifurcated on 1 November, 1966 it fell in Haryana. When the Karnal district, was reorganised and Kurukshetra became a district, it was included in the latter as a tehsil headquarter. In the recent decades, Pehowa has developed rapidly and its population has also increased considerably from 6,159 in 1951 to 11, 366 in 1961 and 17,279 in 1981 with 2,825 occupied residential houses. The growth rate of population from 1961 to 1971 was 84.54% and from 1971 to 1981 it was 51.94%.[139] The population has risen considerably now.

NOTES AND REFERENCES

1. G.C. Mohapatra and Mukesh Singh, "Stratified Occurrence of Lithic Artifacts in the Siwalik Frontal Range of Western Sub-Himalaya", *Panjab University Research Bulletin (Arts)*, Chandigarh, Vol. X, No. 1-2, 1979, pp. 65-77.
2. H. De Terra and T.T Paterson, *Studies on the Ice Age in India and Associated Human Cultures*, Washington, 1939.
3. Mahapatra and Singh, *loc.cit.*
4. *Ibid.*
5. *Indianm Archaeology 1971-72, A Review*, pp. 22-23.
6. G.C. Mohapatra, "Preliminary Reports of the Explorations and Excavations of Stone Age Sites in Eastern Punjab", *Bulletin of the Deccan College Research Institute*, Poona, 1966, pp. 221 ff. and information from Shri J.S. Khatri, Dept. of Archaeology & Museums, Haryana, Panchkula.
7. *Ibid.*
8. *IAR* 1971-72, pp. 22-23.
9. R.N. Khazanchi, "Pit-dwellers of Burzahom", *The Illustrated Weekly of India*, Sept. 5, 1976.
10. Shashi Asthana, "The Dynamics of the Harappan Culture", *Purātattva*, New Delhi, Nos. 13-14, (1981-83), p. 45.
11. Suraj Bhan, "Siswal: A Pre-Harappan Site in Drishadvati Valley", *Purātattva*, No. 5 (1971-72), pp. 42-46; *Excavations at Mitathal (1968) and Other Explorations in the Sutlej-Yamuna Divide*, Kurukshetra, 1975; Suraj Bhan and Jim G. Shaffer, "New Discoveries in Northern Haryana", *Man and Environment*, Vol. II (1978), pp. 59-68; B.B. Lal *et al.* (Eds.), *Frontiers of the Indus Civilization*, New Delhi, 1984, pp. 519 ff.
12. Lal *et al., op. cit.*
13. U.V. Singh, "Sources of the History of Ancient Haryana", in *Sources of the History of India*, ed. S.P. Sen, Vol. II, Calcutta, 1979, p. 82.
14. J.P. Joshi, "A Note on the Excavation at Bhagwanpura", *Purātattva*, No. 8 (1975-76), pp. 178-80.
15. B.B. Lal, "Excavations at Hastināpura and Other Explorations in the Upper Ganga and Sutlej Basins 1950-52", *Ancient India*, New Delhi, Nos. 10 & 11 (1954-55), pp. 150-51.
16. *Ibid.*, p. 23.
17. *Ibid.*, Table I, p. 12A.
18. *Ibid.*, p. 32.

19. R.S. Sharma, "The Later Vedic Phase and the Painted Grey Ware Culture", *Purātattva*, No. 8 (1975-76), p. 67.
20. If the literary evidence is taken on its face value, the foundation of Pehowa will go back to a period anterior to that of the Mahābhārata war. The authenticity and the date of the war are, however, very controversial. For details see, S.P. Gupta and K.S. Ramachandran (Eds.), *Mahabharata: Myth and Reality*, Delhi, 1976; S.B. Roy, *Date of the Mahabharata Battle*, Gurgaon, 1976; G.C. Agrawala (Ed.), *Age of the Bharata War*, Dellhi, 1979.
21. Suraj Bhan, *Pre-historical Archaeology of Sarasvatī and Dṛṣadvatī Vallys*, Ph. D. Dissertation (M.S. University, Baroda, 1972, p. 23.
22. See *infra*, Ch. III.
23. *The Vedic Age* (Eds. R.C. Majumdar and A.D. Pusalkar), Bombay, 1951, p. 246; *Vedic Index*, I, p. 327.
24. *Śatapatha Brāhmaṇa* III.2.3, 15.
25. The *Śāṅkh. Śr. S.* (IV.16.10, 13) states that the Kurus were driven out of Kurukshetra as a result of a sacrificial error.
26. The Pāṇḍavas, the collaterals of the Kauravas, are well-known to have founded Indraprastha (=Inderpat, i.e., Purana Quila, New Delhi) and ruled from there for sometime.
27. For the Paurāṇic accounts in this connection, see F.E. Pargiter, *Purāṇa Text of the Dynasties of the Kali Age*, Oxford University Press, 1913, pp. 4-5.
28. Hemchandra Raychaudhuri, *Political History of India*, 6th ed., Calcutta, 1953, p. 48.
29. *Ibid.*, p. 58.
30. *Aṅguttara Nikāya* (PTS) I.213; *Dīgha Nikāya* II.200; *Mahāvastu* I.84. The Jaina *Bhagavati Sūtra* (XV.1), however, omits Kuru from its list of the sixteen *Mahājanapadas*.
31. *Majjhima Nikāya* (PTS), II.54, 65f. Also see *Theragāthā* commentary II.30.
32. Silak Ram, *Archaeology of Rohtak and Hissar Districts* (Haryana), Ph. D. Dissertation (Ms), K.U., Kurukshetra, 1972, p. 107.
33. Bharadwaj (1986), *op. cit.*, p. 157. D.C. Ahir identifies Thullakoṭṭhita with Sthāneśvara (D.C. Ahir, *Buddhism in the Punjab, Haryana and Himachal Pradesh*, New Delhi, 1971, p. 15). For the Buddhist connections of Thullakoṭṭhita see Devendra Handa, *Buddhist Remains*, Heritage of Haryana II, Department of Archaeology & Museums, Haryana, Chandigarh, 1989, p. 8.
34. B.N. Chaudhari, *Buddhist Centres in Ancient India*, Calcutta, 1969, p. 31.
35. H.A. Phadke, "Buddhism in Kurudeśa", Proceedings of the *International Seminar on Buddhism and Jainism*, Cuttack, 1976, pp. 154-58; Bharadwaj (1986), *op. cit.*, pp. 149-65.
36. *The Jātaka* (Eng. tr. Cowell and Rouse, Cambridge, 1877-97), IV, 444.
37. V.S. Agrawala (1963), *op. cit.*, pp. 49ff.
38. *Ashṭādhyāyī* IV, 1, 178. Manu (VII.193) also endorses this view.
39. Raychaudhuri, *op. cit.*, p. 233.
40. J.W. Mc Crindle, *The Invasion of India by Alexander the Great as Described by Arrian, Curtius, Diodorus, Plutarch and Justin*, Westminster, 1896, p. 121.

41. K.P. Jayaswal, *Hindu Polity*, Part I, 3rd ed., Bangalore City, 1955, p. 67.
42. V.A. Smith, *Journal of the Royal Asiatic Society*, 1897, p. 289.
43. *Journal of the Numismatic Society* of India, Vol. XI, , p. 50.
44. Raychaudhuri, *op. cit.*, p. 371.
45. For numismatic evidence in this connection, see P.L. Gupta, "Chronology of the Post-Kushana Rulers and the Allied Tribes", in *K.P.Jayaswal Commemoration Volume* (Ed. J.S. Jha), Patna, 1981, pp. 291-99.
46. For references, see H.A. Phadke, *Haryana: Ancient and Medieval*, New Delhi, 1990, p. 38. For Indo-Greek coins from Kaithal and Karnal (not mentioned by Phadke), see James Prinsep, *Essays on Indian Antiquities* (Ed. E. Thomas, London, 1858), Vol. I, pp. 24 and 46.
47. Swami Omanand Sarasvati, *Ancient Mints of Haryana*, Jhajjar, V.S 2036, pp. 37 and 109; Devendra Handa, "An Interesting, Yaudheya Seal from Naurangabad", *Journal of the Epigraphical Society of India*, Mysore, Vol. XV, pp. 81-85.
48. See for details Devendra Handa, "Kuninda Coins in Relation to Trade and Economy", *Coinage, Trade & Economy*, The 3rd International Colloquium, Indian Institute of Research in Numismatic Studies, Anjaneri, 1991, pp. 33-35.
49. H.L. Srivastava, *Excavations at Agroha* (Punjab), *MASI*, No. 61, Delhi, 1952; K.K. Dasgupta, *Tribal History of Ancient India—A Numismatic Approach*, Calcutta, 1974, pp. 1-16.
50. *JNSI*, Vol. VIII, pp. 30-32.
51. Devendra Handa, "A New Agacha Coin", *The Journal of Academy of Indian Numismatics & Sigillography*, Indore, Vol. IV (1981-82), pp. 7-8, Pl. I.2.
52. Silak Ram, *op. cit.*, pp. 112 and 253. The illustrations of the coins in the thesis are not clear and the identification is not beyond doubt.
53. G.B. Sharma and Manmohan Kumar, "Mitra Coins from Ghuram (Patiala)", *Numismatic Digest*, Bombay, Vol. III, Part II (December 1979), pp. 4-16.
54. Devendra Handa, *Studies in Indian Coins and Seals*, Delhi, 1985, pp. 52-53.
55. Raychaudhuri, *op. cit.*, p. 437.
56. *Journal of the Royal Asiatic Society*, 1947, pp. 25ff. Also see *JRAS*, 1914, p. 979.
57. Sudhakar Chattopadhyaya, *Early History of North India*, 1958, p. 62.
58. Rodgers, *op. cit.*, p. 2.
59. *CASR*, XIV, p. 69.
60. *Ibid.*, p. 67
61. *Ibid.*, p. 65.
62. Still unpublished (excavated recently from the site).
63. Rodgers, *op. cit.*, p. 2.
64. *Ibid.*, pp. 2-3; Manmohan Kumar, *Archaeology of Ambala and Kurukshetra Districts (Haryana)*, Ph. D. Dissertation (Ms), K.U., Kurukshetra, 1978, pp. 187 and 209-10.
65. R.S. Sharma, *Urban Decay in India*, New Delhi, 1987, pp. 14-20.
66. *Epigraphia Indica*, Vol. VII, pp. 42f.
67. Cf. *JNSI, XXXVII* (1975), p. 134.
68. John Allan, *Catalogue of the Coins of Ancient India*, London, 1936, pp. 270-75.
69. *JNSI*, XXXII, pp. 157-60.

70. A.S. Altekar in *The Vākāṭaka-Gupta Age*, Banaras, 1964, pp. 18-19.
71. This is reflected by their coins of Class 6 bearing the legend *Yaudheya gaṇasya jaya* datable to *circa* third-early fourth centuries A.D. and their distribution. For details see Devendra Handa, "The Yaudheyas and their Coins", *Numismatic Studies*, Vol. I, New Delhi, 1991, pp. 63-77.
72. *Corpus Inscriptionum Indicarum*, Vol. III, p. 8.
73. Handa (1991), *op. cit.*, p. 65.
74. Cf. D. Devahuti, *Harsha: A Political Study*, Oxford, 1970, pp. 58ff. Also see Handa (1985) *op. cit.*, pp. 139-43. Majumdar (*The Classical Age*, Bombay, 1954, p. 97) places the first three Pushpabhūti rulers bearing the title Mahāraja—Naravardhana, Rājyavardhana I and Ādityavardhana—between A.D. 500-80. Their title indicates their feudatory status but it is difficult to determine as to who were their overlords—the Guptas, the Hūṇas or the Maukharis (*EI*, I, pp. 67ff. and IV, pp. 208ff).
75. *Harshacharita* of Bāṇa, edited by K.S. Parab, Bombay, 1892; *Deeds of Harsha* (Eng. tr.) by E.B. Cowell and F.W. Thomas, Delhi, 1961 (Reprint).
76. Thomas Watters, *On Yuang Chwang's Travels in India*, Delhi, 1961 (Reprint), pp. 314 ff.
77. *Vāmana Purāṇa*, Chapters 12-23 (Unless otherwise stated, all references henceforth are from the Critical Edition of A.S. Gupta).
78. Satish Chandra, *Prāchīna Pṛithūdaka*, M.Phil. Dissertation (Ms), K.U., Kurukshetra, 1978, p. 12.
79. B.N. Puri, *History of the Garjara-Pratiharas*, Bombay, 1967, pp. 39ff; Phadke (1991), *op. cit.*, p. 79.
80. *Gauḍavaho* (Ed. S.P. Pandit, Bombay 1887), v. 484.
81. Phadke (1991), *op. cit.*, pp. 79-80.
82. *Rājataraṅgiṇī* (Eng. tr. by K.S. Pandit, New Delhi, 1977), IV. 133-45.
83. *EI*, Vol. XVIII, p. 99, v. 7.
84. *Ibid.*, Vol. XLI, pp. 52 and 56, vv. 5-7.
85. H.A. Phadke, "Haryana and the Gurjara-Pratiharas", *Haryana Research Journal*, Vol. I, No. 3, 1967, pp. 5-10.
86. *EI*, Vol. XVIII, pp. 99-100.
87. Phadke (1990), *op. cit.*, p. 81.
88. *EI*, Vol. I, pp. 184-90.
89. *Ibid.*, pp. 242-50.
90. *Ibid.*, p. 184.
91. *Ibid.*, pp. 184-86, Three other donees were: (1) the temple built by the illustrious Guhāditya at Kanauj (2) the temple built by Kadambāditya at Gotīrtha in Kanauj, and (3) the temple of Vishṇu Garuḍāsana built by the Brāhmaṇa Bhūvaka in Bhojapura near Kanauj.
92. *CASR*, II, p. 225; XIV, pp. 101-02.
93. *EI*, I, p. 243.
94. These three villages have been identified with Jakhepala (Sangrur), Ghaggar and Patran (Dist. Patiala) by Bharadwaj (1986, *op. cit.*, p. 176).

95. *EI*, I, p. 247, v.24, pp. 243-44.
96. *Ibid.*, XLI, p. 50.
97. James Tod, *Annals and Antiquities of Rajasthan*, Delhi, 1971 (Reprint), Vol. I, p. 104; H.C.Ray, *Dynastic History of Northern India*, Delhi, 1973 (Reprint), Part II, p. 1145. See also H.N. Dvivedi, *Dillī ke Tomara*, Gwalior, 1973.
98. *EI*, I, pp. 93-95:
देशोऽस्ति हरियाणाख्यः पृथिव्यां स्वर्गसन्निभः ।
ढिल्लिकाख्या पुरी तत्र तोमरैरस्ति निर्मिता ।।
99. तस्माच्छ्रीचन्दनोभूत्क्षितिपतिभयदस्तोमरेशं सदर्प्पं ।
हत्वा रुद्रेनभूपं समर[भुवि] [ब] लाद्ये[न लब्ध्वा] जयश्रीः ।।
Verse 14
100. Dasharatha Sharma, *Early Chauhan Dynasties*, 2nd revised ed., Delhi 1975, pp. 48-49 and 203-4.
101. *Dvayāśrayakāvya*, Ed. A.V. Kathvate, Bombay, 1915, XVI.8.
102. The Madras were located between the Ravi and the Chenab in the Punjab with their capital at Sākala (Sialkot). See for details Dey, *op. cit.*, p. 116.
103. Details and discussion regarding Vāhīka may be seen in D.C. Sircar, *Studies in the Geography of Ancient and Medieval India*, Delhi, 1960, and M.R. Singh, *Geographical Data in the Early Puranas-A Critical Study*, Calcutta, 1972, pp. 123-27.
104. Devendra Handa, "Arṇorāja's Expedition to the Sindhu and the Sarasvatī", *Haryana Sahitya Academy Journal of Indological Studies*, Chandigarh, Vol. II, 1987, pp. 188-91.
105. *EI*, XXVI, pp. 91-93. See also Devendra Handa, "An Inscribed Image of Chakraswami and New Light on the Tomaras of Delhi", in *Rupanjali in Memory of O.C. Gangoly* (Eds. K.K. Ganguli and S.S. Biswas), Delhi, 1986, pp. 103-05.
106. Edited by Muni Jivavijaya, Bombay, 1953.
107. As quoted by Dasharatha Sharma, *op. cit.*, p. 68, fn.28.
108. Wolseley Haig, *Cambridge History of India* (Reprint, Delhi, 1958), III, pp. 18 ff; R.C. Majumdar (Ed.), *The Struggle for Empire*, Bombay, 1955, pp. 10-11. For original sources, see *Al-Beruni's India* (Ed. Edward Sachau, Delhi, 1989, Reprint), PI, p. 117 & II, p. 103; Al-Utbi's *Kitab-i-Yamini*, (Eng. tr.) James Reynolds, *Memoirs of Mahmud of Ghazni*, London (1858), pp. 393ff: Isami's *Fatuh-us-Salatin* (Ed. Agha Mahdi Hussain, Agra, 1938), I, p. 123; *Tarikh-i-Farishta* (Eng. tr. John Briggs, *The Rise of the Mohammadan Power in India*, Calcutta 1966) I, pp. 29-31; *Journal of Haryana Studies*, Vol. VI, 1974, pp. 26-34, etc.
109. Farishta refers to it as Jagsom.
110. Utbi, *loc.cit.* Also cf. Satish Chandra, *op. cit.*, p. 20.
111. *The Struggle for Empire*, pp. 13ff.; C.V. Vaidya, *History of Medieval Hindu India*, Pune, 1921-26, III, pp. 71ff.
112. Vaidya, *op. cit.*, pp. 92ff. Farishta, *op. cit.*, p. 69.
113. *Ibid.*, p. 70.
114. *Ibid.*, pp. 70-71; *The Struggle for Empire*, pp. 94 ff.
115. *Ibid.*

116. Buddha Prakash, "Kashmir and Haryana in Eleventh Century", *Journal of Haryana Studies*, Kurukshetra, Vol. II (1970), pp. 13-17.
117. Dasharatha Sharma, *Rajasthan Through the Ages*, Vol. I, Bikaner, 1966, p. 260.
118. Mohammad Habib and K.A. Nizami (Eds.), *A Comprehensive History of India*, Vol. V, Delhi, 1970, pp. 197ff; Briggs, *op. cit.*, I, p. 63; K.C. Yadav, *Haryānā kā Itihāsa*, New Delhi, 1981, p. 32.
119. For details, see Phadke (1990), *op. cit.*, pp. 111 ff.
120. S.A.A. Rizvi, *Tughlaq Kālīna Bhārata*, Vol. I, Aligarh, 1956, pp. 48f.
121. A. Mahdi Hussain, *The Rehla of Ibn-Batuta*, (Eng. tr.), Baroda, 1953.
122. Habib and Nizami, *op. cit.*, pp. 118 ff.; Also see K.L. Tuteja, "Timur's Invasion of Haryana and People's Opposition", *Journal of Haryana Studies*, Vol. VI, 1974, pp. 19-21.
123. William Irvine, *Later Mughals* (Ed. J.N. Sarkar), New Delhi, 1971, Vol. II, pp. 334 ff., J.D. Cunningham, *A History of the Sikhs*, New Delhi, 1972 (Reprint); Mahant Banshi Puri, *op. cit.*, last cover page.
124. J.N. Sarkar, *Fall of the Mughal Empire*, Calcutta, 1971, Vol. I, p. 115.
125. Hari Ram Gupta, *Marathas and Panipat*, Chandigarh, 1961, p. 132; "Political History of Haryana 1750 to 1805", *JHS*, III (i), January 1971, p. 20.
126. *Ibid.*, p. 90.
127. *Ibid.*, p. 25; Phadke (1991), *op. cit.*, p. 181.
128. *Ibid.*, pp. 53 ff.
129. Sarkar, *op. cit.*, p. 278.
130. *IGI*, XX, p. 100; Yadav (1971), *op. cit.*, p. 21, Dr. Hari Ram Gupta (*History of the Sikhs*, Vol. IV, Delhi, 1982, p. 96), however, states that Bhanga Singh and his brother Bhag Singh seized the parganah of Pehowa in January 1764 and when they took possession of Thanesar, they divided their territory. Pehowa went to Bhag Singh and Thanesar to Bhanga Singh. In 1767, Bhanga Singh seized the principality of Kaithal from two Afghan chiefs, Bhikbaksh Khan and Neamat Khan (*ibid.*, p. 60).
131. J.D. Cunningham, *op. cit.*, pp. 124-29 and 335-36.
132. K.C. Yadav, "British Rule in Haryana: 1809-56", *JHS*, IV, 1972, p. 28. Cf. Hari Ram Gupta (1982, *op. cit.*, p. 100) who states that Bhag Singh died in 1791 leaving behind four sons of whom only one had a male issue, Jamait Singh, who too died childless in 1834 and Pehowa estate escheated to the British.
133. *IGI*, XX, p. 100.
134. Yadav (1971), *op. cit.*, p. 28.
135. Yadav (1972), *op. cit.*, p. 23.
136. Hari Ram Gupta, *Panjab on the Eve of the First Sikh War* (3rd ed.), Chandigarh, 1975, pp. 129 and 303.
137. *Ibid.*, p. 303.
138. *IGI*, XX, p. 100.
139. *Census of India 1981*, Series-6 Haryana, Part XIII-A & B : Kurukshetra District, pp. 194-95.

3

PLACES OF PILGRIMAGE

Pilgrimage is a place, forest or water (i.e., stream, pond, etc.) associated with great men and thus regarded holy. People visit such holy places with religious devotion.[1] Located on the banks of the Sarasvatī, the river par excellence (Pl. 2), Pehowa is associated with numerous great men and is regarded as the holiest of the holy places.[2] There are various spots, *ghats* (Pl. 3) and temples (Pl. 4) at and around Pehowa which are considered holy because of their association with great kings, sages, warriors, gods and the like and are regarded as *tīrthas*, pilgrimages. An account of these pilgrimages is given below in alphabetic order.

1. AGNI TĪRTHA

Agni *tīrtha* has been referred to in the *Mbh.*[3] and the *Padma Purāṇa.*[4] Cunningham has named it as *Agni-kund* where Agni performed penance. He also states that there were three different pools of this name.[5] Gajānana Śarmā refers to it in the west of Pṛithūdaka, the same as the well-known Devakhāta and Agni *tīrtha.*[6] He has also expressed the probability of the Agni *tīrtha* being located near the Brahma-yoni and Viśvāmitra-*tīrtha.*[7] The Vana Parva too indicates its location between the Kapāla-mochana and Viśvāmitra *tīrthas* and says that by taking a bath at Agni *tīrtha* one obtains the world of Agni and redeems the family.[8] In the Śalya Parva, however, we are told that being afraid of the curse of the sage Bhṛigu, Agni disappeared having reached the womb of a *śamī* tree. All the gods, along with Indra, felt much distressed and started searching him. Having approached the Agni *tīrtha* and seeing him in the *śamī* tree, the gods led by Bṛihaspati, felt very happy but had to return unsuccessful as Agni had become all consuming as a result of Bhṛigu's imprecation.[9]

Dandekar[10] thinks that the myth of the disappearance of Agni in a *śamī* tree has its origin in the *Ṛigveda.*[11]

2. APSARODYA TĪRTHA

King Purūravā, the grandson of Manu and son of Budha and Ilā, is mentioned in the *Ṛigveda*[12] and is generally believed to be a historical figure.[13]

He and his successors Āyu, Yayāti, Pūru, Saṁvaraṇa, Kuru, to mention only a few, were connected with the Sarasvatī and the region of Kurukshetra.[14] He is described in the *Mbh.* as having discovered his lost beloved, the famous *apsarā* Urvaśī in the lotus lake Anyataḥplaksha of Kurukshetra.[15] Cunningham observes that "As the original authority, however, only names the wide field of 'Kurukshetra', the pool of the Apsaras at Pṛithūdaka has the better claim to be identified with the place of Urvaśī's re-appearance".[16]

3. ĀRSHṬISHEṆA TĪRTHA

Ārshṭisheṇa was an excellent *dvija*, twice-born, and was engaged in studies while residing in the *gurukula*. Unable to finish his studies and the Vedas, he felt much grieved but exerted very hard and ultimately mastered the Vedas. Having been successful, the noble sage gave three boons at the *tīrtha*: (1) that any person who will have a dip in the great river at this *tīrtha* will obtain the abundant fruit of the performance of a horse-sacrifice, (2) that there will be no fear from the serpents here, and (3) that one would enjoy here abundant fruits even by only a little effort.[17]

Ārshṭisheṅa's austere penances have been referred to at various places in the *Mbh.*[18] He became a *rājarshi* by his penances.[19] King Jahnu's son Sindhudvīpa and king Pratīpa's eldest son and Śāntanu's elder brother Devāpi, [20] as also Viśvāmitra, attained *brahman*-hood in this very pilgrimage.[21] When Balarāma visited this *tīrtha* during his pilgrimage, [22] he made various gifts of cows, chariots, beds, clothes, ornaments, eatable, drinkables, etc. to the excellent *brāhmaṇas* after having worshipped them.[23] Cunningham does not give any details of this *tīrtha* nor does he mention its location.[24] Since Balarāma reached here from Pṛithūdaka *tīrtha* and went to the hermitage of the sage Dālbhya after visiting it, [26] it may have been located somewhere between these two.

4. ARUṆĀ-SAṄGAMA

This *tīrtha* is located at the junction of the Aruṇā[27] with the Sarasvatī, about 6 km to the north-east of Pehowa. A link road connects it with Pehowa-Ambala road. A new shrine called Saṁgameśvara Mahādeva, marks the old site of the *tīrtha*.[28] Gajānana Śarmā[29] equates it with Vasishṭhāpavāha *tīrtha* at Pṛithūdaka itself as it has been mentioned just after Madhusarva *tīrtha* in the *Padma Purāṇa*.[30] In the *Bṛihannāradīya Purāṇa* (henceforth *Bṛ. P.*) also it has been mentioned after Vasishṭha *tīrtha* which follows Madhusrava.[31] The *Vāmana Purāṇa* locates Vasishṭhodvāha at Madhusrava itself.[32] The sequence of description of the Madhusrava, Devī and Sarasvatī-

Aruṇā-Saṅgama in the Vana Parva, too, indicates that the confluence was to be visited after the Madhusrava.[33] This sequence, however, does not prove the existence of Aruṇā-Saṅgama at Pehowa itself. As noted earlier, Pṛithūdaka included a large number of *tīrthas* and extended over an area from the Aruṇā to (the hermitage of) Maṅkaṇaka sage (i.e., from village Aruṇāya to the village Mangna).[34] The name of the village Aruṇāya is the abbreviated form of '*Aruṇāyaḥ Saṅgamam*'. The village is located on a mound (Pl. 5) which yields PGW. It is thus as old as Pehowa. On the mound is a small shrine dedicated to the sage-Darvi[35] who is said to have brought all the four oceans to this *tīrtha*.[36] The Vana Parva, tells us that one who takes a bath here and lives here for three nights gets absolved of the sin of killing a *brāhmaṇa,* by taking a bath and living here for three nights, gets the merit of Agnishṭoma and Atirātra sacrifices and also delivers seven generations of his family.[37]

It is narrated in the *Vāmana Purāṇa* (henceforth *VP)* that being ordained by Viśvāmitra, the Sarasvatī brought Vasishṭha near him but when the former wanted to kill him, the stream took him away from Viśvāmitra. Enraged at this, Viśvāmitra cursed the Sarasvatī to carry blood, with demons on its banks. Later some sages came there and learnt all this. For the deliverance of the demons, they created the confluence (*saṅgama*) and purified the river. The demons went to heaven after taking a bath there.[38] Aruṇā-Saṅgama was visited by Balarāma during his *tīrtha-yātrā*.[39]

5. ĀŚVIN TĪRTHA

It is said that a devoted pilgrim gains beauty and fame by visiting Aśvin *tīrtha*.[40] It finds mention in the *Padma*[41] and *Bṛ. P.*[42] also. It may have been located between the Koṭi and Varāha *tīrthas.*

6. AUŚANASA TĪRTHA

Auśanasa on the bank of the Sarasvatī is an excellent and well-known *tīrtha* which extinguishes all sins and is regarded as *siddha-kshetra,* field of success or accomplishment.[43] It is dedicated to the planet Venus, Uśanas (also called Śukra), who performed penances on this spot to attain the planetary position.[44] It has been described as unique in the three worlds, त्रैलोक्यापि दुर्लभम्.[45] Those who visit it with devotion obtain highest positions and a person who performs funeral rites at this *tīrtha* is sure to deliver his forefathers.[46] By bathing here one gets delivered from all possible sins of life and goes to Brahma from where he does not come back again.[47]

The *Vāmana Purāṇa* narrates another anecdote of the austerities of Uśanas on the bank of the Aughavatī in the Kurukshetra region. While roaming about to ascertain the cause of the trembling of the earth, Śiva saw Uśanas penancing and asked him the reason of his severe austerities. Uśanas told the former that he was doing so to please him and know the auspicious *Sañjīvinī-vidyā*, knowledge of reanimation. Pleased by his penances, Śiva bestowed him the desired knowledge and Śukra ended his austerities.[48]

Auśanasa *tīrtha* finds mention in *Matsya*, [49] and *Bṛihannāradīya*[50] and *Bhāgavata*[51]*-Purāṇas* also. The Vana Parva and *Padma Purāṇa* (henceforth *PP*) describe it as famous in the three worlds and associate it with gods like Brahmā and sages and also with Kārttikeya.[52] It is also known as Kapāla-mochana as the sage Mahodara (variants Rahodara[53] and Harodara[54]) got emancipated here from a skull which stuck to his thigh. It was here that the war between the gods and demons was planned —

ततः औशनसं तीर्थमाजगाम हलायुधः ।
कपालमोचनं नाम यत्र मुक्तो महामुनिः ॥
महता शिरसा राजन्ग्रस्तजङ्घो महोदरः ।
राक्षसस्य महाराज रामक्षिप्तस्य वै पुरा ॥
तत्र पूर्वं तपस्तप्तं काव्येन सुमहात्मना ।
यत्रास्य नीतिरखिला प्रादुर्भूता महात्मनः ।
तत्रस्थश्चिन्तयामास दैत्यदानवविग्रहम् ॥[55]

Balarāma visited this excellent and the best *tīrtha* and formally gave wealth to the high-souled *brāhmaṇas*.[56] (See also Kapāla-mochana.)

7. AVAKĪRṆA TĪRTHA

The Vana Parva[57] and the *PP*[58] locate the Avakīrṇa *tīrtha* near the Sarasvatī-Aruṇā-Saṅgama and refer to it as the perpetuator of the Kuru family and built by Darbhi because of compassion for the *brāhmaṇas* —

अवकीर्णं च तत्रैव तीर्थं कुरुकुलोद्वहः ।
विप्राणामनुकम्पार्थं दर्भिणा निर्मितं पुरा ॥

We have already noted above that a shrine of Darbhi is located on the mound of Aruṇāya village. The Śalya Parva[59] and the *VP*[60] describe it after Pṛithūdaka *tīrtha* and narrate the myth connected with it. It was here that the sage Baka Dālbhya sacrificed the country of Dhṛitarāshṭra for the sake of an animal. After a twelve-year long sacrifice, the sages of the Naimisha forest approached the ruler of Pañchāla for *dakshiṇā*, sacrificial fee. He gave some animals for them. Leaving those to be divided amongst other sages Baka Dālbhya approached Dhṛitarāshṭra to beg animals (cows). He asked the sage to take away immediately some dead animals at which the latter got enraged and thought of destroying the king. Taking pieces of flesh of the dead animals, he sacrificed with them the country. Dhṛitarāshṭra's dominions suffered diminutions with that sacrifice and having known the cause of his decline, he went to Baka on the Sarasvatī and begged to be excused. Compassionate, the sage sacrificed again and restored his dominions. Having obtained numerous animals, the sage proceeded to the Naimisha forest and the king to his city.[61] The *VP* states that Dhṛitarāshṭra scattered jewels here to please the *brāhmaṇa* (Baka). Having been pleased, he restored the kingdom.[62]

It is said that a person who bathes at this *tīrtha* with devotion obtains the desired fruit —

> तस्मिंस्तीर्थे तु: यः स्नाति श्रद्दधानो जितेन्द्रियः ।
> स प्राप्नोति नरो नित्यं मनसा चिन्तितं फलम् ।।[63]

The *Bṛ. P.* says that one attains the fruit of celibacy by taking a bath at the Avakīrṇa *tīrtha*.[64]

Bṛihaspati, too, had sacrificed here with flesh for the destruction of the demons and the victory of the gods.[65] Balarāma gave horses, elephants, chariots with swift steeds, jewels, plenty of money and grains to the *brāhmaṇas* here.[66]

8. BHĀRGAVA TĪRTHA

This *tīrtha* marks the spot where the sage Bhṛigu performed *tapasyā*, penance.[67] It is located to the west of Pṛithūdaka where the river is curved.[68] A dip here destroys all sins.[69]

9. BRAHMA-YONI TĪRTHA (Pl. 6)

Brahma-yoni is said to have been created by Brahmā himself at Pehowa on the bank of the Sarasvatī. He contemplated here the creation of the four-fold world. The *Brāhmaṇas* were born from his mouth, the *Kshatriyas* from arms, the *Vaiśyas* from thighs and the *Śūdras* from his feet. Seeing the four *varṇas*, sitting in his hermitage, he established the Brahma-yoni *tīrtha* —

> तत्रैव ब्रह्मयोन्यस्ति ब्रह्मणा यत्र निर्मिता ।
> पृथूदकं समाश्रित्य सरस्वत्यास्तटे स्थितः ।।
> चातुर्वर्ण्यस्य सृषट्यर्थमात्मज्ञानपरोऽभवत् ।
> तस्याभिध्यायतः सृष्टिं ब्रह्मणोऽव्यक्तजन्मनः ।।
> मुखतो ब्राह्मणा जाता बाहुभ्यां क्षत्रियास्तथा ।
> ऊरुभ्यां वैश्यजातीयाः पद्भ्यां शूद्रास्ततोऽभवन् ।।

चातुर्वर्ण्यं ततो दृष्ट्वा आश्रमस्थं ततस्ततः ।
एवं प्रतिष्ठितं तीर्थं ब्रह्मयोनीति संज्ञितम् ।।[70]

The *RV* also tells us of the similar birth of the four *varṇas* from the respective limbs of the Brahma (Purusha).[71]

There is a Brahma-yoni-*tīrtha* at Kurukshetra also.[72] The existence of homonymous *tīrthas* at different places is, however, vouched by the *Purāṇas* themselves.[73] The Brahma-yoni at Pṛithūdaka is explicitly stated to have been established on the bank of the Sarasvatī[74] where also exists the Avakīrṇa *tīrtha*.[75]

According to the *Mbh.*[76] and the *PP*,[77] a person who takes bath at Brahma-yoni attains Brahma-loka and sanctifies seven generations. The *VP*[78] lays down that a person desiring deliverance does not see the womb again. Brahma-yoni brings forth all what is desired; it delivers those who remember it, see it or bathe in it and the sins disappear at the very sight of Brahma-yoni as the darkness disappears at sunrise.[79] There is no pilgrimage on this earth like the Brahma-yoni by bathing or taking water where one does not take a birth again.

ब्रह्मयोनि समं तीर्थं नास्ति ब्रह्माण्डलोके
तत्र स्नात्वा च पीत्वा च पुनर्जन्म न विद्यते ।।[80]

It has been mentioned in the *Garuḍa Purāṇa*[81] also.

10. BṚIHASPATI TĪRTHA

It is virtually a part of the Avakīrṇa *tīrtha*. It is known after Bṛihaspati, the *guru* of the gods, as he had performed a sacrifice with flesh here for the victory of the gods :[82]

तत्र तीर्थे महाराज बृहस्पतिरुदारधीः ।
असुराणामभावाय भावाय च दिवौकसाम् ।।
मांसैरपि जुहावेष्टिमक्षीयन्त ततोऽसुराः ।
देवतैरपि संभग्ना जितकाशिभिराहवे ।।

Cunningham describes it as a place 'where the regent of the planet Jupiter performed *tapasya*'.[83] There is, however, no such evidence in the *Mbh.* or the *Purāṇas*.

11. CHANDRA-SAMUDRA TĪRTHA

Chandra-Samudra or "Sea of the Moon" has been listed by Cunningham as one of the pilgrimages at Pṛithūdaka.[84] It has not been mentioned by this name but may be equated with Soma-*tīrtha* (described below) of the *Mbh.* and the *Purāṇas.*

12. CHATUḤ-SAMUDRA TĪRTHA

It may be located at or near the Aruṇā-Sarasvatī-Saṅgama where the sage Darvi is said to have brought the four seas —

समुद्रास्तत्र चत्वारो दर्विणा आहृताः पुरा ।
प्रत्येकं तु नरः स्नात्वा गोसहस्रफलं लभेत् ।।[85]

One gets the merit of (giving) one thousand cows by bathing here. Cunningham records that "There are four pools called respectively the first, second, third and fourth seas".[86] The *PP*[87] and the *Bṛ. P.*[88] also probably refer to these pools — समुद्रास्तत्र चत्वारस्तेषु स्नातो नरः. There is, however, no trace of these pools now.

13. DĀLBHYA TĪRTHA

It is the same as the Avakīrṇa where the sage Dālbhya had sacrificed to destroy Dhṛitarāshṭra and the latter had scattered jewels to please the former. A person who takes a holy dip here with devotion obtains the desired fruit—

तस्मिंस्तीर्थे तु यः स्नाति श्रद्दधानो जितेन्द्रियः ।
सः प्राप्नोति नरो नित्यं मनसा चिन्तितं फलम् ।।[89]

14. DEVĀPI TĪRTHA

Devāpi was the elder brother of Śāntanu. He suffered from some skin disease. When his father king Pratīpa wanted to anoint him, the *brāhmaṇas* and the subjects opposed his anointment whereupon he left the capital and reached Pṛithūdaka where he performed severe austerities and attained *brahman*-hood.[90] It is the same place where Sindhudvīpa and Viśvāmitra also attained similar positions. It is a part of the Auśanasa *tīrtha* described above.[91]

15. DEVĪ TĪRTHA

It has been referred to in the *PP*[92] as देव्यां तीर्थम्. Its exact location is not known but its description after the Madhusrava[93] indicates that it may have been not much distant from that *tīrtha.*

16. DUGDHASRAVA TĪRTHA

Dugdhasravas, or the "milk swelling" pools, in which milk is said to spring up,[94] is connected with the Yayāti *tīrtha*. Yayāti was the son of Nahusha for whom the Sarasvatī flowed with *ghī* and milk—

> यत्र यज्ञे ययातेस्तु महाराज सरस्वती ।
> सर्पिः पयश्च सुस्राव नाहुषस्य महात्मनः ।।[95]

The seeds of the myth can be traced back to the *Ṛigveda* which also refers to this fact.[96]

17. DUSRA-SAMUDRA TĪRTHA

The "Second Sea"[97] was perhaps a part of the Chatuḥ-Samudra described above.

18. GHṚITASRAVA TĪRTHA

The 'ghee-welling' pool, in which *ghee*, or clarified butter, is said to spring up, too, seems to have been a part of the Yayāti *tīrtha*. Cunningham observes that it is one of the holiest places at Pehowa.[98]

19. KAPĀLA-MOCHANA TĪRTHA

Kapāla-mochana, as noted above while describing the Auśanasa *tīrtha*, is another name of the latter. While residing in the Daṇḍaka forest, Rāma killed many demons. The head of one of them fell in the great forest and stuck to the thigh of the sage Mahodara roaming about in that forest. The sage thus could not go to various *tīrthas* and shrines. Being afflicted by excessive pain and with pus oozing, the sage visited all the pilgrimages on earth. Everywhere he went, he narrated to the sages all that had happened to him. Having bathed in all the *tīrthas* he did not get emancipated. He, however, heard from some sages about the famous and excellent Auśanasa *tīrtha* on the Sarasvatī which, being located in sanctified area, mitigated all sins. At the very touch of water in the Auśanasa *tīrtha*, the skull fell down in water and the sage came back to his hermitage diseaseless and pleased, and narrated the whole event to the sages there. Having heard him, they all came to that *tīrtha* and named it as Kapāla-mochana.[99]

Kapāla-mochana has been mentioned in the *Brahma*,[100] *Garuḍa*,[101] *PP*.[102] and *Bṛ. P*.[103] also.

Cunningham says that Śiva was liberated from the sin of cutting off the four heads of Brahmā by bathing in this pool, and hence the name *"Kapali" Mochan*, or the 'Head-liberator'.[104] This myth is found in the *Skanda*

Purāṇa[105] and does not occur in the description and christening of the Auśanasa *tīrtha* in the *Mbh.*, the *Vāmana* and other *Purāṇas* as noted above. Cunningham has also described this *tīrtha* and equated it with a homonymous *tīrtha* located about 16 km south-east of Sadhaura on the Sarasvatī.[106] The *Mbh.* and the *VP*, however, explicitly state that it was the Auśanasa *tīrtha* of Pṛithūdaka which was named Kapāla-mochana. So it cannot be identified with Kapāla-mochana near Sadhaura. We have already observed that *tīrthas* of same names existed at different places. The Kapāla-mochana of Pṛithūdaka has been identified with a *tīrtha* of this name at village Sitaura, about 4 km west of Pehowa.[107]

Kapāla-mochana *tīrtha* is said to be the emancipator of all sins and one gets free of all the sins by taking a bath here —

> कपालमोचनं तीर्थं सर्वपापप्रमोचनम् ।
> तत्र स्नात्वा नरव्याघ्र सर्वपापैः प्रमुच्यते ।।[108]

A man gets rid of even the sin of the murder of a *brāhmaṇa* by taking a dip here.[109] Those who worship this excellent *tīrtha* attain the highest position and the one who performs a *śrāddha* with faith in this *tīrtha,* doubtlessly liberates all his forefathers.[110] A person who worships this holy place on the fifth day of the fortnight becomes affluent पञ्चमम्यां सेवमानस्तु लक्ष्मीवांश्च भवेन्नरः।[111] A man gets rid of all the possible sins of life here and attains salvation.[110] It was visited by Balarāma who gave wealth to the distinguished *brāhmaṇas* here.[113]

20. KĀRŪPĀVANA (KṚIPĀVANA) TĪRTHA

Cunningham has recorded that "This place received its name from Aswathâma, the son of Drona and Kripi, who was also called Kârpâvan after his mother Kripi, the daughter of the nymph Urvasi".[114] Pt. Gajānana Śarmā, however, names it as Kārūpāvana and identified it with Maṁḍhala on the northern end of the Chharauḍa *tālāba* to the east of Pṛithūdaka. Sage Māṇḍavya had set up this *tīrtha* to purify the ploughmen indulging in violence, as also the *brāhmaṇas*.[115] He quotes from the *Brahma Purāṇa* also—

> कारूपावने महापुण्ये पवित्रे चाति निर्मले ।
> तत्रोन्मज्य चित्रकेतुः स वै करमवाप ह ।।[116]

that by bathing in the clear and highly meritorious Kārūpāvana, Chitraketu obtained his (lost) hand.[117]

The healing quality of the *tīrtha* is still believed in and many lepers come to bathe here every year and many of them are even claimed to have been cured.[118]

This *tīrtha* is known as *Brahma tīrtha*[119] also. Now it has four *ghats* and Mahāvīra temple built by the Bairagi *sādhus*.[120]

21. KOṬI TĪRTHA

The *Mbh.* refers to Koṭi *tīrthas* at different places in the Vana Parva[121] but it is the *VP* which tells us of its location on the bank of the Sarasvatī where the twice-born people from Naimisha, Magadha, Sindhu, Pushkara, Daṇḍakāraṇya, Champā, Bhṛigukachchha and those living on the banks of the Devikā[122] came to see Śaṅkara. Assembled in legions, each one said that he will see the god first. Seeing those agitated seers, Śiva showed himself in a crore forms and each saint worshipped him separately. Śiva, thus, became Rudrakoṭi—

ततो भूयः सरस्वत्यास्तीर्थे त्रैलोक्यविश्रुते। कोटितीर्थे रुद्रकोटिं ददर्श वृषभध्वजम् ।
नैमिषेया द्विजवरा मागधेयाः ससैन्धवाः। धर्मारण्याः पौष्करेया दण्डकारण्यकास्तथा ।।
चाम्येया भारुकच्छेया देविकातीरगाश्चये। तत्र ते शंकरं द्रष्टुं समायाताः द्विजातयः ।
कोटिसंख्यातस्तपः सिद्‌ध हरदर्शनलालसाः । अहं पूर्वमहं पूर्वमित्येवं वादिनो मुने ।।
तान् क्षुब्धान् हरो दृष्ट्वा महर्षीन् दग्धकिल्बिषान् ।
तेषामेवानुकम्पार्थं कोटिमूर्तिरभूद् भवः ।।
ततस्ते मुनयः प्रीताः सर्व एव महेश्वरम् ।
संपूजयन्तस्ततस्तस्थुर्वै तीर्थं कृत्वा पृथक् पृथक् ।
इत्येवं रुद्रकोटीति नाम्ना शंभुरजायत ।।[123]

The *Mbh.* also mentions Rudrakoṭi giving almost similar details.[124] It finds mention in the *Brahma,*[125] *Bṛihannāradīya*[126] and *PP* also. The *Bṛihannāradīya,* however, tells us that Śiva had established one crore *tīrthas* here. It is further said that a person who sees the Koṭīśvara-Śiva after bathing in the *tīrtha* here always obtains the merit of five sacrifices. It was here that the gods had installed (an image of) the god Vāmana.[127] The *Mbh.* lays down that a person obtains the merit of a horse-sacrifice and emancipates his family by taking a dip here—

तत्र स्नात्वा नरव्याघ्र रुद्रकोट्यां नरः शुचिः ।
अश्ववमेधमवाप्नोति कुलं चैव समुद्धरेत् ।।[128]

This *tīrtha* was visited by Prahlāda during his *tīrtha-yātrā* where he presented libations to his forefathers and Vasus and from where he proceeded to Kuru-jāṅgala.[129]

22. KUBERA TĪRTHA

The *Mbh.* tells us that Balarāma visited Kubera *tīrtha* after Brahma-yoni. Here Kubera performed penance and obtained abundant boons, the lordship of riches and treasures, friendship with Rudra, divinity, guardianship of the (northern) quarter and two sons named Nala and Kūbara —

ददृशे तत्र तत्स्थानं कौबेरे काननोत्तमे ।
पुरा यत्र तपस्तप्तं विपुलं सुमहात्मना ।।
यत्र राज्ञा कुबेरेण वरा लब्धाश्च पुष्कलाः ।
धनाधिपत्यं सख्यं च रुद्रेणामिततेजसा ।।
सुरत्वं लोकपालत्वं पुत्रं च नलकूबरम् ।
यत्र लेभे महाबाहो धनाधिपतिरञ्जसा ।।[130]

Kubera was anointed here by the Marud-gaṇas and was provided with a vehicle having a beautiful goose, the celestial Pushpaka-vimāna, and divine faculties.[131] From here, Balarāma proceeded to the Badara-pāchana *tīrtha*.[132]

23. MADHUSRAVA TĪRTHA

Madhusrava or the 'honey-welling pool' is a part of the Yayāti *tīrtha* and marks the spot where the Sarasvatī flowed with honey for Yayāti—

मधुश्रवं च तत्रैव तीर्थं पुण्यतमं द्विजाः ।
ययातेर्यजमानस्य मधु सुस्राव वै नदी ।।[133]

One should give the libations of honey for the forefathers here.[134] One who bathes here gets the merit of one thousand cows.[135]

Ghṛitasrava and Dugdhasrava are two of its adjoining *tīrthas*.[136] The mention of the Sarasvatī flowing with *ghee* and milk for Yayāti as described in the *RV*[137] takes back the antiquity of this *tīrtha* to the Vedic period.

It is said that the illustrious sage Kapila also performed austerities here, for which reason it is known as Kapila *tīrtha* also.[138]

Madhusrava is one of the most popular holy places of Pehowa. When Cunningham visited Pehowa during 1878-79, he found it to be a stagnant pool with horrible stench rising from it in the hot weather. His observation recorded below indicates the horrible condition of this pilgrimage and the greed of the *brāhmaṇa* priests. He tells us that "In 1876 a petty Raja was on his way to bathe in this holiest of the pools at Pṛithūdakah; unfortunately the pool was quite dry that year, but the officiating Brahmans, not wishing to lose the anticipated present from the Raja, began to fill the hollow with water drawn from a neighbouring well by a *Charsa*, or 'leather bag'; but the Raja hearing of the trick of substituting common well water contaminated by leather for the holy water of the Sarasvatī pool, turned back indignantly and returned to his home, leaving the disappointed Brahmans to be punished by the laughter of the people".[139] When Rodgers visited it in 1888-89, he found that "It is an ordinary pond in a yard surrounded by ruined houses". He observed further that "This pond had a goodly quantity of town sweepings thrown into it. The water was almost *nil* and what was there was covered with thick green slime".

24. MAṄKAṆAKA ĀŚRAMA

Maṅkaṇaka was born of Sukanyā from the god Vāyu.[140] The hermitage of this sage, endowed with supernatural faculties, was located in the Sapta-Sārasvata *tīrtha* —

> सप्तसारस्वतं तीर्थं ततो गच्छेन्नराधिपः ।
> यत्र मङ्कणकः सिद्धो महर्षिर्लोकविश्रुतः ।।[141]

The myth of Maṅkaṇaka's perfection is narrated twice in the *Mbh.*[142] Once on seeing a sky-clad beautiful woman taking bath, Maṅkaṇaka's semen fell in the Sarasvatī. He collected the semen in a vase wherein it got divided into seven parts from which were born seven sages namely Vāyu-vega, Vāyu-bala, Vāyu-hā, Vāyu-maṇḍala, Vāyu-jvāla, Vāyu-retā and Vāyu-chakra. These sons of Maṅkaṇaka sustain the animate and inanimate world.[143]

Once, when Maṅkaṇaka accidentally cut his finger with the blade of a *Kuśa* grass and plant juice (on which he subsisted) flowed from his wound, he began dancing with boundless joy. Overwhelmed by the powerful skill of his dance, all the creatures and plants began to dance. The gods, however, went to Mahādeva requesting him to stop the dancing sage. Śiva then appeared before the seer and asked him the reason of his ecstatic dance. Maṅkaṇaka showed him the plant juice flowing from his wound and told him that it was the reason for his joy and dancing. Śiva struck his thumb with one of his fingers and snow-white ashes started falling from his wound. The seer fell at the feet of Śiva and worshipped him as the creator and ordainer of the universe. Pleased with Maṅkaṇaka, Śiva gave him the boon that he will be ever present in his hermitage.[144]

Stella Kramrisch has given a philosophic interpretation of this legend. She observes —

> The *sidha ṛṣi* Maṅkaṇaka had absorbed into himself the nourishing juices of the plants of this earth or the Soma juice itself, and the juices retained their purity within the body of the *siddha*. When Maṅkaṇaka saw the plant juice flowing from his body, he felt freed from the bondage of blood. The flow of ashes, however, from the body of the Great God showed a higher degree of rarefication

> than the ṛṣi had achieved, by the transformation of his blood into plant juice. Śiva had absorbed the world into his own self at the time of dissolution.... He showed himself as Kāla and the actuator of Kāla, the fire that burns the world and all its sins.... The elements or sense objects, the senses, mind and its fabric are burned up, one in the other, in the ultimate conflagration that has its symbol in ashes and its Kālāgni-Rudra image in the dance of Śiva when Maṅkaṇaka trembled and bowed his head before the Lord.... He enlightened the sage, allowing him to see beyond the elation of the senses and the mind, when Śiva, the Fire, will dance the cosmos out of existence and nothing will remain but Śiva alone.[145]

The hermitage of Maṅkaṇaka was located in the village Mangna, which name can philologically also be derived from the name of the seer, situated on the southern bank of the Sarasvatī, nearly 10 km north–north-west of Pehowa.[146]

25. MANAS TĪRTHA

Equated with Brahma,[147] Manu[148] and Kārūpāvana[149] *tīrthas*, Manas has been located by Rāmachandra Sarasvatī to the west of the hermitage of Uttaṅka near the Brahma-yoni.[150]

26. MANOJAVA TĪRTHA

It is described in the *Mbh.*,[151] *PP*[152] and the *Bṛ. P.*[153] By taking a bath here, one gets the merit of (the donation of) one thousand cows. It is also identified with the preceding *tīrtha*.[154]

27. MANU TĪRTHA

It has been mentioned in the *Bhāgavata*[155] along with some other *tīrthas* of Pṛithūdaka —

> तस्यां त्रितस्योशनसो मनोश्च पृथोरग्नेरसितस्य वायोः ।
> तीर्थं सुदासस्य गवां गुहस्य यच्छ्राध्ददेवस्य स आसिषेवे ।।

As indicated above it has been identified with Brahma, Manas and Kārūpāvana and located near the Brahma-yoni. Manu is said to have performed sacrifices here.

28. MĀNUSHA TĪRTHA

It is a *tīrtha* in the pool of which the black antelopes turned into human beings, having fallen there injured by a hunter —

> ततो गच्छेत राजेन्द्र मानुषं लोकविश्रुतम् ।

यत्र कृष्णमृगा राजन्व्याधेन परिपीडिताः ।
अवगाह्य तस्मिन्सरसि मानुषत्वमुपागताः ।।[156]

Being told of the importance of this *tīrtha*, the hunters also bathed there and being purified went to heaven.[157] A celibate who has control over his senses also gets purified of all the sins and goes to heaven by taking a bath in this *tīrtha*.[158] A person gets rid of his sins at the very sight of this pilgrimage.[159] Even those who hear with devotion the importance of this *tīrtha* achieve the highest position.[160]

Mānusha-*tīrtha* finds mention in the *Bṛ. P* also.[161] Its exact location has not been mentioned anywhere but it is stated that the river Āpagā flowed one *krośa* (*kos*) east of it.[162] *Pacca ghat* buried under the earth is pointed out to be the spot marking this *tīrtha* at Pehowa.[163]

29. OJASA TĪRTHA

Kārttikeya was anointed as the generalissimo of the forces of the gods at Pṛithūdaka —

पृथूदकमिति ख्यातं कार्त्तिकेयस्य वै नृप ।
तत्राभिषेकं कुर्वीत पितृदेवार्चने रतः ।।[164]

The *VP* names the exact spot as Ojasa and says that one attains Kumārapura by bathing and performing a *śrāddha* there —

कुमारस्याभिषेकं च ओजसं नाम विश्रुतम् ।।
तस्मिन्स्नातस्तु पुरुषो यशसा च समन्वितः ।
कुमारपुरमाप्नोति कृत्वा श्राद्धं तु मानवः ।।[165]

A *śrāddha* performed here on the sixth day of the bright fortnight of Chaitra is as meritorious as the one performed at Gayā or at Saṁnihata during an eclipse. A *śrāddha* performed at Ojasa is undecaying, so one should perform the *śrāddha* there.[166] The forefathers of a person who bathes there with devotion on the sixth of Chaitra remain satisfied for ever.[167]

30. OSHṬISHEṆA TĪRTHA

Cunningham has mentioned this *tīrtha* without giving any details.[168] Nothing is known about it now.

31. PĀPĀNTAKA TĪRTHA (Pl. 7)

Pāpāntaka Tīrtha is located behind the Mahādeva Temple, a little ahead of Avakīrṇa and Bṛihaspati *tīrthas*, where there is a Pīpala tree (known as the Preta-Pīpala) on the Sarasvatī-*ghat*.[169] It is connected with both Śiva and Kārttikeya. The latter was sent here by Vishṇu to undo the sin of killing Krauñcha (a cousin of Kārttikeya).[170]

One gets rid of one's sins and obtains the merit of a horse-sacrifice by taking a dip here.

Cunningham observes that "In this pool the Ganges is said to have bathed to cleanse herself from the load of sin which she had accumulated from the numerous bathers in her own waters. It is one of the holiest places at Pehowa".[171]

32. PRĀCHĪ-SARASVATĪ

Prāchī-Sarasvatī, literally meaning 'Eastern Sarasvatī', has been mentioned in the *Br. P.*[172] *GP*[173] and the *Bh. P.*[174] It was here at Prāchī-Sarasvatī in the Brahmāvarta, the land of Manu, that Pṛithu was anointed with hundred horse-sacrifices.[175] *VP* also refers to it and states that those who perform a *tri-rātra* (three nights) get rid of their misdeeds.[176] Gods including Nara-Nārāyaṇa, Brahmā, Śiva, Sūrya, Indra, etc. always inhabit it and nothing is difficult to be attained in this and the other world by those who perform *śrāddha* here. A person who resorts to Prāchī on the fifth gets affluent.[177] One who is a matricide, patricide or has killed a *brāhmaṇa* or had illicit relations with his teacher's wife also gets purified by taking a bath in the Prāchī-Sarasvatī.[178] It is, however, the *Skanda Purāṇa*[179] which gives a detailed account of the importance of Prāchī-Sarasvatī. Even the deer (or animals) who drink its waters go to heaven like the twice-born who perform sacrifices.[180] Just like a *Chintā-maṇi* (anxiety-allaying jewel) it accomplishes all the desires of men.[181] Like a *Kāma-dhuk* cow which can be milched at will and gives all what is desired, Prāchi-Sarasvatī also provides heaven and salvation.[182] Eighty-eight thousand ascetics had renounced the world here and there is nothing which exceeds Prāchī.[183] It was here that the sage Maṅkaṇaka obtained supernatural faculties and Śiva got rid of Brahma-*hatyā*, the sin of killing Brahmā.[184] When, after the Bhārata war, Arjuna asked Kṛishṇa as to how he could get purified from his sins of killing his relatives and others, he was exhorted to go to the Prāchī-Sarasvatī as the killers of the *Brāhmaṇas*, the drinkers of wine and other sinners get rid of their sins by bathing in the Prāchī-Sarasvatī and the one who resides there for three nights observing fast and bathing thrice, gets emancipated from all one's accumulated sins —

> ब्रह्महाश्च सुरापाश्च ये चान्ये पापकारिणः ।
> तत्र स्नात्वा विमुच्यन्ते यत्र प्राची सरस्वती ।।[185]

The merits of giving donations and performing *śrāddhas* have been referred to at length.[186] The ashes of the dead were also consigned to water in this *tīrtha* as is indicated by a story narrated in the *Bhāgavata Purāṇa*. It is said that Chitraratha, lord of the *gandharvas*, accompanied by many females was once going by his aerial chariot in this area where a *brāhmaṇa* of the Kauśika *gotra* had died earlier. Suddenly he fell down with his chariot and was surprised but was told by the Vālakhilya sages that the reason thereof was that he was crossing over the bones of a *brāhmaṇa*. Chitraratha deposited the bones in the Sarasvatī and then proceeded towards his destination —

> तस्योपरि विमानेन गन्धर्वपतिरेकदा ।
> ययौ चित्ररथः स्त्रीभिर्वृतो यत्र द्विजक्षयः ।।
> गगनान्न्यपतत्सद्यः सविमानो ह्यवाक्शिराः ।
> स वालखिल्यवचनादस्थीन्यादाय विस्मितः ।
> प्रास्य प्राचीसरस्वत्यां स्नात्वा धाम स्वमन्वगात् ।।[187]

The *brāhmaṇa* of this anecdote is said to have lost his life in the 'maru-dhanvan.' The *PP* refers to Prāchī-Sarasvatī in the Pushkara forest.[188] Prāchī-Sarasvatī is described to exist at Patan in Gujarat also.[189] Raychaudhari thought that the very adjective Prāchī presupposes an old Sarasvatī bed to its west.[190] Bharadwaj also thinks that probably a large scale tectonic-seismic-volcanic upheaval led to the disappearance of the Sarasvatī whereafter "the name Sarasvatī was appropriated by the insignificant stream flowing by its side as the name Prāci-Sarasvatī shows".[191] The Pehowa inscription of Bhoja tells us that Bhūvaka had built the Yajñavarāha temple at Pṛithūdaka near the Prāchī-Sarasvatī — पृथूदके प्राचीसरस्वती [सन्निभौ] भूवककारितयज्ञवराय....[192] The description of Prāchi-Sarasvatī as a *tīrtha* in the *Bhāgavata, Skanda* and *Bṛ. P.*[193] indicates that there existed at Pṛithūdaka a particular spot also which was regarded as holy and was known by the name of the stream Prāchī Sarasvatī. In all probability it is the same as Vasishṭha-Prāchī, located near the Sarasvatī distributary where the old bed of the river may still be seen to take an eastward turn. The spot is marked by the existence of the extant Prāchī Śiva temple (Pl. 8).

33. PṚITHŪDAKA TĪRTHA

We have already noted the tradition recorded by Cunningham that Pṛithūdaka marks the spot where Pṛithu is said to have performed the obsequies of his father Vena and offered water to all comers for twelve days.[194] Śrīdharasvāmi (*c.* A.D. 1400) who wrote a commentary on the

Bhāgavata says that it is the place where Pṛithu had performed one hundred horse-sacrifices— पृथूदकं पृथुनाश्वमेधशतेन यत्रेष्टं तत्कुरुक्षेत्रवर्ति.[195] Situated in the Kurukshetra region, it is regarded equal to it in merit[196] and even more in importance.[197] The sage Rushaṅgu, thinking his end to be imminent, came here and exhorted his sons that whosever would die at Pṛithūdaka while uttering his prayers would not be afflicted by death again.[198] Balarāma visited it, bathed here and gave many gifts to the *brāhmaṇas*. It was here that Brahmā created the whole world. Again it was here that Ārshṭisheṇa, Sindhudvīpa, Devāpi and Viśvāmitra attained *brāhman*-hood.[199] It was here that Kārttikeya was anointed.[200] Its importance has been sung by Sanatkumāra and Vyāsa.[201] Situated on the Sarasvatī, Pṛithūdaka removes all sins and is auspicious.[202] It is the only place in Kurukshetra which is the permanent abode of Śiva.[203] It was visited by various gods, kings and sages. Kārttikeya was directed by Vishṇu to visit the excellent *tīrtha* Pṛithūdaka to get emancipated from the sin of sending away (killing) his cousin.[204] A number of sages performed penances and sacrifices and set up their hermitages near it. It is regarded as an excellent *tīrtha* for performing *śrāddha* and giving donations. Those who seek supernatural faculties and salvation also visit it. It is considered to be the best of the *tīrthas*.

34. PṚITHVĪŚVARA TĪRTHA

The present Pṛithvīśvara Mahādeva Temple on the southern bank of the Sarasvatī (at the back of the Pāpāntaka *tīrtha*) represents the spot where Pṛithu established a *liṅga* which is known after him as Pṛithvīśvara.[205] An image of Sūrya and other carved figures and architectural pieces found during the restoration and renovations of the temple indicate that a beautiful fane existed here during the ninth century A.D. It may have been destroyed by Mahmud Ghaznavi in the eleventh century A.D. but subsequently, it was destroyed again by Nadir Shah Abdali and was rebuilt by the Marathas under Sadashiv Rao Bhau in the Mughal style with a dome during the later half of the eighteenth century A.D. During a recent renovation in 1957 relics of as many as sixteen octagonal pillars were seen in the *mahā-maṇḍapa* and many sculptural pieces were also recovered. The renovation was done mainly with the financial help of the Marwari community of Amritsar. Brahmachari Chidanand Swarup got the marble floor laid by selling all his property and Pt. Parmatma Lal Murar got constructed the porch in front of the temple.

Maharaja Ranjit Singh is also said to have got four rooms constructed here for the pilgrims. The well-known Arya Samajist Swami Shraddhanand stayed in this temple for many days. It is now being looked after by Mahanta Banshi Puri.[206]

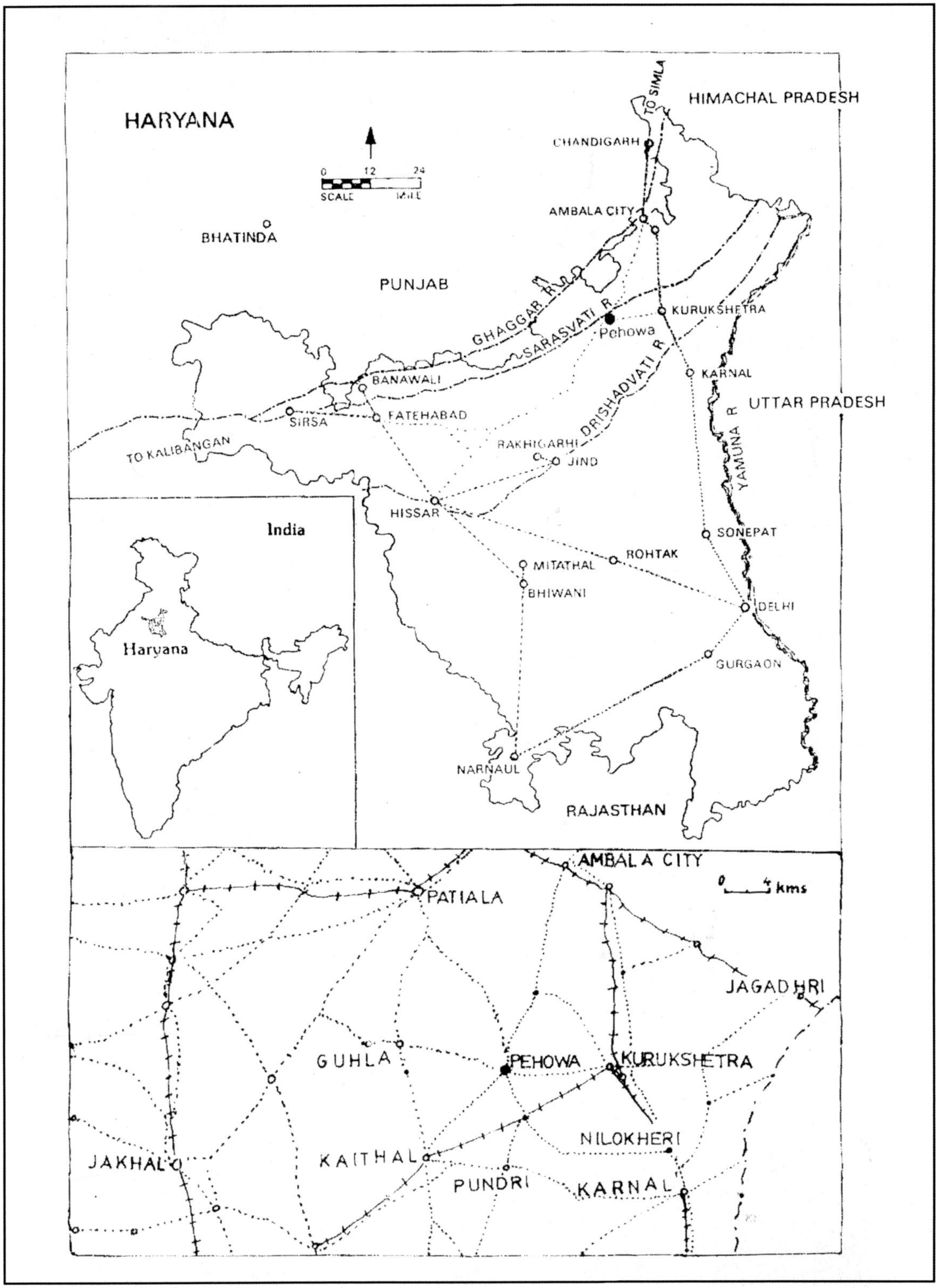

Pl. 1. Map showing the location and road links of Pehowa

Pl. 2. Pehowa on the bank of the Sarasvatī

Pl. 3. Sacred *ghats* on the bank of the Sarasvatī

Pl. 4. Temples on the bank of the Sarasvatī

Pl. 5. Village Aruṇāya, located on an ancient mound

Pl. 6. Brahma-yoni *Tīrtha*

Pl. 7. Pāpāntaka *Tīrtha* with Preta Pīpala

Pl. 8. Prāchī Sarasvatī with Prāchī Śiva Temple

Pl. 9. Viśvāmitra kā Ṭīlā

Pl. 10. Gurudwara Bauli Sahib

Pl. 12. Paśupatinātha (Śravaṇanātha) Temple

Pl. 11. Kāla-Bhairava Temple (Bhaironjī kā Mandira)

Pl. 13. Siddhagir kī Samādhi

Pl. 14. Royal Personage

Pl. 15. Male Figure ,

The Śiva *liṅga* in this temple is regarded as divine.[207]

35. RĀMA TĪRTHA

Rāma *tīrtha* is that holy spot where Paraśurāma performed one hundred Vājapeya and Aśvamedha sacrifices with sage Kaśyapa as his religious preceptor, after killing all the best Kshatriyas and gave the whole earth together with the oceans as sacrificial fee to the *brāhmaṇas* —

शुभं तीर्थवरं तस्माद्रामतीर्थं जगाम ह ।
यत्र रामो महाभागो भार्गवः सुमहातपाः ।।
असकृत्पृथिवीं सर्वां हतक्षत्रियपुगंवाम् ।
उपाध्यायं पुरस्कृत्य कश्यपं मुनिसत्तमम् ।।
अजयद् वाजपेयेन सोऽश्वमेधशतेन च ।
प्रददौ दक्षिणार्थं च पृथिवीं वै ससागराम् ।।[208]

It was visited by Balarāma who also made munificences to the *brāhmaṇas* and after taking leave of the seers proceeded to the Yamunā *tīrtha*.[209] Rāma *tīrtha* is said to be greatly meritorious and destroyer of all sins, by taking a bath where one gets purified even from the sin of *brahma-hatyā*, killing of a *brāhmaṇa*

रामतीर्थं महापुण्यं सर्वकल्मषनाशनम् ।
ब्रह्महत्यादिपापेभ्यस्तत्रस्नाद्विशुध्यति ।।[210]

It is known as Rāma-Prāchī[211] also and is identified with the *ghat* to the north of the turn (end) of Jayagiri's *ghat* up to the Ṭhākurdvārā of Jambu Mahārāja.[212] Rāma *tīrtha* finds mention in *GP*[213] also.

36. RUSHAṄGU'Ṣ ĀŚRAMA

The hermitage of the sage Rushaṅgu was located at the same spot where Ārshṭisheṇa had performed severe austerities and Viśvāmitra had attained *brahman*-hood.[214] When the old pious sage Rushaṅgu realized that his end was near, he asked his sons to take him to Pṛithūdaka. Knowing his imminent death, they took him to that *tīrtha* on the Sarasvatī. Having known the qualities of the *tīrtha* and taken bath, as ordained, he told his sons that a person who leaves his body on the northern bank of the Sarasvatī at Pṛithūdaka while muttering prayers is never afflicted by death in future —

रुषङ्गुर्ब्राह्मणो वृद्धस्तपोनित्यश्च भारत ।
देहन्यासे कृतमना विचिन्त्य बहुधा बहु ।।

ततः सर्वानुपादाय तनयान्वै महातपाः ।
रुषङ्गुरब्रवीत्तत्र नयध्वं मां पृथूदकम् ।।

स तत्र दि[illegible]ना राजन्नाप्लुतः सुमहातपाः ।
ज्ञात्वा तीर्थगुणांश्चैव प्राहेहमृषिसत्तमः ।।

सरस्वत्युत्तरे तीरे यस्त्यजेदात्मनस्तनुम् ।
पृथूदके जप्यपरो नैनं श्वोमरणं तपेत् ।।[215]

The *tīrtha* figures on Balarāma's pilgrimage also where he had bathed and given gifts to the *brāhmaṇas*.[216]

37. SAPTA-SĀRASVATA TĪRTHA

Sapta-Sārasvata is an eminent *tīrtha* of the three worlds where seven streams of the Sarasvatī, viz. Suprabhā, Kāñchanākshī, Mānasa-hradā, Sarasvatī, Oghavatī, Suveṇu, and Vimalodakā flow unitedly —

सप्तसारस्वतं तीर्थं त्रैलोक्यस्यापि दुर्लभम् ।
यत्र सप्तसरस्वत्य एकीभूता वहन्ति च ।।

सुप्रभाकाञ्चनाक्षी च विशाला मानसह्रदा ।
सरस्वत्योघनामा च सुवेणुर्विमलोदका ।।[217]

These seven rivers are described in the *Mbh.* to have been related to Pushkara, Naimisha, Gayā, Uttara Kosala, Gaṅgā-dvāra and Kurukshetra.[218] The fact that the Sarasvatī flowed in seven streams near Pṛithūdaka provided a basis to the concept that it represented different sacred rivers of India, suggesting indirectly first and clearly later that a visit to this *tīrtha* served the purpose of visiting all the places related to those rivers. The *brāhmaṇa* priests, in this way, could attract people from all areas and perhaps could also discourage people of the Kurukshetra and contiguous regions to go to the far off *tīrthas*. Exaggerated account of the sanctity of the Sapta-Sārasvata *tīrtha* also points in this direction.

It is the same *tīrtha* where Maṅkaṇaka obtained supernatural powers —

सप्तसारस्वतं तीर्थं ततो गच्छेन्नराधिप ।
यत्र मङ्कणकः सिद्धो महर्षिर्लोकविश्रुतः ।।[219]

It was here that the gods sent a beautiful nymph (Rambhā or Vapu) to impede Maṅkaṇaka's austerities. Seeing the nymph, the sage could not control himself and his semen fell in the river which when collected in a pot, got divided into seven parts resulting in the birth of seven Marudgaṇas.[220] It was in the Sapta-Śārasvata *tīrtha* that Śiva promised to live with

Maṅkaṇaka in his hermitage permanently and said that a person who will worship him after taking a bath there would attain everything in this and the other world.[221] This *tīrtha* was served by the gods like Brahmā.[222] It finds mention in the *GP* also.[223] As Maṅkaṇaka's hermitage was located at the village Mangna (as detailed above), Sapta-Sārasvata too has to be located there. It is probably one of the oldest *tīrthas* as the Sarasvatī is described as 'Sapta-dhātu' and 'Sapta-thī' in the *RV* also.[224]

38. SARASVATĪ KŪPA

It may have been a well from which the water of the Sarasvatī gushed forth. In the story of Trita, we find the Sarasvatī saving the sage who had fallen in a well by its gushing water.[225] After the desiccation of the river, people may have started believing that the waters of the Sarasvatī appear in the wells and the greedy priests may have woven myths to attract pilgrims. The *VP* describes Sarasvatī-Kūpa as famous in the three worlds by the very sight of which one gets rid of all one's sins and attains salvation—

तत्रापि च सरस्वत्यः कूपं त्रैलोक्यविश्रुतम् ।
दर्शनान्मुक्तिमवाप्नोति सर्वपातकवर्जितः ।।[226]

It was regarded as an important Pitṛi-*tīrtha* where one could obtain undecaying riches by propitiating the gods and the forefathers.[227] *Br. P.* (II.65, 119) also refers to it and gives its second name as Pitṛi-*tīrtha.*

39. ŚATASĀHASRAKA AND SĀHASRAKA TĪRTHAS

The *Mbh.*[228] and the *PP*[229] describe these two *tīrthas*, located on the same place, as famous ones, by bathing where a person obtains the merit of a hundred cows and where the fasts and charities also multiply thousand times —

ततो गच्छेत राजेन्द्र तीर्थं शतसाहस्रकम् ।
साहस्रकं च तत्रैव द्वे तीर्थे लोकविश्रुते ।।
उभयोर्हि नरः स्नात्वा गोसहस्रफलं लभेत् ।
दानं वाप्युपवासो वा सहस्रगुणितं भवेत् ।।

The *VP* names them as Śatasāhasrika and Śatika.[230] These *tīrthas* are located at Sainsa village, nearly 6 km north-east of Pehowa.[231]

40. SINDHUDVĪPA TĪRTHA

Literally meaning the "Sindhu's isle", this name seems to have been given to the place where the sage of this name performed penances at Pehowa.[232] As noted above it is identical with the Auśanasa and Kapāla-mochana *tīrtha.*

41. SOMA TĪRTHA

There were many *tīrthas* of this name in Kurukshetra, one was located near Jayantī (Jind)[233] and another between Ādityāśrama and Dadhīchi *tīrtha* on the Sarasvatī —

> सोमतीर्थे नरः स्नात्वा तीर्थसेवी कुरूद्वह ।
> सोमलोकमवाप्नोति नरो नास्त्यत्र संशयः ।।[234]

The *Mbh.* also refers to a *tīrtha* of this name immediately before Sapta-Sārasvata.[235] The *VP* also describes this Soma-*tīrtha* and tells us that Soma obtained *dvirājya* by penancing here —

> ततो गच्छेत सोमस्य तीर्थं त्रैलोक्यदुर्लभम् ।
> यत्र सोमस्तपस्तप्त्वा द्विराज्यमवाप्नुयात् ।।

Another Soma *tīrtha* has been described after Varāha *tīrtha* where Soma got rid of his malady by performing *tapasyā* —

> ततो गच्छेत विप्रेन्द्राः सोमतीर्थमनुत्तमम् ।
> यत्र सोमस्तपस्तप्त्वा व्याधिमुक्तोऽभवत् पुरा ।।[236]

Prajāpati Daksha had given all his twenty-seven beautiful daughters to Soma (Chandramas) in marriage. Chandramas felt more attracted to Rohiṇī and others, feeling neglected, complained against him to their father. Daksha cautioned Chandramas to be fair to all but the latter behaved as before. Feeling angry, Daksha cursed him to suffer from pulmonary consumption. With his waning, the plants and the people also began suffering whereupon the gods insisted Daksha to revert his imprecation. Daksha exhorted Chandramas to love all his spouses equally, bathe in the western sea where the Sarasvatī enters it and worship Śiva there. By doing so he will regain his resplendence by waning and then waxing for fifteen days. Chandramas went to Prabhāsa *tīrtha* and had a dip in the holy Sarasvatī on Amāvasyā (new moon day) and began illumining the world again.[237]

With the desiccation of the Sarasvatī, the place of the performance of *tapasyā* by Soma, too, seems to have shifted upstream. This probably led to the foundation or belief in the existence of Soma *tīrtha* at various places as the flow went on receding. We have already referred to the belief that all the four oceans were brought to Pṛithūdaka by the sage Darbhi (or Darvi). So the belief in the location of Sarasvatī-Sāgara-Saṅgama in the Kurukshetra region and at Pṛithūdaka is not at all surprising. The *Mbh.* describes this confluence immediately after its description of Rudrakoṭi-*tīrtha*—

तत्र स्नात्वा नरव्याघ्र रुद्रकोट्यां नरः शुचिः ।
अश्वमेधमवाप्नोति कुलं चैव समुद्धरेत् ।।
ततो गच्छेत राजेन्द्र संगमं लोकविश्रुतम् ।
सरस्वत्या महापुण्यामुपासन्ते जनार्दनम् ।।
यत्र ब्रह्मादयो देवा ऋषयः सिद्धचारणाः ।
अभिगच्छन्ति राजेन्द्र चैत्रशुक्लचतुर्दशीम् ।।[238]

The visit of the gods like Brahmā, sages, *siddhas* and *chāraṇas* to this *tīrtha* on the fourteenth of the bright fortnight of Chaitra is also significant as Chaturdaśī is connected with the worship of Śiva.[239] Probably there existed a *liṅga* at the *tīrtha*, called Someśvara.

The *GP* mentions Soma-*tīrtha* immediately after Koṭi-*tīrtha* along with Brahma, Rāma and Agni *tīrthas*-ब्रह्मतीर्थे रामतीर्थे आग्नेये सोमतीर्थके ।[240] The *Bṛ. P.* refers to Soma *tīrtha* thrice: (i) immediately after Koṭi, Aśvi and Varāha *tīrthas*, (ii) between Brahma and Sapta-Sārasvata, and (iii) immediately after Chatuḥ-Samudra.[241] The sequence is repeated almost similarly in the *PP*.[242]

Soma had performed a *rājasūya* sacrifice here with sage Atri as the *hotā* priest. At the end of this sacrifice there took place a fierce war between the gods on one side and the *dānavas* and *rākshasas* on the other, in which Skanda (Kārttikeya) killed Tāraka demon—

यत्राजयद्राजसूयेन सोमः साक्षात्पुरा विधिवत्पार्थिवेन्द्र ।
अत्रिर्धीमान्विप्रमुख्यो बभूव होता यस्मिन् क्रतुमुख्ये महात्मा ।।
यस्यान्तेऽभूत्सुमहान्दानवानां दैतेयानां राक्षसानां च देवैः ।
स संग्रामस्तारकाख्यः सुतीव्रो यत्र स्कन्दस्तारकाख्यानं जघान ।।[243]

The myth of the birth of Skanda and killing of Tāraka by him is narrated in the epics and the *Purāṇas*.[244] The Devāsura war is said to have been planned by Śukra, the preceptor of the demons, at Auśanasa (Kapāla-mochana) *tīrtha* at Pṛithūdaka.[245] Bṛihaspati too is said to have performed a sacrifice at Avakīrṇa at Pṛithūdaka for the destruction of the demons and the victory of the gods.[246] It was here at the Soma *tīrtha* that Kārttikeya was anointed as the commander-in-chief of the divine forces—

सेनापत्यं लब्धवान्देवतानां महासेनो यत्र दैत्यान्तकर्त्ता ।
साक्षाच्चात्र न्यवसत्कार्त्तिकेयः सदा कुमारो यत्र स प्लक्षराजः ।।[247]

This *tīrtha* is thus the abode of Kārttikeya, the precise place of his stay being the Plaksha (Fig) tree.

The *Vāmana* tells us that grieved by Krauñcha-*bhedana*, Kārttikeya was advised by Vishṇu to go to Pṛithūdaka for remorse—

तं प्राह विष्णुर्व्रज तीर्थवर्यं पृथूदकं पापतरोः कुठारम् ।
स्नात्वोघवत्यां हरमीक्ष्य भक्त्या भविष्यसे सूर्यसमप्रभावः ।।[248]

Svāmi Kārttika temple at Pehowa[249] is reminiscent of Kārttikeya's association with Pṛithūdaka and the Soma *tīrtha.*

Soma *tīrtha* was visited by Balarāma[250] and Prahlāda.[251] A dip in the Soma *tīrtha* gets one the merit of a *rājasūya* sacrifice, makes one healthy and free from all vices and leads one to the world of Soma.[252]

42. ŚUKRA TĪRTHA

It is the same as Auśanasa and Kapāla-mochana located at the village Mangna. The *Bṛ. P.*, however, mentions Kapāla-mochana and Śukra *tīrtha* separately.[253]

43. TAIJASA TĪRTHA

It is the same as the Ojasa or Aujasa *tīrtha* identifiable with the Soma *tīrtha* where Kārttikeya was anointed as the generalissimo by Brahmā and other gods—

औजसं वारुणं तीर्थं दीप्यते स्वेन तेजसा ।
यत्र ब्रह्मादिभिर्देवैर्ऋषिभिश्च तपोधनैः ।
सेनापत्येन देवानामभिषिक्तो गुहस्तदा ।।[254]

It is related to god Varuṇa — तैजसं वारुणं तीर्थं.[255]

44. TISRA SAMUDRA

Cunningham has listed Tisra-Samudra, the "Third Sea" amongst the *tīrthas* of Pehowa without giving any details.[256] Evidently, it was one of the four seas said to have been brought to Pṛithūdaka by the sage Darbhi, described above under Chatuḥ-Samudra *Tīrtha.*

45. TRITAKŪPA TĪRTHA

Tritakūpa was visited by Balarāma after Pṛithūdaka and Bindusaras—

पृथूदकं बिन्दुसरस्त्रिकूपं सुदर्शनम् ।
विशालं ब्रह्मतीर्थं च चक्रं प्राचीं सरस्वतीम् ।।[257]

We are told in the *RV*[258] that Trita was thrown into a well and was helped by Bṛihaspati.[259] The *Mbh.* narrates his story at length. Of the three brothers Ekata, Dvita and Trita, the last-mentioned excelled others. He was revered by all. Once they were leading the cattle obtained in a *yajña*, with Trita walking ahead and having his back towards Ekata and Dvita, who under a spell of greed were thinking as to how they both could possess all the kine without Trita. They thought that being an expert in the Vedas and in the sacrifices, Trita will obtain many other cows. Then at night they encountered a wolf. Trita ran along the Sarasvatī and fell into a well. He cried in distress but his brothers abandoned him. He then performed a mental sacrifice which attracted the attention of Bṛihaspati who brought the gods with him to the well. The billowy Sarasvatī shot forth from the well throwing Trita out of the well—

तत्र चोर्मिमती राजन्नुपपात सरस्वती ।
तयोत्क्षिप्तस्त्रितस्तस्थौ पूजयंस्त्रिदिवौकसः ॥

Trita cursed his brothers to become animals for which they had abandoned him.[260]

This *tīrtha* was visited by Balarāma who worshipped the worthy *brāhmaṇas* there and gave them various gifts.[261]

46. UTTAṄKA TĪRTHA

Pt. Gajanana Sarma refers to Uttaṅka *tīrtha* at Pehowa near the Brahma-yoni where the sage Uttaṅka had abandoned his body.[262]

47. VARĀHA TĪRTHA

Varāha-*tīrtha* has been mentioned between Āśvin and Soma *tīrthas*—

ततो गच्छेत धर्मज्ञ वाराहं तीर्थमुत्तमम् ।
विष्णुर्वाराहरूपेण पूर्वं यत्र स्थितोऽभवत् ।
तत्र स्नात्वा नरव्याघ्र अग्निष्टोमफलं लभेत् ॥[263]

Vishṇu appeared here in his Boar form. One gets the merit of an Agnishṭoma sacrifice by taking a dip here. Prahlāda had also visited this *tīrtha* where he lived, bathed in the Sarasvatī, worshipped Nārāyaṇa and saw *Garuḍāsana* (Vishṇu)—

तत्रोष्य नारायणमर्च्य भक्त्या स्नात्वाऽथ विद्वान् स सरस्वतीजले ।
वराहतीर्थे गरुडासनं स दृष्ट्वाऽथ संपूज्य सुभक्तिमांश्च ॥[264]

Some scholars identify it with Barah Kalan situated about 3 km east of the village Basthali (Vyāsasthalī) and 11 km east of Jind.[265] It is, however, clear from the verse quoted above that it was situated on the Sarasvatī. So it cannot be identified with Barah Kalan which lies on the bank of the Chitang, i.e., ancient Āpayā.[263] The Yajñavarāha temple mentioned in the Garibnath Temple inscription of Pehowa must have been built by Bhūvaka at the traditional spot of the Varāha *tīrtha* at Pṛithūdaka on the Sarasvatī. And it has been expressly stated that this temple stood on the Prāchī-Sarasvatī. Varāha *tīrtha* thus may be located on the Prāchī-Sarasvatī at Pṛithūdaka. A door surround now adorning the entrance of the Prāchī Śiva temple, with *Garuḍāsana* Vishṇu as the *lalāṭabimba* indicates the existence here of a temple of Vishṇu (Nārāyaṇa). If this medieval door-frame (and Nārāyaṇa temple which may have existed here) was also built replacing the old ones, the reference to the worship of Nārāyaṇa and seeing of Garuḍāsana at Varāha *tīrtha* as mentioned in the *VP* (*c.* A.D. 700) furnish the corroborative evidence. The description of the Varāha *tīrtha* between the Āśvin and Soma *tīrthas* at Pehowa in the *Mbh.*, *VP*, *Bṛ. P.* and *PP* aṣ referred to above also supports our view that Varāha *tīrtha* under consideration was located at Pṛithūdaka.

48. VASISHṬHĀPAVĀHA TĪRTHA

The legend of Vasishṭhāpavāha, i.e., the taking away of Vasishṭha by the Sarasvatī, is narrated at length in the *Mbh.*[267] and the *VP*[268] and also referred to in the *Bṛ. P.*,[269] *Garuḍa*[270] and *Skanda*.[271]

Because of rivalry in mortification, there was strong enmity between Viśvāmitra and Vasishṭha, whose hermitages lay to the west and east respectively of the Sthāṇu-*tīrtha*.[272] Seeing Vasishṭha's resplendence resultant from his more excessive penances, Viśvāmitra felt jealous and thought that if the Sarasvatī brings him there he will kill Vasishṭha —

> इयं सरस्वती तूर्णं मत्समीपं तपोधनम् ।
> आनयिष्यति वेगेन वसिष्ठं जपतां वरम् ।।
> इहागतं द्विजश्रेष्ठं हनिष्यामि न संशयः ।।

Having determined thus, Viśvāmitra recalled Sarasvatī and asked her to bring Vasishṭha immediately so that he could kill him —

> तामुवाच मुनिः क्रुद्धो वसिष्ठं शीघ्रमानय ।
> यावदेनं निहन्म्यद्य तच्छ्रुत्वा व्यथिता नदी ।।[273]

Fearing imprecation from both, she approached Vasishṭha and apprised him of Viśvāmitra's intention. The compassionate sage Vasishṭha, advised her to carry him immediately to Viśvāmitra and save herself from being cursed —

त्राह्यात्मानं सरिच्छ्रेष्ठे वह मां शीघ्रगामिनी ।
विश्वामित्रः शपेद्धि त्वां मा कृथास्त्वं विचारणाम् ।।[274]

Vasishṭha, however, praised the Sarasvatī as she was taking him away towards Viśvāmitra. Seeing him brought there by the Sarasvatī, Viśvāmitra searched for a weapon to kill Vasishṭha.[275] Seeing him enraged and fearing *brahmahatyā*, the river goddess carried away Vasishṭha swiftly towards the east while talking to them and thus she deceived Viśvāmitra—

तं तु क्रुद्धमभिप्रेक्ष्य ब्रह्महत्याभयान्नदी ।
अपोवाह वसिष्ठं तु प्राचीं दिशमतन्द्रिता ।
उभयोः कुर्वती वाक्यं वञ्चयित्वा तु गाधिजम् ।।[276]

Deceived, Viśvāmitra cursed her to flow blood with villages of demons on her banks. She thus carried water mixed with blood for one year and was ultimately purified by the gods, sages, *gandharvas* and *apsaras* by creating another stream Aruṇā drinking whose water, the demons also went to heaven.[277]

It is said that a person who bathes here in this great *tīrtha* called Vasishṭhodvāha with devotion attains the world of Vasishṭha —

तत्रापि सुमहत्तीर्थं वसिष्ठोद्वाहसंज्ञितम् ।
तत्र स्नात्वा भक्तियुक्तो वासिष्ठं लोकमाप्नुयात् ।।[278]

This *tīrtha* was visited by Balarāma also.[279]

Cunningham had observed that in the list of *tīrthas* available to him, 'Vasishta prâchin' and 'Vasishta dwaha' were said to be two separate shrines but the only one he could hear of "was on the north bank of the Sarasvatī, a short distance above the Visvamitra mound, ...".[280] Now, however, there are four shrines and two *ghats* which represent it. One fane and *ghat* each belong to the erstwhile Nabha State and Siddhagir Gosain, one shrine belongs to Basamar Puri of Pehowa and the fourth one called '*Guphā*' was renovated by Brahmachariji.[281] In the recent years Mahanta Ravi Giri of Prāchī Śiva temple has also got the *ghats* and shrines renovated.

49. VIŚVĀMITRA TĪRTHA

Viśvāmitra was the son of the well-known great *Kshatriya* king Gādhi. Having anointed Viśvāmitra, Gādhi wanted to retire from life but the subjects insisted that he should protect them and should not leave. Having told them that his son will protect the whole world he, however, left for heaven and Viśvāmitra became the ruler. But he was unable to protect the earth in spite of his best efforts.[282]

Then king Viśvāmitra heard of the great alarm of the demons and set out of the city with his fourfold army. He reached the hermitage of Vasishṭha where his soldiers committed many wrongs. Having seen all that and the uprooted forest, the angered sage Vasishṭha asked his cow to produce terrible *śabaras*. The cow did so and the mighty warriors thus produced put Viśvāmitra's forces to rout making him realise the efficacy of penance.[280] Having resorted to the Sarasvatī at this holy spot, he emaciated his body by observing restraints and fasts, living on water, air and leaves and sleeping on ground. He did not stop observing such austerities in spite of the impediments created by gods and thus became resplendent like the sun and ultimately obtained *brahman*-hood —

सोऽस्मिंस्तीर्थवरे राजन्सरस्वत्याः समाहितः ।
नियमैश्चोपवासैश्च कर्शयन्देहमात्मनः ।।
जलाहारो वायुभक्षः पर्णाहारश्च सोऽभवत् ।
तथा स्थण्डलशायी च ये चान्ये नियमाः पृथक् ।।
असकृत्तस्य देवास्तु व्रतविघ्नं प्रचक्रिरे ।
न चास्य नियमाद्बुद्धिरपयाति महात्मनः ।।
ततः परेण यत्नेन तप्त्वा बहुविधं तपः ।
तेजसा भास्कराकारो गाधिजः समपद्यत ।।
तपसा तु तथायुक्तं विश्वामित्रं पितामहः ।
अमन्यत महातेजा वरदो वरमस्य तत् ।।
स तु वव्रे वरं राजन्स्यामहं ब्राह्मणस्त्विति ।
तथेति चाब्रवीद् ब्रह्मा सर्वलोकपितामहः ।।[284]

Viśvāmitra *tīrtha*, where Viśvāmitra attained *brahman*-hood, is mentioned in the *Purāṇas* also. The *VP* calls it a great and well-known *tīrtha*[285] and the *Mbh.*,[286] *Vāmana*,[287] *Bṛihannāradīya*[288] and *Padma*[289] are unanimous to say that one performing ablution in this excellent *tīrtha* obtains *brahmaṇya*.[290]

Balarāma had visited this holy place and given wealth, milch-cows, chariots, beds, clothes, jewellery, eatables and drinks to the *brāhmaṇas* here.[291] It is now represented by a mound known as Viśvāmitra kā Ṭīlā (Pl. 9).[292]

50. YĀYĀTA TĪRTHA

It is known after Yayāti, the second son of king Nahusha. Yayāti had two wives, Devayānī, the daughter of Śukrāchārya, and Śarmishṭhā, the daughter of the demon-king Vṛishaparva. He begot from them five sons, viz., Yadu and Turvaśu from the former and Druhyu, Anu and Puru from the latter. He performed numerous sacrifices.[293] The Sarasvatī flowed with *ghee* and milk where he sacrificed and also gave the *brāhmaṇas* all what they desired and where they were —

> ययौ तीर्थं महाबाहुर्यायातं पृथिवीपते ।।
> यत्र यज्ञे ययातेस्तु महाराज सरस्वती ।
> सर्पिः पयश्च सुस्राव नाहुषस्य महात्मनः ।।
>
> यत्र यत्र हि यो विप्रो यान्यान्कामानभीप्सति ।
> तत्र तत्र सरिच्छ्रेष्ठा ससर्ज बहून्रसान् ।।[294]

The gods and the *gandharvas* felt happy and men surprised at his sacrificial affluence—

> तत्र देवाः गन्धर्वाः प्रीता यज्ञस्य संपदा ।
> विस्मिता मानुषश्चासन्दृष्ट्वा तां यज्ञसंपदम् ।।[295]

A dip in this holy place delivers a person from all sins and he obtains the merit of a horse-sacrifice—

> तस्मिन् स्नातो नरो भक्त्या मुच्यते सर्वकिल्बिषैः ।
> फलं प्राप्नोति यज्ञस्य अश्वमेधस्य मानवः ।।[296]

Yāyāta *tīrtha* includes the Madhusrava, Ghṛitasrava and Dughasrava. It represents the bank of the Sarasvatī from near the Pāpāntaka and the Preta-Pīpala on it to the *maṭha* of Jayagir, now under the extensive *ghats* built by the erstwhile Maharajas of Nabha and Patiala, milkman Rishyani, goldsmith Punumal and the government.[297]

Besides the *tīrthas* enumerated above, there may have been many more at or near Pṛithūdaka as referred to in the great epic and the Purāṇas. The following verse of the *Bhāgavata* reveals that holy places related to Trita, Uśanas, Manu, Pṛithu, Agni, Asita, Sudāsa, Go, Guha and Śrāddhadeva (Pitṛis) existed in close vicinity to each other on the Sarasvatī at Pṛithūdaka —

> तस्यां त्रितस्योशनसो मनोश्च पृथोरग्नेरसितस्य वायोः ।
> तीर्थं सुदासस्य गवां गुहस्य यच्छ्राद्धदेवस्य स आसिषेवे ।।[298]

The scene of the Vasishṭhāpavāha is near Sthāṇu *tīrtha* to the east of which was located the hermitage of Vasishṭha and to its west that of Viśvāmitra. So this Sthāṇu *tīrtha* may have been located between Vasishṭha Prāchī and Viśvāmitra kā Ṭīlā. The *Mbh.* specifically mentions the large number of sages living on the southern bank of the Sarasvatī where the holy places developed into populous towns, particularly in the Samantapañchaka (Kurukshetra region which included Pehowa also) where the best of the *dvijas* resorted to the bank of the river somehow or the other —

ऋषीणां बहुलत्वात्तु सरस्वत्या विशां पते ।
तीर्थानि नगरायन्ते कूले वै दक्षिणे तदा ।।
समन्तपञ्चकं यावत्तावत्ते द्विजसत्तमाः ।
तीर्थलोभान्नरव्याघ्र नद्यास्तीरं समाश्रिताः ।।[299]

Many of the *tīrthas* may have been founded by the lesser known sages also. They may not have been recorded anywhere. Homonymous holy spots on the Sarasvatī and the lack of details about their exact locations also sometimes cause confusion as these *tīrthas* have been described at various places in the Tīrthayātrā Parva and elsewhere. It is thus very difficult to prepare an exhaustive and incontrovertible list of the *tīrthas* of Pṛithūdaka. Most of the *tīrthas* enumerated above, if not all, and perhaps many more, may have belonged to Pṛithūdaka which is said to have been equal to Kurukshetra, both occupying half of the samantapañchaka—

अर्द्धस्तु कुरुक्षेत्रमर्द्धस्तु पृथूदकम् ।

TEMPLES AND OTHER IMPORTANT PLACES

There exist at Pehowa many old and new shrines. No old shrine may, however, be dated to a period anterior to the Maratha occupation of Haryana. There is no doubt that some of these may have been rebuilt on the traditional holy spots as is indicated by antiquarian remains found there. The extant old temples seem to have been restored or built in the eighteenth century after Nadir Shah Abdali's attack. Many new shrines have come up subsequently, some of them very recently even. We give below an alphabetical list of the important shrines of Pehowa—

1. *Baba Dargai Shah Temple* :- It is located in the old bazar. The ownership of the old mound called Viśvāmitra kā Ṭīlā lies with it.
2. *Brahmeśvara Mahādeva Temple* :- It marks the spot of Brahma-yoni. The *liṅga* enshrined in it was known after Brahmā.
3. *Dasanāmī Akhāṛā* :- It is also called Ṭopiyāṁ Mahādeva and has a number of *samādhis* of the *siddhas*. An image of Yama, which may have originally adorned the southern niche of a medieval temple, is preserved in its premises. It has a Śiva *liṅga* also.
4. *Dera Baba Garibnath* :- Located in the town near the Kāla-Bhairava temple, it is well-known because of the inscription of the time of king Bhoja Pratihāra fixed in its wall. Some images and architectural pieces are also fixed in it and many have been removed to various

places from here. Garibnath was a disciple of Gorakhnath and the *dera* is in possession of *Kanphaṭā jogīs* called *Nātha-panthīs*.

5. *Gurudwara Bauli Sahib* (Pl. 10) :- Located near the bus stand of Pehowa, this elegant *gurudwara* is said to have been built to commemorate the visit of Guru Nanak here. It has a huge pond in front of it and a large number of rooms for the pilgrims.
6. *Hanumān Temple* :- It marks the spot of Māṇḍavya *tīrtha* where the sage of this name had performed austerities. Chitraketu's lost hand was also restored here.[300] It is known for its huge image of Hanumān.
7. *Kāla-Bhairava Temple* (Pl. 11) :- It is located near the Garibnath Temple. Old images of Sūrya and some architectural pieces are fixed in its southern wall and a pillar stands nearby. An image of Bhairava in touchstone is enshrined in it.
8. *Kṛishṇa-Yadhishthira Temple* :- Located on the main *ghat* near the Sarasvatī temple, this shrine is said to have been built on the spot where Yudhishṭhira, as advised by Kṛishṇa, performed *śrāddha* of all those who died in the Great War and thus obtained satisfaction and peace.[301] It was built by the Brāhmaṇa Pañchāyata of Pehowa and is looked after by Śrī Sarasvatī Sewa Dal.
9. *Lakshmī-Nārāyaṇa Temple* :- It is a new but elegant shrine to be visited by the pilgrims.
10. *Mahāmṛityuñjaya Temple* :- Newly built beautiful fane.
11. *Māṇḍavya Tīrtha* :- The same as Hanumān Temple described above. It is located on the Madhusrava.
12. *Nava-Durgā Temple* :- Dedicated to Nava-Durgā, it is a newly built shrine and is managed by the *Tīrtha* Sudhar Sabha of Pehowa.
13. *Paraśurāma Temple*.[302]
14. *Paśupatinātha Temple* (Pl. 12) :- Also known as the temple of Bābā Śravaṇanātha, it is the biggest temple of Pehowa built during the Maratha occupation. It stands on a high platform and is quintet (*pañchāyatana*) on plan. The sanctum enshrines a huge Chaturmukha-*liṅga* of touchstone, the like of which is enshrined in the Paśupatinātha Temple of Kathmandu, Nepal. The domed *maṇḍapa* in front has beautiful old murals on its ceiling. The temple is being managed by a trust which runs a school also.
15. *Prāchī-Śiva Temple* (Pl. 8) :- It marks the holy spot of Vasishṭhāpavāha and is located to the north-west of the Viśvāmitra kā Ṭīlā. The old bed of the Sarasvatī flowing from west to east may still be seen near this temple, also called Vasishṭheśvara because of the *liṅga* named after the sage enshrined in it. The present shrine may have been built by the Marathas or during their occupation. The shrine has

two *samādhis* on either side of the sanctuary. There were some murals showing mythological scenes but unfortunately they have been concealed under the whitewash done recently.

Near it stands the *guphā*, a subterranean shrine with a *liṅga* in it, clearly indicating it to have been an old Śaiva shrine. A small Pratihāra door-frame is fitted to the entrance of this *Guphā* and a mound stood before it which has also been levelled recently. Old brick foundations indicated the existence of old shrines here.

It is now being looked after and renovated by Mahant Ravi Giri.

16. *Preta-Pīpala* (Pl. 7) :- This Pīpala tree is seen at the Pāpāntaka *tīrtha* by bathing where Kārttikeya got rid of the sin of killing his cousin. It is believed that a person who bathes in the Sarasvatī at the Pāpāntaka *tīrtha* near the Pṛithveśvara Mahādeva Temple on the fourteenth of the black fortnight of Chaitra and offers the obsequial rice-balls (पिण्ड-दान) is not afflicted by evil spirits.[303] Some people[304] connect it with the Aśvattha tree under which Nārada saw the dual between Narasiṁha and Śarabha where Vishṇu appeared on being eulogised by Nārada and told him that he will ever live at the root of that tree and whosoever will worship the Pīpala tree will not see the terrific god of death.[305] The pilgrims usually wind a cotton thread around the Pīpala tree for avoiding affliction from the ghosts and also offer the libation of milk, water and sesamum seeds, particularly on the fourteenth of the black fortnight of the month of Chaitra.
17. *Rāma-Lakshmaṇa-Sītā Temple.*
18. *Saṅgameśvara Mahādeva Temple* :- It is located at Aruṇāya near the confluence of the Sarasvatī and Aruṇā and is managed by the Pañchāyatī Akhāṛā.
19. *Santoshī Mātā Mandir* :- It is a new temple built on the Avakīrṇa *tīrtha*.
20. *Sarasvatī Temple* :- Built on the Sarasvatī river near the main *ghats*, it is one of the most sacred temples with an old Pratihāra door-surround found from Viśvāmitra kā Ṭīlā[306] fitted at its entrance. The temple was renovated in 1909 at the instance of M.L. Lord, the then Deputy Commissioner of Karnal district.
21. *Satya-Nārāyaṇa Temple* :- This new temple contains an old image of Mahishāsuramardinī.
22. *Siddhagir ki Samadhi* (Pl. 13) :- It is located a little to the east of the Prāchī Śiva temple and is built in the style of a Nāgara temple. Architecturally, it belongs to the Maratha period. Siddhagir's *haveli* is situated in the midst of bazaar in the south-east quarter of the

city in the wall of which was fixed Mahendrapāla's *praśasti* when Cunningham visited it.[307]

23. *Ṭhākuradvārā* :- It is located on the Brahma-yoni *tīrtha* and is built in Maratha style.
24. *Tripura-Bāla-Sundarī Temple* :- Located on the northern bank of the Sarasvatī, it was in this temple of Tripura-Bālā-Sundarī, it is believed, that before the Great War, Yudhishṭhira and Arjuna received the blessings of the goddess for victory.
25. *Uśaneśvara Mahādeva Temple* :- It marks the spot of the perfection of Uśanas (Śukra) to become a planet and is also known as Auśanasa, Śukra, Kapāla-mochana and Asita *tīrtha*. It is situated in the village Sitaura. It is said to have been built more than 400 years ago but the lakhauri bricks used in its construction indicate that it may have been built in the time of Jahangir or afterwards. There are some beautiful murals in its porch depicting Durgā, Bhairava, Śeshaśāyī Vishṇu, Rāma-Lakshmaṇa with Hanumān, Hanumān lifting Gandha-mādana mountain, Dāna līlā, Śiva on horseback and Arjuna in a chariot driven by Kṛishṇa.

IMPORTANCE OF PILGRIMAGES

"All religions have laid great emphasis on the sacredness of certain localities and have either enjoined or recommended with great insistence pilgrimages to them".[308] The Muslims consider it as an incumbent religious duty to visit Mecca and Madina; the Buddhists visit Lumbinī, the Christians regard Jerusalem to be the holiest place and have undertaken in historic times, several great military pilgrimages even.[309] Similarly, rivers, mountains, forests, lakes and ponds, hermitages and places connected with great men and heroes have always been venerated as sacred and played a very important part in India. They have tended to foster in the different communities and kingdoms, otherwise divided into cults and castes, an idea of the essential and fundamental unity of our country and culture. They have disciplined the people, the rich and the poor alike, by the scriptural injunctions to behave and live in a particular way, keeping purity of body and mind. The association of the holy and philosophic men with pilgrimages have raised higher the spiritual level of the pilgrims and inculcated in them certain enduring moral and spiritual values.[310] They have drawn ordinary mortals away from selfish pursuits and made the affluent make charities to keep a harmonious economic balance. They have thus played a very important role in the life of Indians and still continue to do so. The Haryana government, known for its tourism development endeavours, will do well to develop Pehowa also as a tourist centre, which has remained neglected so far, perhaps because of its vicinity to Kurukshetra. It is, however, to be kept in mind that Pehowa too, has got a great touristic potential and is as important as Kurukshetra — अर्द्धस्तु कुरुक्षेत्रमर्द्धस्तु पृथूदकम्।

NOTES AND REFERENCES

1. Cf.
   न तीर्थतां जलस्याहुर्न स्थलस्य वनस्य वा।
   यदध्यासितं महद्भिस्तद्वै तीर्थं विदुर्बुधाः ।।
2. *Supra,* chapter I.
3. *Mbh.* (unless otherwise indicated, all references are from the Cr. ed.) III.81, 119 & IX. 46, 16-21.
4. *PP* I. 27, 27. *Bhāgavata Purāṇa* (III.1, 22) also mentions it.
5. *CASR,* XIV, p. 102.
6. It has also been identified with Devakhāta to the west of Pehowa (*PM,* p. 58).
7. *Ibid.,* p. 109. *Mbh.* (IX.46, 20) tells us that Balarāma had gone to Brahma-yoni from the Agni-tīrtha.
8. *Mbh.* III.81.119:
   अग्नितीर्थे ततो गच्छेत्तत्र स्नात्वा नरर्षभ।
   अग्निलोकमवाप्नोति कुलंचैव समुद्धेरत् ।।
9. *Mbh.* IX.46, 16-20.
   भृगोः शापाद्भृशंभीतो जातवेदाः प्रतापवान् ।
   शमीगर्भमथासाद्य ननाश भगवांस्ततः ।।
   प्रनष्टे तु तदा वह्नौ देवाः सर्वे सवासवाः ।
   अन्वेषन्त तदा नष्टं ज्वलनं भृशदुःखिताः ।।
   ततोऽग्नितीर्थमथासाद्य शमीगर्भस्थमेव हि ।
   ददृशुर्ज्वलनं तत्र वसमानं यथाविधि ।।
   देवाः सर्वे नरव्याघ्र बृहस्पतिपुरोगमाः ।
   ज्वलनं तं समासाद्य प्रीताभून्सवासवाः ।
   पुनर्यथागतं जग्मुः सर्वभक्षश्च सोऽभवत् ।।
   भृगोः शापान्महीपाल यदुक्तं ब्रह्मवादिना ।
   तत्राप्याप्लुत्य मतिमान्ब्रह्मयोनिं जगाम ह ।।
10. As quoted by Satish Chandra, *Prāchīna Pṛithūdaka,* p. 37.
11. X.51, 12.
12. I.31, 4.
13. F.E. Pargiter, *Ancient Indian Historical Tradition,* Delhi, 1972 (Reprint), p. 23; H.C. Raychaudhuri, *Political History of India,* p. 25; P.L. Bhargava, *India in the Vedic Age,* Lucknow, 1956, pp. 66 & 77; R.Morton Smith, *Dates and Dynasties in Earliest India,* Delhi, 1973, pp. 1, 11, 445, etc.

14. O.P. Bharadwaj (1986), *Studies in the Historical Geography of India*, p. 54.
15. *Śatapatha Brāhmaṇa* XI.5.1, 4. *Vāyu Purāṇa* (91, 31-32) refers to it as Plaksha-*tīrtha*.
16. *CASR*, XIV, p. 102
17. पुरा कृतयुगे राजन्नार्ष्टिषेणो द्विजोत्तमः ।
    वसन्गुरुकुले नित्यं नित्यमध्ययने रतः ।।
    तस्य राजन्गुरुकुले वसतो नित्यमेव ह ।
    समाप्तिं नागमद्विद्या नापि वेदा विशांपते ।।
    स निर्वण्णस्ततो राजंस्तपस्तेपे महातपाः ।
    ततो वै तपसा तेन प्राप्य वेदाननुत्तमान् ।।
    Mbh. IX.38, 3-5
18. यत्र तप्तं तपो घोरमार्ष्टिषेणेन भारत ।
    Mbh. IX.38, 22.
    आर्ष्टिषेणस्य राजेर्षराश्रमं ददृशुस्तदा ।
    ततस्तं तीव्रतपसं कृशं धमनिसंततम् ।।
    पारगं सर्वधर्माणमार्ष्टिषेणमुपागमत् ।
    Mbh. III.156, 89-90.
    आर्ष्टिषेणस्य राजर्षेः प्राप्य भूयस्त्वाश्रमम् ।
    Mbh. III.159, 10.
19. *Ibid.*
20. For details about him, see V.S. Agrawala, *Mahābhārata kā Nāmānukramaṇikā* (Hindi), Gorakpur, V.S. 2016, p. 153.
21. *Mbh.* IX, 39, 10-11.
    तस्मिन्नेव तदा तीर्थे सिन्धुद्वीपः प्रतापवान् ।
    देवापिश्चैव महाराज ब्राह्मण्यं प्राप्तुमर्हत् ।।
    तथा च कौशिकस्तात तपो नित्यं ञ्जितेन्द्रियः ।
    तपसा वै सुतप्तेन ब्राह्मण्यमवाप्तवान् ।।
22. *Mbh.* IX.29-53.
23. *Mbh.* IX.39, 30-31:
    तस्मिंस्तीर्थवरे रामः प्रदाय विविधं वसु ।
    पयस्विनीस्तथा धेनूर्यानानि शयनानि च ।।
    तथा वस्त्राण्यलंकारं भक्ष्यं पेयं च शोभनम् ।
    अददान्मुदितो राजन्पूजयित्वा द्विजोत्तमान् ।।
24. He names this *tīrtha* as Arishtasrena or Arishtisena which both are misspelt names (*CASR*, XIV, p. 102).
25. *Mbh.* IX.38, 29-31.
26. *Mbh.* IX.39, 32.
27. Cunningham (*CASR*, XIV, p. 102) identifies Aruṇā with the Markanda.
28. For details see *Śrī Saṁgameśvara Mahādeva-Aruṇāya*, published by Digambara Śaraṇapurī Mahanta Gaṅgāpurī, 2nd ed., Aruṇāya, 1989. Cf. *PM*, p. 145 where this *tīrtha* is identified with Vasishṭhāpavāha at Pehowa.
29. *PM*, p. 147.

30. *PP*, I.27, 39.
31. *Br. P.* II.65, 109.
32. मधुस्रवं च तत्रैव तीर्थं पुण्यतमं द्विजाः।
 तस्मिन्स्नात्वा नरो भक्त्या मधुना तर्प्पयेत् पितृन्।।
 तत्रापि सुमहत्तीर्थं वसिष्ठोद्वाहसंज्ञितम्।
 तत्र स्नातो भक्तियुक्तो वासिष्ठं लोकमाप्नुयात्।।
 VP (SM) XVIII, 39-40.
33. *Mbh.* III.81, 130-31:
 मधुस्रवं चं तत्रैव तीर्थं भरतसत्तम।
 तत्र स्नात्वा नरो राजन्गोसहस्रफलं लभेत्।।
 ततो गच्छेन्नरश्रेष्ठ तीर्थं देव्या यथाक्रमम्।
 सरस्वत्यरुणायाश्च संगमं लोकविश्रुतम्
34. अरुणायाः पश्चिमे भागे यावन्मंकणको मुनिः।
 तावत्पृथूदकं क्षेत्रं सर्वदेवैरलंकृतम्।।
35. Satish Chandra, *op. cit.*, p. 68.
36. *VP (SM)* XX.1.
37. *Mbh.* III. 81, 132:
 त्रिरात्रोपोषितः स्नात्वा मुच्यते ब्रह्महत्यया।
 अग्निष्टोमातिरात्राभ्यां फलं विन्दति मानवः।
 आसप्तमं कुलं चैव पुनाति भरतर्षभ।।
 Cf.*VP (SM)* XIX.41-42:
 अरुणायाः सरस्वत्याः संगमे लोकविश्रुते।
 त्रिरात्रोपोषितः स्नातो मुच्यते सर्वकिल्बिषैः।।
 प्राप्ते कलियुगे घोरे अधर्मे प्रत्युपस्थिते।
 अरुणासंगमे स्नात्वा मुक्तिमाप्नोति मानवः।।
38. ततस्ते राक्षसाः सर्वे स्नाताः पापविवर्जिताः।
 दिव्यमाल्याम्बरधराः स्वर्गस्थिति समन्विताः।।
 VP (SM), XIX, 43.
39. *Mbh.* III.81, 131-32.
40. *VP. (SM)* XIII.31:
 अश्विनोस्तीर्थमासाद्य श्रद्धावान् यो जितेन्द्रियः।
 रूपस्य भागी भवति यशस्वी च भवेन्नरः।।
41. *PP.* I.26, 15.
42. *Br. P.* II.65, 30.
43. *Mbh.* IX.38, 16:
 सरस्वत्यास्तीर्थवरं ख्यातमौशनसं तदा।
 सर्वपापप्रशमनं सिद्धक्षेत्रमनुत्तमम्।।
44. *VP (SM)* XVIII.1
 उशना यत्र संसिद्धो ग्रहत्वं च समवाप्तवान्।
 and *Ibid.*, XXI.25

उशना यत्र संसिद्ध आराध्य परमेश्वरम् ।
ग्रहमध्येषु पूज्यते तस्य तीर्थस्य सेवनात् ।।
Also see P.V. Kane, *History of Dharmaśāstra*, Vol. IV, Poona, 1953, p. 736.

45. *VP (SM)* XX1.24.
46. *VP (SM)* XXI.25-26:
एवं शुक्रेन मुनिना सेवितं तीर्थमुत्तामम् ।
ये सेवन्ते श्रद्दधानास्ते यान्ति परमां गतिम् ।।
यस्तु श्राद्धं नरो भक्त्या तस्मिंस्तीर्थे करिष्यति ।
पितरस्तारितास्तेन भविष्यन्ति न संशयः ।।
47. *VP (SM)* XVIII.2:
तस्मिन् स्नात्वा विमुक्तस्तु पातकैर्जन्मसम्भवैः ।
ततो याति परं ब्रह्म यस्मान्नावर्तते पुनः ।।
48. *VP (SM)* XXXVI.40-44:
ततः पर्यचरच्छूली कुरुक्षेत्र समन्ततः ।
ददर्शौघवतीतीरे उशनसं तपोनिधिम् ।।
ततोऽब्रवीत्सुरपतिः किमर्थं तप्यते तपः ।
जगत्क्षोभकरं विप्र तच्छीघ्रं कथ्यतां मम ।।
तवाराधनकामार्थं तप्यते हि महत्तपः ।
संजीवनीं शुभां विद्यां ज्ञातुमिच्छे त्रिलोचन ।।
तपसा परितुष्टोऽस्मि सुतप्तेन तपोधन ।
तस्मात् संजीवनीविद्यां भवान् ज्ञास्यति तत्त्वत्तः ।।
वरं लब्ध्वा ततः शुक्रस्तपस सब्यवर्त्तत ।।
तथापि चलते पृथ्वी साब्धिभूभृन्नागावृता ।।
49. XXII.31.
50. II.65, 105.
51. III.1, 22.
52. *Mbh.* III. 81, 116-17; *PP* I, 27, 24-25:
ततस्त्वौशनसं गच्छेत्त्रिषु लोकेषु विश्रुतम् ।
यत्र ब्रह्मादयो देवा ऋषयश्च तपोधनाः ।।
कार्त्तिकेयश्च भगवांस्त्रिसंध्यं किल भारत ।
सानिध्यकरोत्तत्र भार्गवप्रियकाम्यया ।।
53. *VP (SM)* XVIII, 3.
54. *PM*, p. 54.
55. *Mbh.* IX. 38, 4-6.
56. *Mbh.* IX. 38, 7:
तत्प्राप्य च बलो राजस्तीर्थप्रवरमुत्तमम् ।
विधिवद्धि ददौ वित्तं ब्राह्मणानां महात्मनाम् ।।
57. *Mbh.* III.81, 1333. The *tīrtha* is, however, named as Avatīrṇa here.
58. *PP* I. 27, 41.
59. *Mbh.* IX.40. The *tīrtha* is named as Ākīrṇa.

60. *VP (SM)* XVIII. 25-36.
61. *Mbh.* IX.40, 1-25.
62. *VP (SM)* XVIII.28-35.
ऋषयो नैमिषेया ये दक्षिणार्थं ययुः पुरा ।
तत्रैव च बको दाल्भ्यो धृतराष्ट्रमयाचत ।।
तेनापि तत्र निन्दार्थमुक्तं पश्वनृतं तु यत् ।
ततः क्रोधेन महता मांसमुत्कृत्य तत्र ह ।।
पृथूदके महातीर्थे अवकीर्णेति नामतः ।
जुहाव धृतराष्ट्रस्य राष्ट्रे नरपतेस्ततः ।।
हूयमाने तदा राष्ट्रे प्रवृत्ते यज्ञकर्मणि ।
अक्षीयत ततो राष्ट्रं नृपतेर्दुष्कृतेन वै ।।
ततः स चिन्तयामास ब्राह्मणस्य विचेष्टितम् ।
पुरोहितेन संयुक्तो रत्नान्यादाय र्सवशः ।।
प्रसादनार्थं विप्रस्य ह्यवकीर्णं ययौ तदा ।
प्रसादितः स राज्ञा च तुष्टः प्रोवाच तं नृपम् ।।
ब्राह्मणा नावमन्तव्याः पुरुषेण विजानता ।
अवज्ञातो ब्राह्मणस्तु हन्यात् त्रिपुरुषं कुलम् ।।
एवमुक्त्वा स नृपतिं राज्येन यशसा पुनः ।
उत्थापयामास ततस्तस्य राज्ञो हिते स्थितः ।।
63. *VP (SM)* XVIII.36
64. *Br. P.* II.65, 107
अवकीर्णे नरः स्नात्वा ब्रह्मचर्यफलं लभेत् ।।
65. *Mbh.* IX.40, 26-27:
तत्र तीर्थे महाराज बृहस्पतिरुदारधीः ।
असुराणामभावाय भावाय च दिवौकसाम् ।।
मांसैरपि जुहावेष्टिमक्षीयन्त ततोऽसुराः ।
देवतैरपि संभग्ना जितकाशिभिराहवे ।।
66. *Ibid.*, IX 40, 28-29:
तत्रापि विधिवद्दत्वा ब्राह्मणेभ्यो महायशाः ।
वाजिनाः कुञ्जरांश्चैव रथांश्चाश्वतरीयुतान् ।।
रत्नानि च महार्हाणि धनं धान्यं च पुष्कलम् ।
ययौ तीर्थं महाबाहुर्यायातं पृथिवीपते ।।
67. *CASR*, XIV, p. 102.
68. *PM*, p. 59:
पृथूदकतः पश्चिमे यत्र नदी वक्रा तदेव तदेव भार्गवतीर्थम् ।
69. *Ibid.*
70. *VP (SM)* XVIII.39, 21-23. See also *Mbh.* (Gita Press ed.) IX. 47, 22-24.
71. *RV* X. 90, 12:
ब्राह्मणोऽस्य मुखमासीद् बाहु राजन्यः कृतः ।
ऊरु तदस्य यद् वैश्यः पद्भ्यां शूद्रोऽजायत ।।

72. *CASR*, XIV, p. 105; *PM*, p. 88.
73. The *Mbh.* refers to three different Devī-*tīrthas* in Kurukshetra (III.81, 41) at Śaṅkhiṇī, III.81.79 at Madhuvaṭī and III. 81, 86 after Mṛigadhūma. See also V.S. Agrawala, *loc.cit.*, pp. 153-54); *Bṛ. P.* refers to Soma *tīrtha* (II.65, 32; II.65 103 and II.65, 111), Sūrya-*tīrtha* (II.65, 49 & II.65, 97), *Koṭi-tīrtha* (II.65, 27, II.65, 90 and II. 65, 95), Brahma-*tīrtha* (II.65, 102 and II.65, 122) at different places. And so also the other Purāṇas.
74. *VP* XVIII. 39, 21.
75. *Ibid.*, XVIII.39, 25; *Mbh. IX*.40, 1.
76. *Mbh.* III.81, 121:
ब्रह्मयोनिं समासाद्य शुचिः प्रयतमानसः ।
तत्र स्नात्वा नर व्याघ्र ब्रह्मलोकं प्रपद्यते ।
पुनात्यासप्तमं चैव कुलं नास्त्यत्र संशयः ।।
77. *PP I.* 27, 29-30.
78. *VP (SM)* XVIII. 25:
तत्र स्नात्वा मुक्तिकामः पुनर्योनिं न पश्यति ।
79. Śaṅkaropādhyāya as quoted in *PM*, p. 86:
ब्रह्मयोनिरियं सूते सर्वानर्थान्मनोगतान् ।
स्मरणाद्दर्शनात्स्नानान्मुक्तिदात्री न संशयः ।।
तस्याः किं वर्णनीयं हि ब्रह्मयोनेस्तु दर्शनात् ।
पापानि विलयं यांति तमः सूर्य्योदये यथा ।।
80. *Ibid.*
81. *GP* 83.24 & 30. See also *PP* I. 26, 66; I.27, 2; *Bṛ. P.* II.65, 61, 102 and 122; *CASR*, XIV, p. 102.
82. *Mbh.* IX.40, 26-27.
83. *CASR*, XIV, p. 104.
84. *Ibid.*, p. 102.
85. *VP* XX, 1.
86. *CASR*, XIV, p. 102.
87. I.27, 44.
88. II.65, 110.
89. *VP* XVIII, 36.
90. V.S. Agrawala (V.S. 2036), *op. cit.*, p. 153 and *Mbh.* IX.39, 32.
91. See also *CASR*, XIV, p. 102.
92. *PP.* I.27, 39. Another Devī-*Tīrtha* (*ibid.*, I.26, 93) lay in the Kurukshetra region.
93. *Mbh.* III.81, 131. For other Devī-*Tīrthas* in Kurukshetra, see *supra* fn.73.
94. *CASR*, XIV, p. 102
95. *Mbh.* IX. 40, 32.
96. *RV* VII. 95, 2:
एकाचेतत् सरस्वती नदीनां शुचिर्यती गिरिभ्य आ समुद्रात् ।
रायश्चेतन्ती भुवनस्य भूरेर्घृतं पयो दुदुहे नाहुषाय ।।
97. *CASR*, XIV, p. 102.
98. *Ibid.*, p. 103.

99. *Mbh.* IX. 38, 9-20:
पुरा वै दण्डकारण्ये राघवेण महात्मना ।
वसता राजशार्दूल राक्षसास्तत्र हिंसिताः ।।
जनस्थाने शिरश्छिन्नं राक्षसस्य दुरात्मनः ।
क्षुरेण शितधारेण तत्पपात महावने ।।
महोदरस्य तल्लग्नं जङ्घायां वै यदृच्छया ।
वने विचरतो राजन्नस्थि भित्त्वास्फुरत्तदा ।।
स तेन लग्नेन तदा द्विजातिर्न शशाक ह ।
अभिगन्तुं महाप्राज्ञस्तीर्थान्यायतनानि च ।।
स पूतिना विस्रवता वेदनार्तो महामुनिः ।
जगाम सर्वतीर्थानि पृथिव्यामिति नः श्रुतम् ।।
स गत्वा सरितः सर्वाः समुद्रांश्च महातपाः ।
कथयामास तत्सर्वमृषीणां भावितात्मनाम् ।।
आप्लुतः सर्वतीर्थेषु न च मोक्षमवाप्तवान् ।
स तु शुश्राव विप्रेन्द्रो मुनीनां वचनं महत् ।।
सरस्वत्यास्तीर्थवरं ख्यातमौशनसं तदा ।
सर्वपापप्रशमनं सिद्धक्षेत्रमनुत्तमम् ।।
स तु गत्वा ततस्तत्र तीर्थमौशनसं द्विजः ।
तत औशनसे तीर्थे तस्योपस्पृशस्तदा ।
तच्छिरश्चरणं मुक्त्वा पपातान्तर्जले तदा ।।
ततः स विरुजो राजन्पूतात्मा वीतकल्मषः ।
आजगामाश्रमं प्रीतः कृत्यकृत्यो महोदरः ।।
सोऽथ गत्वाश्रमं पुण्यं विप्रमुक्तो महातपाः ।
कथयामास तत्सर्वमृषीणां भावितात्मनाम् ।।
ते श्रुत्वा वचनं तस्य ततस्तीर्थस्य मानद ।
कपालमोचनमिति नाम चक्रुः समागताः ।।
VP (SM) (XVIII.5-13) repeats the same story almost verbatim but names the sage as Rahodara.
100. II.65, 105-06 and 121.
101. 52.6.
102. I.27, 24-26.
103. III.65, 106. For a philosophic interpretation and significance of the episode given in the *Mbh.* and *VP*, see V.S. Agrawala (1964), *op. cit.*, pp. 73ff.
104. *CASR*, XIV, p. 103.
105. *Skanda Purāṇa*, ch.89. See also *VP*, chapters 3-4.
106. *CASR*, XIV, pp. 75-78. See also Devendra Handa, "Kapāla Mocana: An Ancient Holy Place", *Purāṇa*, Vol. X, No. 2, July, 1968, pp. 148-53.
107. Cf. *PM*, p. 54.
ततः सतौड़ाग्रोम किंचिद्दूरे उत्तरभागे वटाश्वत्थभागे
पश्चिमवाहिन्यां सरस्वत्याम् भग्नसोपानादिचिन्हचिन्हितम्
कपालमोचनापरनामकमौशनसं तीर्थं सरस्वत्याम् ।

108. *Mbh.* III.81, 118; *PP* I.27, 26.
109. *GP* XLII, 6.
110. *VP (SM)* XXI, 26-27:
एवं शुक्रेण मुनिना सेवितं तीर्थमुत्तमम् ।
ये सेवन्ते श्रद्दधानास्ते यान्ति परमां गतिम् ।।
यस्तु श्राद्धं नरो भक्त्या तस्मिंस्तीर्थे करिष्यति ।
पितरस्तारितास्तेन भविष्यन्ति न संशयः ।।
111. *Ibid.*, XLI, 24.
112. *Ibid.*, (Veṅk. Pr. Edn.) XXXIX, 2:
तस्मिन्पुण्ये कुरुक्षेत्रे पातकैर्जन्मसम्भवैः ।
मुक्तो याति परं ब्रह्म यतो नावर्तते पुनः ।।
113. *Mbh.* IX.38, 16.
114. *CASR*, XIV, p. 103.
115. *PM*, pp. 106-7. He also gives the literal explanation of the word Kāru-Pāvana as the one which purifies the bad, anti-Vedic person. This explanation is, however, not much convincing.
116. *Brahma Purāṇa* as quoted in *PM*, p. 107.
117. See also *Bh.P.* IX.11, 12 and X, 61, 12. For references to Chitraketu in the *Mbh.*, see S. Sorensen, *An Index to the Names in the Mahābhārata*, Reprint, Delhi, 1978, p. 176.
118. *PM*, p. 107.
119. Cf. *PP* I. 27, 2 and *Bṛ.P* II.65, 102 & 122.
120. Satish Chandra, *op. cit.*, p. 77.
121. *Mbh.* III.80, 68, and 81, 14.
122. For its identification with Deeg in the Punjab, see F.E. Pargiter, *The Mārkaṇḍeya Purāṇa*, (Eng. tr.), Bibliotheca Indica, Calcutta, 1904, p. 292 and Jagannath, "Further light on the identification of the river Devikā", *Journal of the U.P. Historical Society*, Lucknow, Vol. 17, Pt. 2, December 1944, p. 78.
123. *VP* LVII, 34-39.
124. *Mbh.* III.81, 124-27:
ततो गच्छेत धर्मज्ञ रुद्रकोटिं समाहितः ।
पुरा यत्र महाराज ऋषिकोटिः समाहिता ।
प्रहर्षेण च संविष्टा देवदर्शनकाङ्क्षया ।।
अहं पूर्वमहं पूर्वं द्रक्ष्यामि वृषभध्वजम् ।
एवं संप्रस्थिता राजन्नृषयः किल भारत ।।
ततो योगेश्वरेणापि योगमास्थाय भूपते ।
तेषां मन्युप्रणाशार्थमृषीणामग्रतः स्थिता ।।
सृष्टा कोटिस्तु रुद्राणामृषीणामग्रतः स्थिता ।
मया पूर्वतरं दृष्ट इति ते मनिरे पृथक् ।।
There was probably another Rudrakoṭi near Kaithal (Kapishṭhala) which has been described in the *VP* XV, 22-23.
125. *Brahma P.* II. 65, 27. *GP* (LXXXIII.23) also mentions it.

126. *PP*. I. 12, 9; 17, 8ff; 24, 14 and 26.95.
127. *Bṛ. P*. III.65, 27-29:
कोटितीर्थं ततो गच्छेद्यत्र रुद्रेण मोहिनि ।
कोटितीर्थान्युपाहृत्य स्थापितानि महात्मना ।।
तत्र तीर्थे दृष्ट्वा कोटीश्वरं हरम् ।
पचंयज्ञभवं पुण्यं तत्प्रभृत्याप्नुयात्सदा ।
तत्रैव वामनो देवः सर्वदेवैः प्रतिष्ठितः ।।
VP (SM) (XIII, 28-30) also gives similar details.
128. *Mbh*. III. 81, 129 and III. 80, 68 which also mentions Mahākāla, probably the temple at this *tīrtha*.
129. *VP* LVII, 40:
तं ददर्श महातेजाः प्रह्लादो भक्तिमान् वशी ।
कोटितीर्थे ततः स्नात्वा तर्षयित्वा वसून्पितृन् ।
रुद्रकोटिं समभ्यर्च्य जगाम कुरुजाङ्गलम् ।।
130. *Mbh*. IX.46, 24-26.
131. *Ibid*., IX.46, 27
अभिषिक्तश्च तत्रैव समागम्य मरुद्गणैः ।
वाहनं चास्य प्रदत्तं हंसयुक्तं मनोरमम् ।
विमानं पुष्पकं दिव्यं नैर्ऋतैश्वर्यमेव च ।।
132. *Ibid*., IX.46, 28-29.
133. As quoted in the *PM*, p. 104 from the *VP*. The critical edition of the *VP*, however, has the following verse:
तत्र तीर्थं सुविख्यातं यायातं नाम नामतः ।
यस्येह यजमानस्य मधुसुस्राव वै नदी ।।
134. *VP (SM)*, XVIII. 39:
मधुस्रवं च तत्रैव तीर्थं पुण्यतमं द्विजाः ।
तस्मिन् स्नात्वा नरो भक्त्या मधुनातर्पयेत् पितृन् ।।
135. *Mbh*. III.81, 130:
तत्र स्नात्वा नरो राजन्गोसहस्रफलं लभेत् ।।
Also *PP* I.27, 38 which names the *tīrtha* as Madhupura. *Bṛ.P* II.65, 108 names it as Madhusrava. *PM* (p. 104) quotes the following verse from *VP:*
मुच्यते सर्वपापेभ्यो गोसहस्रफलं लभेत् ।
फलं प्राप्नोति यज्ञस्य ह्यश्वमेधस्य मानवः ।।
136. Devendra Handa, "Pehoa—The Ancient Pṛthūdaka", *Purāṇa*, Vol. IX, No. 2, July 1967, p. 302.
137. *RV* VIII. 95, 2.
138. *PM*, p. 104.
139. *CASR*, XIV, p. 103.
140. For details see V.S Agrawala (V.S. 2036), *op. cit.*, p. 240.
141. *Mbh*. III.81, 97.
142. *Mbh*. III. 81, 97-115 and IX.37, 34-49. It is repeated in the *PP* (I.27, 4-23), also *Kūrma P*. (Ed. A.S. Gupta, Varanasi, 1971) II.34, 44-53 gives a different version.

143. *Mbh.* IX. 37, 30-32. The *VP (SM)* XVII. 2-7 gives this myth with more specificity:
कश्यपस्य सुतो जज्ञे मानसो मङ्कणको मुनिः ।
स्नानं कर्तुं व्यवसितो गृहीत्वा वल्कलं द्विजः ।।
तत्र गता ह्यपसरसोरम्भाद्याः प्रियदर्शनाः ।
स्नायन्ति रुचिराः स्निग्धास्तेन सार्धमनिन्दिताः ।।
ततो मुनेस्तदा क्षोभाद्रेतः स्कन्नं यदम्भसि ।
तद्रेतः स तु जग्राह कलशे वै महातपाः ।।
सप्तधा प्रविभागं तु कलशस्थं जगाम ह ।
तत्रर्षयः सप्त जाता विदुर्यान् मरुतां गणान् ।।
वायुवेगो वायुबलो वायुहा वायुमण्डलः ।
वायुज्वालो वायुरेतो वायुचक्रश्च वीर्यवान् ।।
एतेह्यपत्यास्तस्यर्षेर्धास्यन्ति चराचरम् ।
See also *VP* XLVI, 71-75.
144. *Mbh.* III. 81, 97-115.
145. Stella Kramrisch, *The Presence of Siva*, Delhi, 1988 (Ist Indian ed.), pp. 278-81.
146. *PM.*, p. 45:
अथ मंकणग्रामे सप्तसारस्वतं तीर्थम् । तत्र मांगणाग्रामस्थलोकानां जलाहरणघट्टोपलक्षितसरस्वत्येव सप्तसारस्वतं तीर्थं ज्ञेयम् । सोपानादितीर्थचिन्हचिन्हितत्वात् प्रायशो मांगणास्थलोकानां जलाहरणघट्टतो नैमिषसीमपर्य्यंतं घट्टत उत्तरे वटनिकटे निकटस्थ प्राचीमूलपर्य्यंतं सरस्वती सप्तसारस्वतं सम्भावितम् । तत्र प्राचीमूले परपारे वटाश्वत्थसमुदायमध्ये महादेवस्य लिङ्गं स्थितं तत्र मंकणतीर्थे (सप्तसारस्वते) स्नानादिकं विधाय ध्यानेन शिवं प्रत्यक्षीकृत्य पूजयेत् ।
147. *GP* 53.24; *Br.P* II.65, 102 and 122.
148. *PM*, p. 60.
149. *Supra*, No. 19.
150. As quoted in *PM*, p. 60. It is said that a pilgrim who bathes here attains the merit of a horse-sacrifice.
151. *Mbh.* III.81, 78:
मनोजवे नरः स्नात्वा गोसहस्रफलं लभेत् ।।
152. *PP* I.26, 87.
153. *Br.P.* II.65, 82:
ततो व्यासवने गत्वा स्नात्वा तीर्थे मनोजवे ।
154. *PM*, pp. 59-60.
155. III.1, 22. It has also been mentioned in X.79, 21:
प्रविष्य रेवामगमद्यत्र माहिष्मती पुरी ।
मनुतीर्थमुपस्पृश्य प्रभासं पुनरागमत् ।।
156. *Mbh.* III. 81, 53; *PP* I.26, 60-61. The *VP (SM)* XIV. 51-53 give more details:
पुरा कृष्णमृगास्तत्र व्याधेन शरपीडिताः ।
विगाह्य तस्मिन् सरसि मानुषत्वमुपागताः ।।
ततोव्याधाश्च ते सर्वे तानपृच्छन् द्विजोत्तमान् ।
'मृगा अनेन वै याता अस्मामिः शरपीडिताः ।।

निमग्नास्ते सरः प्राप्य क्व ते याता द्विजोत्तमाः ।
तेऽब्रुवस्तत्र वै पृष्टा वयं ते च द्विजोत्तमाः ।।

157. *VP (SM)* XIV.54-55.
158. *Mbh.* III.81, 54:
तस्मिंस्तीर्थे नरः स्नात्वा ब्रह्मचारी जितेन्द्रियः ।
सर्वपापविशुद्धात्मा स्वर्गलोके महीयते ।।
PP I. 26, 62 also repeats this verse.
159. *VP (SM) XIV*, 50:
ततो गच्छेत श्रद्धावान् मानुषं लोकविश्रुतम् ।
दर्शनात्तस्य तीर्थस्य मुक्तो भवति किल्बिषैः ।।
160. *Ibid.*, v.56:
एतत् तीर्थस्य माहात्म्यं मानुषस्य द्विजोत्तमाः ।
येश्रृण्वन्ति श्रद्धानास्तेऽपि यान्ति परां गतिम् ।।
161. *Bṛ.P.* II.65, 57-58.
162. *Mbh.* III.81, 55; *VP (SM)* XV, 1; *PP* I.26, 63.
163. Satish Chandra, *op. cit.*, p. 77. Some scholars identify Mānusha with Manas, a village located about 5 km to the west of Kaithal (see Bhargava, *op. cit.*, p. 32; Bharadwaj, 1986, *op. cit.*, p. 194).
164. *Mbh.* III.81, 122. See also *Mbh.* IX. 43-45.
165. *VP (SM)* XX, 6-7.
166. *Ibid.*, vv. 8-10.
167. *Ibid.*, v. 11:
यस्तु स्नानं श्रद्धानश्चैत्रषष्ठ्यां करिष्यति ।
अक्षय्यमुदकं तस्य पितृणामुपजायते ।।
168. *CASR*, XIV, p. 163.
169. The following verses from the *Mbh.* and *VP* have been quoted in the *PM* in this connection:
भवतीर्थं तु विख्यातं पापांतं नाम नामतः ।
तस्मिन्स्नातो नरो भक्त्या मुच्यते सर्वकिल्बिषैः ।।
अश्वमेधस्य यज्ञस्य फलं प्राप्नोति मानवः ।
तत्रापि विधिवद्दत्वा ब्राह्मणेभ्यो महायशाः ।।
We have, however, not been able to locate these verses in the editions of these works available to us.
170. *VP* XXXII, 86-115.
171. *CASR*, XIV, p. 103. We have not been able to find any epic or Paurāṇic reference to substantiate Cunningham's observation.
172. II.65, 120.
173. LXXXI.5.
174. IX.19 1; VI.8, 38-40 and X.78, 19.
175. *Ibid.*, IV. 19, 1:
अथादीक्षत राजा तु हयमेधशतेन सः ।
ब्रह्मावर्ते मनोक्षेत्रे यत्र प्राची सरस्वती ।।

176. *VP (SM)* XXI, 20-21:
प्राचीसरस्वती पुण्या अपि दुष्कृतकर्मणाम् ।
त्रिरात्रं ये करिष्यन्ति प्राचीं प्राप्य सरस्वतीम् ।।
न तेषां दुष्कृतं किञ्चिद् देहमाश्रित्य तिष्ठति ।
177. *Ibid.*, vv.21-24.
178. *Ibid.*, vv.18-19:
मातृहा पितृहा यश्च ब्रह्महा गुरुतल्पगः ।
स्नात्वा शुद्धिमनाप्नोति यत्र प्राची सरस्वती ।।
179. *Skanda Purāṇa* (Nāg Publishers, Delhi, 1982), Prabhāsa Khaṇḍa, ch.36.
180. *Ibid.*, v.9:
प्राचीं सरस्वतीं ये तु पिबंति सततं मृगाः ।
तेऽपि स्वर्गं गमिष्यन्ति यज्ञैर्द्विजवरा यथा ।।
181. *Ibid.*, v.10.
सर्वकामप्रपूर्त्यर्थं नृणां तत्क्षेत्रमुत्तमम् ।
चिंतामणिसमा देवी यत्र प्राची स्रस्वती ।।
182. *Ibid.*, v.11:
यथा कामदुघा गावः सर्वकामफलप्रदाः ।
तथा स्वर्गापवर्गाभ्यां प्राची देवी सरस्वती ।।
183. *Ibid.*, v.12:
अष्टाशीतिसहस्राणि मुनीनामूर्ध्वरेतसाम् ।
यत्र स्थितानि संन्यासं तस्मात्किमधिकं स्मृतम् ।।
184. *Ibid.*, v.13:
यत्र मंकणकः सिद्धः प्राचीने नियतात्मवान् ।
ब्रह्महत्याव्रतंचीर्णं मया यत्र वरानने ।।
185. *Ibid.*, vv.30-33.
186. *Ibid.*, vv.44-58.
187. *Bhāg.P.* VI.8, 39-40.
188. I.18, 220:
पुष्करारण्यमासाद्य प्राची यत्र सरस्वती ।
189. *Indian Antiquary*, Vol. VI, p. 192.
190. H.C. Raychaudhuri, *Studies in Indian Antiquities*, Calcutta, 1958, p. 129.
191. Bharadwaj (1991), *op. cit.*, pp. 24ff.
192. *EI*, I, pp. 187-88. Also cf. *VP* XXIII.43:
तस्यैव मध्ये बहुपुण्य युक्तः पृथूदकः पापहरः शिवश्च ।
पुण्या नदी प्राङ्मुखतां प्रयाता यत्रौघयुक्तस्य शुभा जलाढ्या ।।
193. II.65, 120:
स्नात्वा प्राचीसरस्वत्यां श्राद्धं कृत्वा विधानतः ।
दुलर्भं प्राप्नुयात्कामं देहान्ते स्वर्गतिं लभेत् ।।
194. *CASR*, XIV, p. 101.
195. *Bhāg.P.* X.78, 19, p. 588.
196. अर्द्धस्तु कुरुक्षेत्रमर्द्धस्तु पृथूदकम् , *PM*, p. ख.

197. पुण्यमाहुः कुरुक्षेत्रं कुरुक्षेत्रात् सरस्वतीम् ।
सरस्वत्याश्च तीर्थानि तीर्थेभ्यश्च पृथूदकम् ।।
198. *Mbh.* IX. 38, 29.
199. *Ibid.*, vv. 30-32.
200. *Ibid.*, v. 122:
पृथूदकमिति ख्यातं कार्त्तिकेयस्य वै नृप ।
तत्राभिषेकं कुर्वीत पितृदेवार्चने रतः ।।
201. *Ibid.*, v.127:
गीतं सनत्कुमारेण व्यासेन च महात्मना ।
वेदे च नियतं राजन्नभिगच्छेत्पृथूदकम् ।।
202. *VP* XXIII, 43.
203. पृथूदकसमं तीर्थं नाम्ना पापप्रमोचनम् ।
कुरुक्षेत्रगतं नान्यद्यत्र शंभोः सदास्थितिः ।।
204. *VP* XXXII, 114.
205. In ancient times, Śiva *liṅgas* and Vishṇu temples were known after the persons who got them established or built.
206. Mahanta Banshi Puri, *loc.cit.*
207. *PM*, pp. 98-99.
208. *Mbh.* IX. 48, 6-8. See also III. 81, 22-30; *VP (SM)* XIV, 1-14; *Bṛ.P*II.64, 15-17; *Skanda P.* (More ed.) V. 218, 27-57; (Veṅk. Pr. ed.) VI.66, 1;69, 27;VII. 49, 1-16.
209. *Mbh.* IX.48.9-10:
रामो दत्त्वा धनं तत्र द्विजेभ्यो जनमेजय ।
उपस्पृश्य यथान्यायं पूजयित्वा तथा द्विजान् ।।
पुण्ये तीर्थे शुभे देशे वसु दत्त्वा शुभाननः ।
मुनींश्चैवाभिवाद्य यमुनातीर्थमागमत् ।।
210. *PM*, p. 109.
211. Since the Sarasvatī flows southwards from the *ghat* of Jambu Mahārāja, the identification of Rāma-*tīrtha* with Rāma-Prāchī is doubted by some (*PM*, p. 107). It is believed by others that the Agni-*tīrtha* here may be actually the Jamadagni-*tīrtha*. Jamadagni was Paraśurāma's father. Paraśurāma's *tīrtha* known as Rāma-Prāchī being located to the north of the *Agni-tīrtha* where the stream takes a southward bend is thus quite possible. See also *Mbh.* III.83, 14:
ततो महेन्द्रमासाद्य जामदग्न्यनिषेवितम् ।
रामतीर्थे नरः स्नात्वा वाजिमेधफलं लभेत् ।।
212. *Ibid.*, p. 108. Satish Chandra (*op. cit.*, p. 78) seems to have confused it with Rāma-hrada *tīrtha* which is generally identified with Ram Rai in district Jind. See also *VP (SM)* XIV.1ff.
213. LXXXIII. 24, 33 & 64. It is said that a person gets (the merit of) hundred cows by bathing in the Rāma-*tīrtha* (v.64).
214. *Mbh.* IX.38, 21-22:
जगाम वृष्णिप्रवरो रुषङ्गुराश्रमं तदा ।
यत्र तप्तं तपो घोरमार्ष्टिषेणेन भारत ।

ब्राह्मण्यं लब्धवांस्तत्र विश्वामित्रो महामुनिः ॥

VP (SM) XVIII. 16-20 repeats this story but tells us that Rushangu shifted to Prithūdaka from Gangādvāra and became a *siddha* here.

215. *Ibid.*, vv. 24-29.
216. *Ibid.*, v. 30.
217. *VP (SM)*. XVI, 17-18.
218. *Ibid.*, vv. 19-40; *Mbh.* IX.37, 3-29.
219. *Mbh.* III. 81, 105; IX.36, 63; *PP* I.27, 4; *VP (SM)* XVI.40, *Br. P.* III.65, 103-4, etc.
220. *Mbh.* IX.37, 29-33; *VP* XLVI, 71-75.
221. *Mbh.* III.81, 113-15; IX.37, 48-49; *PP* I.27, 21-22; *VP (SM)* XVII, 21-22; XXXVI. 45-58; *Kūrma P.* II.35, 44-76; *Skanda P.* VI.40, 27-52; VII.270, 1-46.
222. *Kūrma P.* II. 35, 44-76.
223. *GP* LXXXI, 5.
224. *RV* VI. 61, 10 & 12; VII. 36, 3.
225. *Mbh.* IX.35, 7-51.
226. *VP (SM)* XXI.16-17.
227. *Ibid.*, vv.17-18:
     यस्तत्र तर्पयेद् देवान् पितृंश्च श्रद्धयान्वितः ।
     अक्षय्यं लभते सर्वं पितृ तीर्थं विशिष्यते ॥
228. *Mbh.* III.81, 137-38.
229. *PP* I. 27, 45-47.
230. *VP (SM)* XX, 3.
231. Satish Chandra, *op. cit.*, p. 75.
232. *Mbh.* IX. 38, 32; 39, 10.
233. *Mbh.* III.81, 16.
234. *Ibid.*, v. 162. *VP (SM)* XX.4 mentions one Soma-*tīrtha* after Śatasāhasrika and Śatika:
     सोमतीर्थं च तत्रापि सरस्वत्यास्तटे स्थितम् ।
     यस्मिन् स्नातस्तु पुरुषो राजसूयफलं लभेत् ॥
235. *Mbh.* III. 81, 96. See also *VP (SM)* XVI.15.
236. *VP (SM)* XIII.33 & LVII.53.
237. See for details *Mbh.* IX. 34, 38-77; *Śiva P.* (*Veṅk. Pr.*) III. 6, 56-62 & IV.14, 1-62; *Skanda P.* VI.63 and VIII. 21, 35; 22, 115.
238. *Mbh.* III.80, 129-31.
239. *VP (SM)* XIII.34.
240. *GP* LXXXIII, 24.
241. *Br. P.* II.65, 32, 103 and 111.
242. *PP* I.26, 17; 27, 3 & 72.
243. *Mbh.* IX. 42, 39-40.
244. *Brahmāṇḍa, Devī Bhāgavata, Liṅga, Matsya, Padma, Śiva, Skanda, Varāha* and *Vishṇu Purāṇa* contain the accounts of Skanda's birth and Tāraka *vadha*, besides the epics. For detailed references, see A.S. Gupta, *The Vāmana Purāṇa*, Varanasi, 1967, p. 770.

245. *Mbh.* IX. 38, 6.
246. *Mbh.* IX.40, 26-27.
247. *Mbh.* IX.42, 41.
248. *VP* XXXII, 114.
249. The present shrine is not very old architecturally but may have been built on the traditional spot. The image of Kārttikeya in this temple being covered by a thick coat of oil and vermilion is beyond recognition. Two lamps keep burning in the temple continuously and women are not allowed to visit it.
250. *Mbh.* IX. 42, 38.
251. *VP* LVII, 12.
252. *Mbh.* III.81, 16, 96 & 162; *VP (SM)* XIII, 34; XX, 4, etc.
253. *Bṛ. P.* II.65, 106 & 121.
254. *Mbh.* III.81, 143; *PP* I.27, 52-53.
255. *Ibid.*
256. *CASR*, XIV, p. 103.
257. *Bh. P.* X.78, 19.
258. *RV*. I.105, 17:
    त्रितः कूपेऽवहितो देवान् हवत ऊतये ।
    तच्छुश्राव वृहस्पतिः कृण्वन्नंहूरणादुरु वित्तं मे अस्य रोदसी ।।
259. *Nirukta* IV.6. See also Kane, *op. cit.*, p. 814.
260. *Mbh.* IX.35, 7-50.
261. *Ibid.*, vv. 52-53.
    तत्राप्यतिविक्रान्तः स्पृष्ट्वा तोयं हलायुधः ।
    दत्त्वा च विविधान्दानान्पूजयित्वा च वै द्विजान् ।।
    उदपानं च तं दृष्ट्वा प्रशस्य च पुनः पुनः ।
    नदीगतमदीनात्मा प्राप्तो विनशनं तदा ।।
262. *PM*, pp. 76 and 87. See also V.S. Agrawala (V.S. 2016), *op. cit.*, pp. 40-41 for details regarding Uttaṅka and his activities.
263. *Mbh.* III.81, 15. *VP (SM)* XIII.32 also maintains the same sequence but says that one gets high position by bathing here with devotion. The *Bṛ. P.* (II.65, 31) and *PP* (I.26, 15-16) also describe these *tīrthas* in the same sequence. *G.P.* (LXXXI.14) also refers to it. It is to be noted that there were various *tīrthas* of this name which have been described in the *Mbh.* and the *Purāṇas*. For details, see Kane, *op. cit.*, p. 818.
264. *VP* LIII, 5.
265. H.A. Rose, "A Note on Kurukshetra", *Indian Antiquary*, Vol. XXXIII(1904), p. 299. See also B.K. Muztar, *Kurukshetra: Political and Cultural History*, Delhi, 1978, p. 113.
266. Bharadwaj (1991), *op. cit.*, p. 55.
267. *Mbh.* IX. 41.
268. *VP (SM)* XIX, 1-43.
269. *Bṛ. P.* II.65, 108.

270. *GP* LXXXIII, 65.
271. *Skanda* (*Veṅk. Pr.*) VI.172, 1 and 173, 16.
272. *Mbh.* IX.41, 4 & *VP (SM)* XIX, 3:
आश्रमो वै वसिष्ठस्य स्थाणुतीर्थेऽभवन्महान् ।
पूर्वतः पश्चिमश्चासीद्विश्वामित्रस्य धीमतः ।।
273. *Ibid.*, v. 16.
274. *Ibid.*, v. 23.
275. *Ibid.*, v. 33 & *VP (SM)*. XIX.18:
तमानीतं सरस्वत्या दृष्ट्वा कोपसमन्वितः ।
अथान्वेषत्प्रहरणं वसिष्ठान्तकरं तदा ।।
276. *Ibid.*, vv. 34 and 19 respectively.
277. *Mbh.* IX. 42; *VP (SM)* XIX, 20-43.
278. *VP (SM)* XVIII.40.
279. *Mbh.* IX.40, 35:
ततस्तालकेतुर्महाधर्मसेतुर्महात्मा कृतात्मा महादाननित्यः ।
वसिष्ठापवाहं महाभीमवेगं धृतात्मा जितात्मा समभ्याजगाम ।।
280. *CASR*, XIV, p. 103.
281. Satish Chandra, *op. cit.*, pp. 66-67.
282. *Mbh.* IX. 39, 12-16:
गाधिर्नाम महानासीत् क्षत्रियः प्रथितो भुवि ।
तस्य पुत्रोऽभवद्राजन्विश्वामित्रः प्रतापवान् ।।
स राजा कौशिकस्तात महायोग्य भवत्किल ।
स पुत्रमभिषिच्याथ विश्वामित्रं महातपाः ।।
देहन्यासे मनश्चक्रे तमूचुः प्रणतः प्रजा ।
न गन्तव्यं महाप्राज्ञ त्राहि चास्मान्महाभयात् ।।
एवमुक्तः प्रत्युवाच ततो गाधिः प्रजास्तदा ।
विश्वस्य जगतो गोप्ता भविष्यति सुतो मम ।।
इत्युक्त्वा तु ततो गाधिर्विश्वमित्रं निवेश्य च ।
जगाम त्रिदिवं राजन्विश्वमित्रोऽभवन्नृपः ।
न च शक्नोति पृथिवीं यत्नवानपि रक्षितुम् ।।
283. *Ibid.*, vv. 17-22.
284. *Ibid.*, vv. 23-28.
285. *VP (SM)* XVIII, 14.
286. *Mbh.* III. 81, 120.
287. *VP (SM)* XVIII, 15.
288. *Bṛ. P.* II. 65, 106.
289. *PP* I. 27, 28.
290. *VP (SM)* XVIII, 15 adds that a *brāhmaṇa* of a pure soul obtains high position by bathing here:
ब्राह्मणस्तु विशुद्धात्मा परं पदमाप्नुयात् ।

291. *Mbh.* IX. 39, 30-31:
तस्मिंस्तीर्थवरे रामः प्रदाय विविधवसु।
पयस्विनीस्तथा धेनूर्यानानि शयनानि च ॥
तथा वस्त्राण्यलंकारं भक्ष्यं पेयं च शोभनम्।
अददान्मुदितो राजन्पूजयित्वा द्विजोत्तमान्॥
292. *CASR*, XIV, p. 103.
293. The *Mbh.* gives details of his life and activities at various places. For references, see V.S Agrawala (*V.S.* 2016), *op. cit.*, pp. 264-66.
294. *Mbh.* IX.40, 29-33. *VP (SM)* XVIII, 37 refers to the flowing of honey in the stream at his sacrifice:
तत्र तीर्थं सुविख्यातं यायातं नाम नामतः।
यस्येह याजमानस्य मधु सुस्राव वै नदी॥
295. *Mbh.* IX.40, 34.
296. *VP (SM)* XVIII, 38.
297. *PM*, pp. 102ff; Satish Chandra, *op. cit.*, pp. 58-59.
298. *Bh.P.*, p. X.1, 22.
299. *Mbh.* IX. 36, 41-42.
300. *Supra* Rāma *Tīrtha*.
301. *PM*, p. ग, : Mahanta Baṃsī Puri, *op. cit.*, p. 8. Cf. *Skanda Purāṇa* VII.36.
302. Pt. Upendra Śarmā Chakrapāṇi, *Pṛithūdaka (Pihovā) Tīrtha Mahātmya* (Hindi), Pīhovā, n.d., p. 60.
303. Cf. चैत्रकृष्णचतुर्दश्यां यः स्नायात् शिवसन्निधौ।
न प्रेतत्वमाप्नोति पिण्डदानात्पृथूदके॥
and
चैत्रकृष्णचतुर्दश्यां यमुद्दिश्य पृथूदके।
पिण्डं हि दीयते सो वै प्रेतभावाद् विमुच्यते॥
as quoted in *PM*, p. 100.
304. Mahanta Baṃsī Puri, *op. cit.*, pp. 2-4.
305. The myth is narrated in the *VP (SM)* XV, 29-36 at the Anyajanma *tīrtha* whose identity with Pṛithūdaka cannot be established. The verse quoted in this connection *VP (SM)* XV. 38 is—
अश्वत्थस्य तु यन्मूलं सदा तत्र वसाम्यहम्।
अश्वत्थवन्दनं कृत्वा यमं रौद्रं न पश्यति॥
The *tīrtha* mentioned in the succeeding verse is Nāga-hrada which is generally identified with Nagdu.
306. *CASR*, XIV, p. 103.
307. *Ibid.*, Vol. II, p. 225 and XIV, p. 101. Later, this inscription was removed to the Lahore Museum where it is preserved still.
308. Kane, *op. cit.*, p. 552.
309. *Ibid.*
310. *Ibid.*, p. 553.

4

ANTIQUARIAN REMAINS

Being an important and old holy place, Pehowa has yielded some antiquarian remains which are described below.

POTTERY

As noted in Chapter I, the earliest archaeological relics found from Pehowa are the Painted Grey Ware sherds.[1] B.B. Lal had obtained these sherds 'from the throw-out of manure-pits located near the southern and south-eastern periphery of the town' which is located on an old mound. He had tentatively associated PGW with the Mahābhārata people and dated it to *circa* 1100-800 B.C.[2]

Since almost the whole of the extensive old mound is under habitation, no PGW sherds or the pottery of the subsequent periods has come to light in the subsequent years[3] though the mound, when excavated, is quite likely to yield such remains. Sherds of medieval red ware, of thin-sectioned bowls in particular, may, however, still be picked up from the mound near the *Guphā* and the Prāchī Śiva Temple. Even this mound has been levelled recently. The thin-sectioned red ware bowls are known from numerous medieval sites in the Punjab-Haryana region and may be dated to *circa* ninth-tenth centuries A.D. on stratigraphic evidence. They may thus belong to the Gurjara-Pratihāras whose two inscriptions, too, furnish evidence of their sway at Pehowa.

COINS

The only coins known from Pehowa were procured by Rodgers. One belongs to the Kuṇinda king Amoghabhūti, one to Kanishka and one probably to Huvishka or some other Kushāṇa ruler.[4]

The following details of these coins may be gathered from Rodgers' account and other known specimens.

Amoghabhūti

Metal	:	Copper
Shape	:	Round

Size	:	0.65 inch
Weight	:	28.5 grains (1.846 gm)
Obverse	:	Deer to right, female figure (Lakshmī)[5] standing, holding lotus in right hand, tree-in-railing over the hind quarters of deer, crescented *chaitya* below the deer and a *śrīvatsa* symbol above the horns. Brāhmī legend around *Rājña(ḥ) Kuṇindasa Amoghabhutisa Mahārājasa.*
Reverse	:	In circle, tree on right, six-arched *chaitya* surmounted by an umbrella, and a *triratna* symbol in the centre, triangle headed standard with a *svastika* above it on left, a wavy line below and traces of Kharoshṭhi legend *Raña Kuṇindasa Amoghabhutisa Maharajasa.*

Kuṇinda coins of this type are assigned to first century B.C.[6] It is difficult to ascertain whether Amoghabhūti held sway over Pehowa or not[7] but the coin is important as it indicates the continuing existence of Pehowa in the first century B.C.

Kanishka

Metal	:	Copper
Shape	:	Round
Size	:	0.65 inch
Weight	:	58.5 grains (3.79 gm)
Obverse	:	King clad in coat and trousers, and cloak, standing to left by fire altar, holding spear in left hand, right hand extended over altar, Greek legend *PAO KA....*
Reverse	:	Male deity (Moon) to left with right hand extended in front, long sceptre in left hand, sword at waist, and a monogram to left, Greek legend MAO

Huvishka?

Metal	:	Copper
Shape	:	Round
Size	:	0.8 inch
Weight	:	134.7. grains (8.727 gm)
Obverse	:	Bust of king and Greek legend[8]
Reverse	:	Draped figure to left

The exact attribution of this coin is difficult as the legend is not fully deciphered and intelligible.

The importance of these coins, however, lies in the fact that they furnish evidence that Pehowa continued to exist during the Kushāṇa period.

It is strange that old coins from Pehowa have not been obtained by anybody after Rodgers during the last more than a century. Maybe that the old coins found from this ancient site made their way to the goldsmiths or metal dealers and were not preserved by anybody.

TERRACOTTAS

Royal Personage (Pl. 14)

Cunningham[9] had obtained from Pehowa the terracotta figure of a seated royal personage. Even though the left hand of the figure is broken off, the piece is fairly well preserved. Cunningham took the figure to be a seated king.[10] R.C. Agrawala, however, observes that the terracotta "depicts a royal personage seated on a throne in a majestic pose. He appears to wear a full-sleeved upper garment resembling the well known *colaka* which covers his arms to the wrists; the collar covering his neck. Apparently, he also wears trousers reaching his ankles. Besides this, a transparent cloth (*cādara*) has been spread over his arm, chest and thighs, and even hangs a bit below the right knee".[11] The figure bears *tilaka* on the forehead and wears a jewelled garland hanging up to the navel. The wig-like headdress, studded with round jewels, is typical of the Gupta period.[12]

The tip of the nose is slightly damaged and the eyes are open. R.C. Agrawala thinks that the upper garment of the figure suggests foreign association and observes that "From artistic point of view this is really an interesting product of the *Gandhāra Art*".[13]

Nobody knows the whereabouts of this terracotta now.

Male Figure (Pl. 15)

Another terracotta plaque obtained from Pehowa by H.A. Phadke and now housed in the Archaeological Museum, Department of Ancient Indian History, Culture and Archaeology, Kurukshetra University, Kurukshetra,[14] is a fine specimen of the classical Indian art tradition. It shows a male figure standing almost frontally with the middle part of the body slightly inclined towards his left, wearing close-fitting upper garment and having frizzled locks of hair falling on the shoulders in an attractive way. Both the hands and the portion below the knees are broken but the damaged portion on the right thigh indicates that the right hand rested on it. The waistband shows a floral pattern in front and circlets around. Twisted part of the *dhotī* with its free end falling gracefully on the outer side of the left thigh may also be seen clearly. A small dagger is tucked up in the waistband on the right thigh. Both the *Kañchuka* and the *dhotī* have been bedecked by a triangular triple circlet pattern[15] whereas the necklace, below a thick twisted and another sturdy golden necklet, is also marked by circlets.

The figure is characterised by a long face with broad forehead, bow-like eyebrows, eyes with heavy eyelids, sturdy nose, full cheeks, long-drawn mouth, thick lower lip and a prominent chin. Circular ear ornament may also be seen clearly. Broad chest and muscular rounded arms, together with the facial features, show him to be in the prime of his life. Shukla feels that "The feeling of contentment and joy is revealed on its facial expression".[16] The absence of a staff in his hand and the style of standing, however, make it difficult to agree to Shukla in regarding it as a doorkeeper.

The figure is carved on a brick-panel which seems to have formed part of a brick temple at Pehowa in the Gupta period. Rodgers had seen carved bricks near the Prāchī Śiva Temple.[17] During one of our exploratory visits, we had seen carved bricks at Viśvāmitra kā Ṭīlā also. So there seem to have existed brick temples at Pehowa during the Gupta period. We do not know the precise place from where Cunningham picked up his terracotta. The plaque in the Kurukshetra University was collected by Phadke from the north of the town some quarter century ago[18] indicating that a brick temple may have existed at or near the Viśvāmitra kā Ṭīlā during the Gupta period.

INSCRIPTIONS

As already noted, Cunningham had discovered two inscriptions at Pehowa, one fixed in the wall of the Garibnath Temple and the other fixed in the wall of a dwelling house called *Siddhagir-ki-Haveli* in the midst of the bazaar in the south-east quarter of the city.[19]

Garibnath Temple Inscription, Pehowa (Pl. 16)

The inscription, [20] incised on a reddish buff sandstone slab measuring 67.5 x 40 cm, is still fixed in the outer wall of the sanctum, facing east, a little to the (viewer's) right of the entrance, in the Garibnath Temple, which is located in the western lower part of the city, near the Kāla-Bhairava temple, a small distance south of the Sarasvatī. The temple belongs to the *Kanphata* Gorakhpanthi *jogis* who also live in it. The inscription consists of seventeen lines, the last of which is nearly one-fourth of others in length. Besides the initial and final letters in the lower half part of the slab, lines 7, 8, 9, 13 and 15 have also suffered some damage. The inscription, however, is beautifully engraved and is in a good state of preservation. Repeated whitewashing, too, has obscured some letters, on the margins of the slab in particular. The inscription is engraved in the northern Nāgarī characters of the ninth century and is in Sanskrit prose showing contemporary dialectal impact. Among the orthographic peculiarities, the use of *va* for *ba* and *m* for *ṁ* in *Samvatsara* is notable.

The inscription records that 33 or 34 pious horse-dealers hailing from Chūṭavārshika, Utpalika, Salavaṇapura, Baladevapura, Śāraṅgaḍika, Sīhabhadrakkaka, Ttreghāṭaka, Ghaṁghaka and [Aśvala] Uḍovaka in various countries, who met at the horse-fair held at Pehowa – Pṛithūdaka on the fourteenth day of the half-month preceding the bright half of Vaiśākha, agreed to impose upon themselves and upon their customers, certain taxes or tithes, the proceeds of which were to be distributed among the following donees: (1) the temple built by the illustrious Guhāditya at Kanauj; (2) the temple built by Kadambāditya at Go-*tīrtha* in Kanauj; (3) the temple of Vishṇu Garuḍāsana built by Brāhmaṇa Bhūvaka in Bhojapura near Kanauj; (4) the temple of Vishṇu in his Yajñavarāha or boar-incarnation form built by Bhūvaka at Prāchī-Sarasvatī in Pehowa – Pṛithūdaka; (5) the *Pūjaka* or temple priest of the latter deity; and (6) the *sthāna* or sanctuary of Pṛithūdaka.

The tax or the tithe imposed was—

1. Two *dharmas*, to be deducted from the sale proceeds by the dealer for each animal sold in Pṛithūdaka to the king and to any subject, or sold in Ttreghāṭaka and the other places where the dealers traded, to the king.
2. One *dharma* to be paid by the buyer of each animal in addition to the stipulated price.

Bühler takes *dharma* to mean a religious gift, the amount of which was settled by custom.[21] The allotment of the shares was as follows—

S.No.	*Share from the tax paid by merchants*	*Share from the tax paid by customers*
1.	7/24	-
2.	7/24	-
3.	7/24	-
4.	1/24	6/12
5.	1/24	2/12
6.	1/24	4/12

The distribution of the charity was entrusted to the *Goshṭhikas*, i.e. members of a committee or Pañch, who had also to look to the collection of money, स्वत: परतश्च निर्वाह: कर्त्तव्य: ।

The date of the inscription *Saṁvat* 276 was rightly taken by Cunningham to refer to the Harsha era of A.D. 606-07. The ruling king mentioned in the record (line 1) is Bhoja (Pratihāra), son of Rāmabhadra.

The inscription is an important document of the social, cultural, economic and religious history of the reign of Bhoja as also of Pehowa city which seems to have been an important commercial and religious centre then. People from far off places used to visit it for the same and purchase of horses, and perhaps other animals also, as well as for earning religious merit. It is notable that an animal fair is still held at Pehowa every year on the date mentioned in the inscription.

Text[22]

Line 1. [सिद्धम्][23] परमभट्टारक-महाराजाधिराज-परमेश्वर श्री ***रामभद्रदेव***-पादानुध्यात-परमभट्टारक-महाराजाधिराज-परमेश्वर-श्री ***भोजदेव***-पादानामभिप्रवर्द्धमान-क

2. ल्याण-विजयराज्ये सम्वत्सर[24] शतद्वये षट्सप्तत्यधिके वैशाख-मास शुक्लपक्ष-सप्तम्यां सम्वत्[25] २७६ वैशाख शुदि ७ अस्यां सम्वत्सर[26] मास-दिवस-पूर्व्वा-

3. यां तिथाविह श्री**पृथूदका**धिष्ठाने पिशाची-चतुर्द्दश्यां-घोटक-यात्रायां समायात[27] चूटवार्षिकेत्य भट्ट-**वीरुक**-सुत **वन्द** तथा **राज्यव(ब)ल** तथा **वल्लुक[र]ाणुक**-सुत **राज्यसीह उत्प-**

4. **लिकेत्य भल्लुक**-सुत[28] [**माहुक**][29] **चिण्ह** (-) सुत [30] **सेणराक**[31] तथा **चिक्करि सलवण** [32]-पुरीय [**दड**][33] -सुत[34] **कल्लुक** एतत्सुत **जयराक विष्णु**-सुत **आदित्यराक रज्जुक**-सुत **चिण्ह** तथा **रङ्गक कल्लुक-**

5. सुत **वामुक व(ब)लदेव**-पुरीय **खम्भट**-सुत **भोट्ट**[35] **मृगाङ्क**-सुत[36] **विड्डक केशव**-सुत **धामुक खड्ग** [37]-सुत **वामुक** [38] **मणिक्क**-सुत **उए-हरि शारङ्गडिकेत्य**[39] **नार**-सुत **लाहट**[40]

6. तथा **शङ्कर वल्लुक**-सुत **ईश्वरादित्य सीहभद्रक्क**केत्य[41] **उल्लूक**[42]-सुत **वच्छक जयध-राक**-सुत **रणिक सूर**-[सुत][43] **प्रगट** [44] **त्रेघाटकीय**[45] **धारट**-सुत **चन्द एकगौरक**[46]-सुत **सव्व**

7. **देव-शर्म्म**-सुत **फम्फ वग्गुक**-सुत **कम्मिक घंघकेत्य लल्लिक**-सुत **स्वामिराक सिंघुक**-सुत **सी [-] दामोदर**-सुत **पोम्भ हल्लुक**-सुत **दन्धु [क?** तथा] **कशिलि माण-सुत [ख]**[48] **ज्जि अ-**

8. **[श्व]ल उडोवकेत्य**[49] **उसूह**-सुत **वद्ध** एवमेतत्प्रमुख-नाना-देशागत-हय-वृक-व्युवहरक[50] [वे] शी[51] श्री**पृथूदकीय**-[स्थानाय][52] पत्त्रं प्रयच्छति यथा[ऽ]*स्माभि:

9. श्री**कन्यकुव्(ब्)जे** श्री **गुहादित्य**-कारित-देवाय तथा तत्त्रैव **गो-तीर्थे कदम्व** (-) **(ब)ादित्य**-कारित-देवाय च तथा श्री **कन्यकुव्(ब्)**जा[सन्न][53] श्री **भोजपुरे गङ्गा**-तीरे नागर-

10. भट्ट-**प्रभाकर**-सुत **भूवक**-कारित गरुडासन-देवाय तथा श्री **पृथूदके प्राची-सरस्वती**-सन्निधौ **भूवके**नैव [का]रित-यज्ञवराहाय च **पृथूदके** घोटक[54]-

11. [घोटिका-वे][55] ग-सर-रूपादि-विक्रयस्य राजकीयोपक्रये **ठक्कुर**-जनपदाद्युपक्रये च तथा **त्रेघाटका**दिस्थानेषु[56] केवलं राजकीय एवोपक्रमे [रूपं प्र-]

12. [ति-धर्म्म-हे]तो[57] र्यद्धर्म्मद्वयमस्माभिरक्षयनीव्यां प्रदत्तं तच्चतुर्व्विन्शति भिव्(ब्)र्भागै:[58] परिकल्प्य भागास्सप्त श्री **गुहादित्य**-कारित-देवाय त[था भागास्सप्त]-

13. [**कदम्व(ब)ा]दित्य**-कारित-देवाय[59] तथा भागाः सप्त **भूवक**-कारित गरुडासनाय तथा [भा]गैकः **पृथूदके भूवक**-क[ारि]त[60] यज्ञवराहाय तथा भागैकस्तत्पूज[का][61]-

14. [य तथा भा]गैक:[62] **पृथूदक**-स्थानाय[63] तथा घोटक[64]-संग्राहकै-र्घोटकं प्रति प्रदत्त-धर्म्मैकस्य कल्पित-भागाना[-]द्वादशानां मध्यात् पृथूदके प्राची-सरस्वती-

15. [सन्निधौ] **भूवक**-कारित-यज्ञ-वराय[65] भागा:[66] [षट् त][67] था तत्पूजकाय च भाग-द्वयं तथा श्री पृथूदकीय-स्थानस्य· भागाश्चत्वारो[ऽ]*स्माभिः प्रतिपादि [तास्तद][68]-

16. [नुमान्यं घोटक][69]-विक्रेतृभि[:] क्रेतृभिश्च ।[70] [चन्द्राक्कर्-का][71] लं यावत्[72] यथोद्दिष्ट-स्थित्या गोष्ठिकैः सद्भिः स्वतः परतश्च निर्व्वाहः कर्त्तव्यः ।। [एते च भागा यथोद्दिष्ट][73]-

17. [स्थित्या गोष्ठिकैः कल्पयि]तव्याः ।।[74]

Translation

[Siddham!][75] During the increasing, auspicious and victorious reign of *Paramabhaṭṭāraka Mahārājādhirāja, Parameśvara,* the illustrious king **Bhoja**,[76] who meditated on the feet of *Paramabhaṭṭāraka, Mahārājādhirāja, Parameśvara,* the illustrious king **Rāmabhadra**, in the year two hundred exceeded by seventy-six, on the seventh (lunar day) of the bright half of the month of Vaiśākha - Saṁvat 276 Vaiśākha Śudi 7- on this lunar day, month and year, as specified above, the following persons who had come at the horse-fair[77] on Paiśāchī-chaturdaśī[78] (met) here[79] in the famous town of **Pṛithūdaka**: Bhaṭṭa **Vīruka**'s sons **Vanda** and **Rājyabala** and **Valluka**, as well as **Rāṇuka**'s son **Rājya-siṁha**, from **Chūṭavārshika**; **Bhalluka**'s son **Māhuka** and **Chiṇha**'s son **Seṇarāka**[81] and **Chikkari**[82] from **Utpalika**; **Daḍa**'s son **Kalluka**, his son **Jayarāka**, **Vishṇu**'s son **Ādityarāka**, **Rajjuka**'s sons **Chiṇha** and **Raṅgaka**, **Kalluka**'s son **Vāmuka** from **Salavaṇapura**; **Khambhaṭa**'s son **Bhoṭṭa**, [83] **Mṛigāṅka**'s son **Viḍḍaka**, **Keśava**'s son **Dhaṇuka**, **Khaḍga**'s[84] son **Vāmuka**, **Maṇṇika**'s (**Mānikya**'s) son **Ue-hari** of **Baladevapura**; **Nāra**'s son **Lāhaṭa** and **Śaṅkara**, **Valluka**'s son **Īśvarāditya** from **Śāraṅgaḍika**;[85] **Ulūka**'s[86] son **Vachchhaka**, **Jayadharāka**'s son **Raṇika**, **Sūra**'s son **Pragaṭa**[87] from **Siṁhabhadraka**;[88] **Dhāraṭa**'s son **Chanda**, **Ekagauraka**'s[89] son **Sarva**, **Deva-śarmma**'s son **Phampha**, **Vagguka**'s son **Kammika** (**Kārmika**) of **Ttreghāṭaka**;[90] **Lallika**'s son **Svāmirāka**, **Siṅghuka**'s son **Sī-**, **Dāmodara**'s son **Pombha**, **Halluka**'s son **Dandhu(ka?)**[91] (and) **Kaśili**[92] **Māṇa**'s son **Khajji** [-/and] **Aśvala**[93] from **Ghaṅghaka** (and) **Usūha**'s son **Vaddha** from **Uḍovaka**.[94] The chief amongst these horse-dealers (as mentioned above), hailing from different countries give a charter to the famous **Pṛithūdaka** Temple to the following (effect): To the (temple of the) god[96] built by the illustrious **Guhāditya** in famous **Kanyakubja** and to (the temple of) the god built by **Kadambāditya** in the **Go-*tīrtha*** at that very place, and to the (temple of the god Vishṇu (riding on Garuḍa) built by **Bhūvaka**, son of Nāgara Bhaṭṭa **Prabhākara**, on the bank of the **Gaṅgā** in celebrated **Bhojapura** near famous **Kanyakubja**, and to the (temple of the) Yajña-Varāha (sacrificial Boar)[98] built by the same **Bhūvaka** in famous **Pṛithūdaka** near the **Prāchī-Sarasvatī**, we have given on the sale of horses, mares, mules and other animals[99] in **Pṛithūdaka** in the case of a governmental purchase as well as in the case of a purchase by the **Ṭhakkuras**, the provincials, etc., and in **Ttreghāṭaka**[100] and other places in the case of governmental purchase only – for the sake of spiritual merit two *dharmas*[101] per animal as a perpetual endowment;[102] and dividing that into twenty-four shares, we have assigned seven shares to the (temple on the) god built by the illustrious **Guhāditya**, and seven shares to the (temple of the) god built by **Kadambāditya**, and seven shares to the Garuḍāsana (Temple) and one share to Yajña-Varāha (Temple) built by **Bhūvaka** in **Pṛithūdaka**, and one share to the temple-priest of the latter, and one share to the **Pṛithūdaka** Temple; of the twelve supposed shares of each *dharma* given by the purchasers of horses we have assigned six shares to the Yajña-Varāha (Temple) built by **Bhūvaka** in **Pṛithūdaka** near the **Prāchī-Sarasvatī** and two shares to its priest, and four shares to the famous **Pṛithūdaka** (Temple). This should be approved by the sellers and buyers of horses, (and) the noble Goshṭhikas[103] should thus manage on their own part and on behalf of others, according to the rule laid down above as long as the sun and the moon exist. And the Goshṭhikas should divide these shares as prescribed (above).

Pehowa *Praśasti* of Mahendrapāla (Pls. 17 & 18)

This inscription, along with the horse-dealers' grant, was first discovered by Mr. Bowring at Pehowa[104] and both of these are published partially by Rajendralal Mitra.[105] The stone slab on which it was incised was fixed close to the door wall of *Siddhagir ki Haveli* in the bazaar where Cunningham also saw it and even tried to take it out of the wall as it was used as a seat and was likely to wear away.[106] Rodgers who got this inscription extracted from the wall with the help of J.R. Drummond, the then Deputy Commissioner of Karnal, has observed that "Near the highest part of the town is *Siddhagīr's Havelī*. In the doorway is a stone, used for people to sit upon, with a Sanskrit inscription on its upper surface. It contains 20 2/3 lines. Eleven inches of the stone to the left are embedded in the wall. There is margin of two inches on the right. Two bottom lines are injured. The left hand upper corner has been ill-treated with a chisel. The stone is 3′ 3″ by 1′ 11″.[107] This stone was obtained by Rodgers and sent to the Lahore Museum where two estampages of the inscription were prepared by J.L. Kipling and sent to Burgess who forwarded them to Bühler to edit them.[108]

Bühler observed that "Judging from the impression, the slab on which the inscription is incised measures 36" x 24". The stone-mason has done his work with great care; for there are very few Indian epigraphical monuments which show an equal amount of neatness and artistic finish in their execution. Owing to the rough treatment which the stone has undergone, a certain number of letters have, however, been either obliterated or become indistinct. Lines 3-7 have lost from four to seven letters at the beginning; in lines 1-6, the letters 17-21 on the left-hand side have been partly rubbed out, and lines 20-21 have lost a piece out of the middle. Moreover, a number of single letters and small groups have been defaced in various places on the right-hand side of the inscription. It is, however, fortunately possible to restore most of the lost signs with some degree of certainty by conjecture".[109]

The inscription is in very good Sanskrit and metrical throughout except the opening invocation. In all, there are 27 verses with the following metres: Śārdūlavikrīḍita 1, 6, 7, 9; Mandākrāntā 2, 17, 20; Vasantatilakā 3, 12, 23; Sragdharā 4; Praharshiṇī 5, 14, 18; Mālinī 8; Āryā 10; Śālinī 11; Anushṭubh 13, 21, 22, 24, 26, 27; Pṛithvī 15, 19; Drutavilambita 16 and Vidyullekhā 25. The script used is the Nāgarī of Northern and Western India of ninth-tenth centuries with ornamental superscribed *mātrās* and sometimes tails of some letters also. The orthographic peculiarities include the frequent use of *Jihvāmūlīya* and *Upadhmānīya, va* for *ba, d* for *dd* (ll. 4, 12 etc.), unusual *sandhi* of *sa śrīmān* as *saśśrīmān* (l. 5.), etc.

The object of the inscription is to record the building of a triple temple of Vishṇu by Gogga, Pūrṇarāja and Devarāja, the three sons of Jajjuka, himself son of Vajraṭa and a scion of Jāula, of the Tomara clan. The inscription recorded the names of the three villages assigned for the *bhoga* of the three deities in the triple shrine as Yakshapālaka, Gejjara and Pāṭala which have been identified with Jakhepala (Dt. Sangrur), Ghaggar and Patran (Dt. Patiala) by Bharadwaj.[110] The architect was Achyuta, son of Rāma, a native of Kāmboja. The poet (name lost) was the son of Bhaṭṭa Rāma, the *sūtradhāra* was Durlabhāditya and the engraver Bālāditya(?).

The epigraph is not specifically dated but refers to king Mahendrapāla, the successor of Bhoja. The earliest dated inscription of Mahendrapāla is the Una Grant of A.D. 893.[111] As the script of this inscription resembles that of the preceding record, it cannot be far removed from that in date.[112]

Text[113]

Line 1. ओं[114] नमो माधवाय ।।
याते यामवती-पतौ शि[खरिषुक्षामे]षु सर्वात्मना
ध्वस्ते ध्वान्त-रिपौ जने विघटिते स्रस्ते च तारा-गणे ।
भ्रष्टे भू-वलये गतेषु च तथा रत्नाकरेष्वेकता-
मेको यस्स्वपिति प्र-
2. धान-पुरुष≍ पायात्स वः शार्ङ्गभृत् ।। [१।।]*
दृष्टि≍ [पायात्त्रिजग]दखिलं शार्ङ्गिणX कान्त-मुर्त्तेX
कान्ता सद्भ्रू-स्फारित-सुभग-स्निग्ध-ताराभिरामा ।
उद्यत्तीव्र-स्मर-जलनिधौ मज्जतश्श्री-मुखेन्दु-
स्फार-ज्योत्स्ना भव[115]-
3. ⌣⌣ [रुचः][116] स्मेर-गण्ड-स्थलस्य ।। [२ ।।]*
क्षेत्रं कुरो[र्विविध-पाप-][117] मलाभिघात-
दक्षं क्रियादुदयमस्त-समस्त-तापम् ।
अद्ध्यासितं मुनि-गणैरुदितात्म-वो(बो)ध-
प्रद्ध्वस्त-गाढ-तिमिर-प्रकट-प्रमोदैः ।। [३ ।।]*
पोत-
4. [स्संसार-सिं]*[118] धौ सुर-पथ-गमने स्यन्दनस्साधु-[वर्ग]-
- - - -[119]त-ह्ने≍ प्रलय-जलधरस्सम्पतत्सान्द्र-धारः ।
नाना-व्याधि-प्रव(ब)न्ध-प्रचुरतम≍ पङ्क-विद्ध्वंस-भानु-
नीर्ऱ्ञ्चैतत्समन्ता[द]* द्ययु-दुरित-
5. [गुणं चारु]*[120] **[स]रस्वतं** वः ।। [४ ।।]*
यश्शक्तः स्वकुल⌣—⌣—⌣[121] मृद्ध्या[122]
भिन्दान≍ पर-व(ब)ल-मानस[123] समन्तात् ।
सश्श्रीमाञ्जयति **महेनद्रपालदेवः**
शान्तारिश्शशधर-सुन्दरः शरण्यः ।। [५ ।।]*
आसी**त्तोमर**-तुङ्ग-वंश-ति-
6. [लकश्चण्ड-प्र]तापोज्व(ज्ज्व)लो
राजा-रंजित[124]-साधु-वृत्त- [हृदयो दु-]र्वृत्त-शैलाशनिः ।
नाम्ना **जाउल** इत्यपूर्व-चरित-ख्यातो दयालंकृति-
स्तम्वा(त्त्वा)लोकि-विलोकित-क्षितिपति-व्यापार-लब्धोदयः ।। [६।।]*
येन ज्ञाति-कुलं क-
7. [—⌣⌣⌣—नी]तं परां संपदं
छिन्नाराति-करीन्द्र-कुम्भ-शकलैX कृत्वोपहारं भुवः ।

कीर्त्या (र्त्त्या) यस्य च नाक-नाग-निकर-व्यासङ्गतः सङ्गमा-
*द्व्योमन्ध्र स्फुरदिन्दु-सुन्दर-रुचा स्वस्सिन्धु-लीलायितम् ॥ [७॥]**
प्रतिदिश-
8. *[ममरा]णां मन्दिराण्युच्छ्रिताग्र*
स्थगित-शशधराणि स्फारमारोपितानि ।
जगति वितत-भासा येन दूरं विभान्ति
*स्वयश इव निरोद्धुं शङ्कवो दिङ्निखाता ॥ [८॥]**
तत्सन्तान-महोदधे॒ प्रमुदित-प्रोद्यद्भुजङ्गाश्र- या
9. *दुर्ल्लङ्घाद्घन-मौक्तिकांशु-निकर-स्फारीभवत्सम्पदः ।*
प्रख्यातादजनि स्ववङ्शतिलकः[126] *श्री**वज्रटाख्य**॒ प्रभु॒*
*प्राप्ताशेष-मनोरथश्शुभतर-व्यापार-तुङ्गोन्नतिः ॥ [९॥]**
तस्य स्फुरदिन्दु-रुचिः शौरेरिवजल-
धि-कन्यका जाता ।[127]
10. *नाम्ना मङ्गलदेवी जाया गिरिजेव गिरिशस्य ॥[१०॥]**
तस्मात्तस्याज्जज्जुक॒ प्रादुरासीदुच्चैश्शान्तस्सत्सु निर्मत्सरेषु ।
*क्रूर X केतुर्द्दुद्धरारातिं चक्रे क्रुद्ध्यत्सेना-कुञ्जर-द्ध्वान-रौद्रे ॥ [११॥]**
तस्य
11. *स्फुरन्निशित-खड्ग-निकृत्त-शत्रो-*
स्त्रस्तान्ध-दीन-निकरोद्धरणोरु-कीर्तेः (र्त्तेः) ।
सद्वृत्त-रक्त-वनिता-तिलकाङ्क कल्पे
*कान्ते व(ब)भूवतुरदार-शशाङ्क-कान्ते ॥ [१२॥]**
एका ***चन्द्रे****ति विख्याता द्वितीया* ***नाइ(यि)के****ति च [।]**[128]
विशि-
12. *ष्ट-गुण-निर्माणा [द्]* द्वे एव सदनं श्रियः ॥ [१३॥]**
चन्द्रा*यास्समजनि* ***गोग्ग****-नामधेयो धीराणां धुरि*
धीराणां धुरि विनिवेशितो विधात्रा ।
भूनाथो द्विषदिभ-कुम्भ-भेद-निर्य-
न्मुक्ताभि [र्महत्[129] *महीतल]श्शितासिः ॥ [१४॥]**
असूत च वि-[130]
13. *चक्षणं क्षत-विपक्ष-पक्ष-प्रभं*
प्रभाकर-करोत्करं स्वव(ब)ल-सैनिकाम्भोरुहाम् ।
अधर्म-परिपन्थिनं तदनु ***पूर्णराजं*** *सुतं*
स्ववंश-गगनोदरे तुहिन-[दीधितिं ***नायि]का*** *॥ [१५॥]**
करतल-स्थगिताधर-पल्ल-

14\. वा≍ प्रतनु-कान्ति-कपोल-तलोदरम् ।
सिषिचुरस्रु (श्रु)जलैर्यदरिस्त्रियस्सरलित-प्रचुरालक-जालकाः ॥ [१६॥]*
    तस्य भ्राता गुण-निधि[र]भूत्सोदरो **देवराजः**
स्फुर्जत्तेज [≍][131] प्रविहत-पर-स्फार-सेनान्धकारः ।
    स्था- नं क्षान्तेः क्षत-कलि-मलः क्षिप्त-रागादि-दोषः
15\. स्निग्धच्छायास्तरुरिव ततस्सत्फलानम्म्र (म्र) मूर्तिः (र्त्तिः) ॥ [१७॥]*
नामापि प्रकटतरं निशं(श)म्य यस्य
    क्रुद्धस्य भ्रुकुटि-तरङ्गिताननस्य ।
दृप्तानां युधि विकसद्विगाढ-भासां
16\. सस्रंसे करतलतः कृपाण-दण्डः ॥ [१८॥] *[132]
यदास्य-सरसीरुहं सरसमर्थिनां पश्यता-
    न्नितान्तमगमत्क्षणात्क्षयमुपद्रवो मानसः ।
व्यघूर्णत च सम्भ्रमात्प्रतिभट-द्ध्वद्दन्तिनां
    घटा-विघटनोन्मुखी
17\. समिति यस्य सद्य≍ पुरः ॥ [१९॥]*
इत्युद्दाम-प्रकटित-गुणोद्गार-रम्या X क्रमेण
    प्राप्त-श्रीकाश्शुभतर-धियस्साधु-रक्तास्त्रयो(ऽ)* पि ।
विष्णो[133] स्सौधान्यतुलमहस X कारयामासुरत्र
    त्रस्तास्ती[व्राद्भव-जल]-निधेर्दुर्ग[मा]-
18\. न्मन्द-वो (बो)धैः ॥ [२०॥]*
गोग्गेन कारितं मध्ये **पूर्णराजेन**[134] पृष्ठतः ।
    पुरतो **देवराजेन** घनान्ध-तमस-छि (च्छि) दे ॥ [२१॥] *[135]
चतुस्समुद्र-सीमांकं यावदेतन्महीतलम् ।
    इदमायतं तावद्विभातु सदनं श्रियः ॥ [२२॥]*
धन्वन्तरि-[प्र]-
19\. तिनिधिश्श्रुत-सार-मूर्ति (र्त्ति)-
    स्सद्व (ब) **न्धुरच्युत** इति प्रकटाभिधानः
काम्वो (बो) जज≍ प्रभु-मन X कमल-द्विरेफो
    रामस्य सूनुरिह कारयिता व(ब)भूव ॥ [२३॥]*
यक्षपाल-नामैको द्वितीयो **गेज्जरा**भिधः ।
    पाटला[ख]यस्तृती[यो(ऽ)* पि ग्रा-]
20\. मो भेगाय कल्पितः ॥ [२४॥]*
अत्रार्यैः क्ष्मा-नाथैः श्रेयो [ऽ]* र्थं देहस्य ।
    संसारं दृष्ट्वोचैः(च्चैः)कर्त(र्त्त)व्या सद्वु(ब)द्धिः ॥ [२५॥]*
स्वकुल-गगन-भ[ानुः]-ि⌣— ार-प्रसक्तः

श्रुत-विनय-विदग्धो **भट (द्ट) राम** X *किलासीत् ।*
अकृत मधुर-[व (ब)न्धां मु]⌣⌣स्तस्य
सूनु-
*स्सरस-ललित-सारांल्ली (ली) लयेमां प्रशस्तिम् ।। [२६।।]**
व (ब)भूव सूत्रधारो [ऽ] त्र* **दुर्लभदित्य**-*संज्ञितः ।*
xxxx⌣— — [व **(ब)**][136] **ग्लादित्येन** *धीमता ।। [२७।।]**

Translation

Om! Salutation to Mādhava!

Verse :-

1. May that Chief Male, the holder of the Śārṅga-bow (Vishṇu), protect you; He, who alone sleeps, when the lord of the night (Moon) has disappeared, when the mountains have completely been singed, when the foe of darkness (Sun) has been destroyed, when mankind has been disintegrated, when the host of stars has fallen off, when the terrestrial globe has decayed, and thus the oceans have become one.[137]
2. May handsome Vishṇu's beautiful eye, pleasing with its lovely brow and expanded, charming, affectionate and delightful pupil, protect all the three worlds—(the eye) of him who is immersed in the surging and impetuous ocean of love, whose lustre is increased by the great splendour of Lakshmī's moon-like face, whose cheeks are radiant with smiles.
3. May **Kurukshetra** (literally 'the field of Kuru') effect your exaltation free from all troubles, —(Kurukshetra) which is capable of removing the impurities of various kinds of sins, which is inhabited by hosts of sages, who have destroyed the dense darkness (of ignorance) with the knowledge of the self (and hence) are filled with evident delights.
4. And may that (beautiful) water of the **Sarasvatī** cut your (bonds of) misery—(that water which is) a ship for crossing the ocean of mundane existence, a chariot for travelling along the path of the gods (i.e., heaven), a cloud which appears on the destruction of the world, pouring copious showers on the fire (of miseries?) of the virtuous people, and a sun which destroys the slushy darkness of a concatenation of various diseases.
5. Victorious is the illustrious king **Mahendrapāla**, who is able to bless his race with prosperity and to destroy the courage of the armies of his enemies all around, whose foes are extinguished, who is handsome like the moon and affords protection.[138]

6. There was a king, **Jāula** by name, the front ornament of the exalted Tomara race, resplendent with fierce valour, who gladdened the hearts of the virtuous, who was a thunderbolt to the mountains in the form of the wicked people, who was well-known for his unprecedented deeds, adorned with compassion (and) acquainted with truth, who gained eminence by looking after the affairs of his sovereign.
7. By whom the race of his kinsmen was led to the highest prosperity..., after having made an offering of the pieces of the severed temples of the elephants of his foes to the earth; and whose fame, possessing the fair splendour of a glittering moon, simulated the heavenly stream (i.e., Gaṅgā) by having come into contact with the host of celestial elephants and united with the sky.
8. By him, whose lustre spread all over the world, were built in every region numerous temples of the gods, which obscured the moon with their lofty summits, and which look from afar like the darts fixed at the quarters of the horizon in order to set limits to his fame.
9. From his famous ocean-like race, which is the resort of joyful and prospering intimates, as the ocean is of the serpents, difficult to overcome, and possessing treasures, ever increasing with the clustered rays of big pearls, sprung a lord, called the illustrious **Vajraṭa**, the front ornament of his family, who obtained all his wishes and gained an enormous rise through his auspicious business transactions.
10. Charming like the glittering moon, (a lady) called **Maṅgaladevī** became his wife, like the daughter of the Ocean (Lakshmī) that of Śauri (Vishṇu) and the daughter of the Mountain (Pārvatī) that of Girīśa (Śiva).
11. He begot by her **Jajjuka**, who was exceedingly peaceful among good men who are free from envy, (but) a terrible comet for the army of his invincible foes who inspired terror through the trumpeting of the angry war elephants.
12. He (i.e., Jajjuka), who cut down his enemies with his sharp and flashing sword and gained widespread glory by rescuing the timid, the blind and the miserable, had two wives who were lovely like the full moon and were the front ornaments of the virtuous and sporting women.
13. One was famed as **Chandrā** and the second as **Nāyikā**, being created out of the most excellent qualities, they were both abodes of excellence (or beauty or prosperity).

14. From **Chandrā** was born a prince, named **Gogga**, who was placed by the creator at the head of the courageous men, who possessed a sharp sword and honoured the earth with the pearls issuing from the rents in the temples of the elephants of his foes.
15. And afterwards **Nāyikā** gave birth to a clever son **Pūrṇarāja**, a destroyer of the splendour of the ranks of his enemies, a multitude of the rays of the sun for lotuses, (i.e.) the soldiers of his own army, a foe of unrighteousness, and a moon on the firmanent of his own race.
16. The wives of his foes, covering their lips (red) like young shoots, with their hands, moistened with the water of their tears, their hollow cheeks that had lost their lustre and the straightened abundant multitude of locks of hair.[139]
17. **Devarāja**, a store of virtues, was his uterine brother; he who destroyed the dense darkness, (i.e.) the armies of his foes, with a sudden burst of his brilliant courage, (he who was) the abode of forbearance, destroyed the impurity of the Kali age, cast off the evil passions of attachment, etc., and resembled a tree providing agreeable shade and bending under good fruit.
18. When the arrogant foes whose exceeding lustre blossomed in the battle merely heard the more illustrious name of that (warrior) who angrily furrowed his face with frowns, their strong swords fell from their hands.
19. When the supplicants looked at his lotus-face with rapture, their mental disturbance completely disappeared in an instant and the hostile troops of trumpeting elephants reeled before him in battle, ready to disperse.
20. All the three (brothers), lovable on account of the free manifestation of their virtues, who gradually rose to prosperity, who were very pure-minded and attached to holy men, caused to be built here temples of Vishṇu, who is endowed with unmatched greatness, because they are afraid of the dreadful ocean of mundane existence that is difficult to cross for men of little wisdom.
21. (The temple) in the middle has been built by **Gogga**, that at the back by **Pūrṇarāja**, and the one in front by **Devarāja**, in order to destroy the dense and deep darkness (of sin).
22. As long as the earth is bounded by four oceans, so long may this temple shine as an abode of magnificence.[140]
23. The architect (*Kārayitā*) here was **Achyuta**, of famous name, the son of **Rāma**, born in **Kamboja**, a representative of Dhanvantari,[141]

embodiment of the quintessence of learning, a friend of the virtuous, and a bee on the lotus of the heart of his master.

24. One village called **Yakshapālaka,**[142] a second named **Gejjara,**[143] and a third named **Pāṭala,**[144] have been assigned for the enjoyment (of the god).[145]
25. With respect to this (endowment), the (future) noble kings, keeping in mind the mundane existence, must maintain a highly virtuous disposition for the welfare of their body.
26. There was, indeed, a **Bhaṭṭa Rāma**, the sun on the firmament of his family, attached to... learned and modest; his son **Mu**... composed as if in sport (i.e., easily) this eulogy of sweet composition, the essence of which lies in its poetic sentiment and elegance.
27. Here was a mason (*sūtradhāra*) named **Durlabhāditya**. (This epigraph has been engraved) by (his son?) the wise **(Bā)lāditya**.

A Fragmentary Inscription on an Architrave (Pl. 19)

Besides the well-known preceding two inscriptions at Pehowa, there is another one engraved on the architrave of a door-frame now fitted upside-down in an almirah of the Garibnath Temple complex. Faint traces of the carvings on its extremities indicate that an earlier stone slab was utilised to form the architrave of a small Sun Temple as is borne out by the *lalāṭa-bimba* depicting Sūrya holding lotuses in his two hands. That the inscription existed on this slab before the *lalāṭa-bimba* was carved is revealed by the letters which stand truncated by the figure. The extant inscription shows three lines. The third line may be made out only by a few traces and some letters which have survived on the proper left hand side of the Surya.

The record is in a very indifferent state of preservation and it is difficult to read it, or even to photograph it or prepare its estampage. It seems to begin with a symbol (*Siddham*), followed by *Svasti*. There are faint traces of the date in the beginning but it is difficult to decipher it properly. The script seems to be late variety of the Northern Brāhmī or the early medieval Nāgarī. Nothing, however, can be made out clearly. The inscription may tentatively be dated to *circa* tenth-eleventh century A.D.[146]

TEMPLE REMAINS

The literary and epigraphic evidence leaves little doubt to Pehowa being an important holy place studded with religious edifices. The terracotta figures described above indicate that some beautiful brick temples may have existed at Pehowa during the Gupta period. Excavations of the Viśvāmitra kā Ṭīlā and the mound in the vicinity of Prāchī Śiva Temple are likely to

Pl. 16. Garibnath Temple Inscription

Pl. 17. Pehowa *Praśasti* of Mahendrapāla (Photograph)

Pl. 18. Pehowa *Praśasti* of Mahendrapāla (Estampage)

Pl. 19. Fragmentary inscription on an Architrave

Pl. 20. Doorway from Viśvāmitra kā Ṭīlā fitted in the Sarasvatī Temple

Pl. 21. Yamunā with her attendants

Pl. 22. *Uttaraṅga* of the doorway

Pl. 23. Doorway of the *Guphā*

Pl. 24. Architrave

Pl. 25. Unfinished doorway fitted in the Prāchī Śiva Temple

Pl. 26. *Lalāṭa-bimba*: Garuḍavāhī Vishṇu

Pl. 27. Door-frame, Durgā Temple, Prāchī Complex

Pl. 28. Socle of a Vaishṇava Temple showing Garuḍa

Pl. 29. Gaṅgā with a male attendant

Pl. 30. Door jamb

Pl. 31. Door jamb

Pl. 32. Architectural piece

Pl. 33. Pilaster

reveal the foundations of the Gupta and early medieval shrines. Cunningham's observation regarding the Viśvāmitra *Tīrtha* is worth noticing: "This is situated on the south bank of Saraswati, on a mound rising 40 feet above the bed of the river. Here are the remains of a fine temple, of which only the stone doorway of the sanctum is now left standing. There is a mass of solid bricks, with numerous fragments of carved bricks. Over the doorway there is a male figure with two arms seated with hands in lap, and with a small elephant on each side anointing him. To his left were the *Navagraha,* or nine planets, and to the right the *Ashta-Sakti,* or eight female energies of gods".[147]

Rodgers also recorded that "In the walls of the houses of the town I noticed fragments of large bricks some 5" thick, and some few carved bricks".[148] Taking note of the doorway, noticed earlier by Cunningham, and other relics, Rodgers thought that "Pehoa had in olden times 3 stone temples of great beauty".[149] It is, however, difficult to agree with him in his observation that "Some were undoubtedly Jaina, perhaps all were so: but there was an admixture of Hinduism".[150] Rodgers certainly erred in his judgment. No Jaina images or temple-remains have been found from Pehowa.

The doorway mentioned by Cunningham is now fitted in the Sarasvatī Temple on the bank of the river (Pl. 20). It is 1.75 metre high and 1.40 metre broad. The inner height of the door-opening is 1.40 metres and its breadth is nearly 0.70 metre, the jambs being about 35 cm wide (each).[151] The bottom portions of the jambs show the river goddesses with their female and male attendants, Gaṅgā on the proper right hand side and Yamunā on the corresponding left. Their vehicles, *makara* (crocodile) and *kūrma* (tortoise) respectively, are carved below the lotus *pīṭhas* on which they stand. The female attendants also stand on the lotus seats under which are carved the foliated tails of the mounts. The male attendants on the extremes, however, stand on pedestals under which are carved half-diamond (*ardha-ratna*) designs. The river-goddesses, together with their female acolytes stand under the canopies of inverted flowers. Their dresses and ornaments are also similar. They bear *dhammilla* coiffures adorned with jewels, circular earrings, pearl necklets and necklaces, the latter with long strings falling from between their rotund breasts with the pendents touching their left thighs, *keyūras, valayas, uttarīyas, mekhalas, adhovastras* and *nūpuras*. The free ends of their waistbands fall on their thighs which are also covered with sashes. The river-goddesses stand very gracefully with their *kaṭi* portions accentuated and turned towards the door opening, holding lotus flowers (damaged in both the cases) in their hands towards the door and the ends of the *uttarīyas* in their other *pralamba-hastas*. The female attendants with similar attributes stand cross-legged with their inner thighs parallel to those of the river-goddesses. The posture of the male attendants are also similar to those of the river-goddesses but their necklaces are smaller and they wear sacred threads and long garlands also. Rings in their fingers may also be seen. They bear *karaṇḍa-mukuṭas* adorned with front jewels and support the free ends of the sashes in their outer hands. The male attendant of Gaṅgā holds a lotus flower in his left hand. The right hand of the corresponding male figure is broken (Pl. 21).

The doorway consists of five *śākhās*: "The innermost is scroll. The next is a series of panel each containing an image. The middle band consists of alternate large and small panels each containing two figures. Then follows a narrow band of scroll work. The outside band has alternate large and small panels like the middle band".[152]

Cunningham had wrongly described the *lalāṭa-bimba* as a male figure with two arms and anointed by the elephants. Rodgers rightly pointed out that "In the centre of the lintel is a four-armed image seated cross-legged on two lions".[153] Two hands are folded in front. The upper right hand holds the *gadā* and the left a lotus flower.[154] The deity, thus, may certainly be identified as Yoga-Nārāyaṇa.[155] The god is showed in a pedimented *rathikā* which has got three ornamental ribbings on its pillars. There are no elephants on each side anointing the god but an outward facing rampant animal on each side, the *gaja-śārdūla* motif. The central band of the lintel shows four musicians on each side of the central figure, two male and two female. At the ends of these bands of musicians is a large female figure, one on each side. These female figures are reminiscent of the river-goddess figures which occupied these positions in Gupta temples (Pl. 22).[156]

The uppermost band of the lintel shows *navagrahas* on the proper right hand side and *Sapta-mātṛikās* on the left. The *navagraha* figures are clearly identifiable with Sūrya holding lotus flowers in his two hands followed by Soma, Maṅgala, Budha, Bṛihaspati, Śukra and Śani, each seated in *sukhāsana,* holding water-pot in the left hand and allaying fear (*abhayamudrā*) with the right. Next to Śani is the big head of Rāhu followed by the serpentine Ketu. The *sapta-mātṛikās* on the left hand side are accompanied by Vīrabhadra and Gaṇeśa. The fifth *mātṛikā* is Vārāhī, shown as sow-faced.[157]

Yoga-Nārāyaṇa on the *lalāṭa-bimba* and the innermost *Nāga-śākhā* of the doorway[158] indicate[159] that this doorway belongs to a Vaishṇava temple. Rodgers has observed that "This is the most elaborate doorway, entire, in the whole Panjab. Perhaps there were other portions of this temple of stone, for there are huge stones lying about and worked up into the building".[160]

Stylistically, it is a typical Pratihāra door-frame which may have certainly adorned a Pratihāra temple.

As indicated above, this doorway was found at Viśvāmitra kā Ṭilā which is located a short distance south of the Prāchī-Sarasvatī. As such, we feel inclined to its having been a part of the Yajña-Varāha Temple built by Bhūvaka near the Prāchī-Sarasvatī at Pṛithūdaka— श्रीपृथूदके प्राची-सरस्वती-सन्निधौ भूवकेनैव कारित यज्ञ-वराहाय— during the reign of Bhoja Pratihāra.

Amongst the numerous other remains noticed at Pehowa by Rodgers, "The most interesting is a carved doorway in a building or rather a ruin on a small mound about 20 feet high about a mile up the Saraswati from Pehoa, on its left bank. The building was after the fashion of a house and not a temple, and it seems to have been used by a faqir as his residence. There was a temple here once, however, for many of the bricks on the mound and in the walls of the house are carved. The place was uninhabited when I was there and I strongly advocate the removal of the doorway before it is utterly ruined by neglect. For months the mound is cut off from the outer world by the water of the river".[161] The doorway mentioned by Rodgers is still to be seen fitted in the same building called *Guphā* near the Prāchī Śiva Temple. This doorway (Pl. 23) is smaller in size, 1.40 x 0.70 metre. The original *udumbara*, door-sill, is missing. The doorway is of *pañcha-śākhā* variety like the one described above. The innermost band is the *nāga-śākhā* with an adoring serpent at the base. The upper half portion of this *nāga* is anthropomorphic, canopied by snake-hoods, and the lower half is anguine, coiled beautifully and covering the remaining part of the band. The next band consists of a series of panels each containing an image, either dancing or playing on some musical instrument. The middle band represents *mithuna-śākhā* and consists of alternate large and small panels showing the couples in different postures. Then follows the *gaṇa-śākhā* with dwarfish figures dancing in different poses. The outermost band shows exquisite scroll work. The *pedyās*, bases of jambs, show the river-goddesses with their female and male attendants. Gaṅgā on the proper right-hand side stands in *dvibhaṅga*, double flexion, posture slightly turned to her left, supporting a vase in her left hand at the level of the shoulder while her suspended right hand holds the dangling end of the scarf. Wearing earrings, *ekāvalī* (single stringed necklace) with a long pendent strand falling from between her breast to the waist, armlets, wristlets, scarf and a lower garment held in position by an elaborately carved girdle, she stands under the canopy of an inverted flower. The goddess is followed by a female attendent, probably a fly-whisker, under a similar canopy and wearing similar dress and ornaments. The male attendant, with necessary difference of dress and ornamentation which include a sacred thread and a long garland, also stands under lotus canopy, almost to front, in double flexion pose, holding in his left hand an object which looks like a flower, with the suspended left touching the thigh. The vehicle of the goddess is not visible because of the weathering of the stone below her feet. Yamunā on the other side stands almost symmetrically accompanied by identical attendants.

The positioning of the architrave on the side jambs (Pl. 24) clearly indicates that it has been fitted into its present position after its removal from somewhere. The *lalāṭa-bimba* shows a male deity seated on a lotus *pīṭha* in *Yogāsana,* with two hands placed in the lap over the soles of the feet, in a pillared pedimented niche. The *rathikā* is adorned with an *udgama* (pediment) of *chaitya* (dormer window) motif which shows *ardharatna* (half-diamond) in the centre and *makara-mukhas* (crocodile faces) with rampant leogryphs outside the ribbed pillars. The attributes in the upper hands of the deity of the *lalāṭa-bimba* are not very clear but seem to have been the same as in the preceding example.[162] As such, the deity may be identified as the Yoga-Nārāyaṇa.

Except the middle band which shows a *kīrti-mukha* (face of glory) at the level of the lintel on each side, all other bands continue on the lintel and terminate on either side of the *lalāṭa-bimba.* Strangely enough, the dancers and musicians on the second and the fourth jambs are shown horizontally on the lintel. This must have been necessitated by the available width of the jambs. In the case of the *mithuna-śākhā,* however, the ingenuity of the artist is to be seen. As noted above, a *kīrṭi-mukha* has been introduced just below the topmost panel of the vertical sides because otherwise the height of the panels would have rendered that much space as blank. On the horizontal part of this jamb on either side of the central piece, however, are depicted *gandharva* and *vidyādhara* figures, five on each side, in flying postures. Starting from the central piece on the proper right hand side, may be seen a garland bearing *vidyādhara* followed by his spouse holding lotus flowers by their stalks in both the hands. Another couple follows showing the male figure with a sword in his right hand and some indistinct object (arrows?) in the left, the female holding perhaps a drinking cup in the left and a lotus in the right hand. The last female figure is depicted as holding a long lute across her body in both her hands. On the corresponding other side we have the garland bearing male followed by his spouse in *añjali-mudrā,* another couple similar to that of the proper right hand side followed by a male figure with a long lute held similarly across the body. All these figures have been carved turned towards the *lalāṭa-bimba.* It is, however, the sur-lintel which is very interesting. On the proper right hand side of the pediment of the *rathikā* are the *navagrahas* with Rāhu in a sacrificial pit and Ketu as the hybrid figure with human bust and serpentine tail. On the left of the pediment are Ashṭa-Vasu, all two-handed, holding a water-pot in the left hand placed on the knee with right hand disposed in fear allaying pose. They are all bull-headed and seated in *sukhāsana*. The depiction of the eight Vasus on the sur-lintel is very interesting and no other similar example is known to us.

It is one of the most elaborate and complete doorways which are but very rare in the whole region. A very look at it and its dimensions, however, makes it clear that it cannot be the doorway of any main shrine. We, therefore, think that it may have belonged to the subsidiary shrine of some *pañchāyatana* (quincunx) temple. Stylistically, it is quite close to the Sarasvatī Temple doorway and belongs to the mature Pratihāra idiom. It may be assigned to the late ninth-early tenth century A.D.[163]

Another door-frame recovered from the mound of Viśvāmitra has now been fixed in the main extrance of the Prāchī Śiva Temple (Pl. 25). It is, however, an unfinished door-frame showing the river goddesses accompanied by their female and male attendants on the *pedyās*, hybrid *nāga* figure in *añjali-mudrā* on the bases of the innermost *śākhā*, the outermost *patra-śākhā* and the *lalāṭa-bimba* depicting Garuḍāsana Vishṇu. All the other vertical bands and the *uttaraṅga* have been left plain. This door-frame is not different from those described above in conception but for the fact that it shows Garuḍavāhī Vishṇu as the *lalāṭa-bimba* and is unfinished.

The vehicles of the river-goddesses are also missing. In place of the original door-sill the slabs of the *vedibandha* mouldings still showing *chaitya*, *ardha-chaitya* and *ardha-ratna* decorations have been used upside-down. Garuḍāsana Vishṇu as the *lalāṭa-bimba* is, however, interesting. The god sits in *lalitāsana* on an anthropomorphic vehicle. He wears a *kirīṭa-mukuṭa*, ear ornaments, *ekāvalī*, *yajñopavīta*, *vanamālā*, *keyūras*, pearl bracelets, *adhovastra* secured by a pearl band and anklets (Pl. 26). The stalk in the front right hand indicates that it held the lotus. The rear right and left hands support the *gadā* and *chakra* respectively. Though the normal left hand is damaged yet it may be presumed unmistakably to have held a conch. Garuḍa is depicted in *vīrāsana* to his left and a diminutive devotee is carved before him in profile with folded hands. It is, however, difficult to agree with Shukla that "The profuseness of ornaments lacking sharpness in depiction makes the whole scheme of form as a fossilised one".[164] There is no profusion of ornamentation as noted above though the sharpness of lines is absent in the entire carving. The lively posture of Garuḍa negates the fossilisation as conceived by Shukla.

Though unfinished yet this door-frame is very important as it indicates that architectural pieces, and presumably sculptures also, were carved at

Pehowa itself and were not imported ready-made. Garuḍāsana Vishṇu as the central piece reminds us of the Garuḍāsana Vishṇu Temple built by Bhūvaka at Bhojapura near Kanauj—

> श्री भोजपुरे गङ्गातीरं नागर-भट्ट-प्रभाकर-
> सुत-भूवक-कारित गरुडासनदेवाय ।

Probably he got this form carved in his Yajña-Varāha Temple at Pehowa also and it was copied in the present example as well. It is just a surmise as one can never be sure of it in the absence of any definite evidence. The style and roughness of execution, however, indicate that this door-frame must have been carved in the first half of the tenth century A.D., probably not much later than Bhūvaka's Yajña-Varāha temple. It is, however, somewhat enigmatic as to why it was left unfinished. It may have been the sudden death of the builder and/or lack of patronage.

Another door-frame (Pl. 27) now fitted in a small shrine dedicated to Durgā near the Prāchī Śiva Temple shows beautifully carved river-goddesses holding water-pots and accompanied by male attendants, but with plain upper bands. A part of the *vedibandha* stone showing a *ratna* in a pedimented niche is also fixed in this Durgā shrine to serve as the pedestal for the Devī.

The existence of a Pratihāra Vaishṇava temple in the present Prāchī Śiva Temple complex is evidenced by a large part of the socle of that temple now fixed in the newly built shrine of the complex. It measures 87.5 x 37.5 cm and represents Garuḍa in *vīrāsana* holding serpent in left hand and right hand raised above the head, in a beautiful *rathikā* having *chaitya-udgama* and centrally ribbed pillars with rampant *gaja-śārdūla* motifs on the sides. There are two female fly-whiskers also carved in separate niches on the sides (Pl. 28).

A very roughly carved *pedyā* depicting Gaṅgā with a male attendant fixed elsewhere in the Prāchī complex (Pl. 29) is indicative of yet another door-frame of a Vaishṇava temple. Its height of 25 cm, however, betrays its association with some sub-shrine. Yet another *pedyā* in the same complex, showing Gaṅgā with Śaṅkhapurusha (30 x 27.5 cm) further corroborates the evidence.

A fragment showing a female supporting a *kalaśa* (river-goddess),[165] a *nāgara-kūṭa*,[166] door jambs,[167] and other architectural and sculptural fragments obtained many years back from the Prāchī mound[168] furnish evidence to the existence of some temples at this site. A beautifully carved jamb (Pl. 30) shows Gaṅgā standing over her vehicle, the crocodile, under the canopy of an inverted flower, supporting the water-pot in her left hand and the dangling end of the *uttarīya* in the *pralamba* right hand, accompanied by a male attendant holding a lotus by its stalk (Padma-purusha?), also under a similar lotus canopy. Both wear usual dress and ornaments. The innermost *śākhā* above shows beautiful scroll work with a hybrid hooded *nāga* at its base. The second hand is carved with exquisite *bakula* flowers. The third *śākhā* shows vertical panels, the lowermost depicts a seated male figure (*gaṇa?*), then a *mithuna*, a *kīrtimukha*, a *mithuna* again, two *bhāra-putras* supporting the superstructure and then again a *mithuna* (at the top). The outermost hand is carved with lotus-leaf pattern. Another jamb (Pl. 31) betrays comparatively rough execution and shows Yamunā and her male attendant standing under flower canopies with *latā*, *nṛitta-gaṇa* and *patra śākhās* above. An elaborately carved fragment depicts a male figure holding a lotus in his right hand and wearing a *vanamālā* in the central *rathikā* flanked by female figures at the extant lower portion with *gaṇa śākhā* showing the dwarfish figures either dancing or playing some musical instrument, *mithuna* panels with intervening smaller panel of celestial musicians and the *gaja-vyāla śākhā* with musicians' panel continuing over the first panel. At the top is the square abacus with foliage motif (Pl. 32). A fragmentary pilaster with *kīrtimukha* spewing pearl strings and *gaja-vyāla* figues on the side (Pl. 33) is also worthy of note. A lintel with Gaṇeśa, made of brownish sandstone, measuring 65.5 x 15 cm was also recovered from the Prāchī Śiva Temple.[169] A complete door-sill (Pl. 34) from the same complex shows the earth-goddess adored by hybrid *nāga* couples against the background of lotus stalks, buds and flowers on the *mandāraka*, the central projection of the sill. The *mandāraka* is flanked on either side by a female and a male figure followed by *Udadhi-kumāras* and the garland bearing *vidyādharas* hovering in the sky. Outward moving lions with hind portions in profile and foreparts facing have been carved at the back of the *Udadhi-kumāras*. On the extreme ends are two male figures, one on either side. The execution of this sill indicates that it must have belonged to an elegant Pratihāra temple.

Another door-sill (Pl. 35) now fixed in a recently built wall of the same complex betrays comparatively poorer workmanship. The *mandāraka* shows lotus motif. Bird-legged *Udadhi-kumāras*, garland bearing hovering *vidyādharas* and outward moving lions have also been depicted. Near it is fixed on the same wall the shaft of pillar with a Vaishṇava *pratihāra* (Pl. 36). The *kīrṭamukuṭa* on his head and *gadā* and *chakra* in the rear right and left hands may still be made out. The figure is adorned with exquisite dress and ornamentation and is accompanied by miniature attendant figures. The flutings of the shaft are capped by inverted lotus petals.

Much more elegant, however, is another part of a pillar (Pl. 37) fixed in a corner of the compound of the Prāchī Śiva Temple. It shows exquisitely carved *pūrṇa-ghaṭa*, *kīrtimukha* and *ardha-padma* motifs. A *kīrtimukha* (Pl. 38) and many more architectural and sculptural relics from this complex have been acquired recently by the Department of Archaeology and Museums, Haryana, Chandigarh.[170]

During one of our visits to Pehowa on 18 December, 1989, we saw the area before the *Guphā* near Prāchī Śiva Temple being levelled. Very wide walls and foundations, indicative of some huge and magnificent temple, made of bricks of 39 x 22.5 x 5 cm and 30 x 21 x 4 cm, being exposed. These bricks may be dated to the Pratihāra period. On the evidence of a very large number of architectural and sculptural remains found from the Prāchī complex, we feel inclined to believe that the triple temple built by the Tomara brothers Gogga, Pūrṇarāja and Devarāja, was located here.

Pehowa must have virtually been littered with temples during the Pratihāra period. A century back, Rodgers had seen two sculptured fragments in the fields to the south-east of the town: "One is part of the capital of a pillar 2' 9" long and 12" square. It is very deeply carved. The other stone is part of the superstructure of a building. It is 2' 4" x 1'. There are a central figure and some mouldings on it".[171] Rodgers had also seen and drawn fragments from Garibnath and Bhairon temples.[172] Though some of them seem to have been taken away, yet a few of them may still be seen. Of these, the pillar in the yard of the temple of Bhaironji still stands on the place where Rodgers saw it (Pl. 39): "It is 4' 2' high and 11" square. The shaft is 20" high only, the capital is 2' 6". It is an exquisite example of this type of pillar".[172] A *nāgara-kūṭa* and two Sūrya images also lie fixed in the southern wall of Bhaironji's shrine (Pl. 40).

A door-jamb showing Yamunā and Chakrapurusha on the *pedyā* and *nāga, bakula, mithuna* and *patra śākhās* above and a *chaitya* motif with an ascetic in the *gavāksha* window (Pls. 41 and 42) were preserved in the Śravaṇanātha Temple at Pehowa till sometime back.[174] Evidently they belonged to some temple in a nearby locality.

Rodgers had seen some architectural relics in Siddhagīra's *havelī* also. He observed, "The sill of the door of the *havelī* is made of two fragments of sculpture, one a portion of a pilaster with scrolls, the other part of a lintel of a doorway. Inside the *havelī* is a piece of stone from a temple. It is 22 1/2" square and 17 1/2" thick. There are two figures in a panel, outside of which are deeply cut mouldings".[175] The two fragments in the field, mentioned above, probably belonged to a temple on the site of Siddhagīra's *havelī*. Another existed near it as Rodgers records—

> On the way to Siddhgir's haveli I noticed *an old gurgoyle lying*. It is 5' 9" long and 10" square. The head had horned eyes and large tusks. The orifice was 2" in diameter. From all this we may infer that here was a second temple near Siddhgir's haveli....[176]

Pl. 34. Door-sill

Pl. 35. Door-sill fitted in Prāchī Śiva Temple

Pl. 36. Pillar shaft and other fragments

Pl. 37. Part of a pillar in Prāchī Śiva Temple

Pl. 38. *Kīrtimukha*

Pl. 39. Pillar, Bhaironjī kā Mandira

Pl. 40. *Nāgara-kūṭa* and Sūrya images in the wall of Bhairon Temple

Pl. 41. Door jamb, Paśupatinātha Temple

Pl. 44. Chakrapurusha

Pl. 42. *Chaitya* arch, Paśupatinātha Temple

Pl. 43. Gaṇeśa

Pl. 45. Bhūdevī (?) and Garuḍa

Pl. 46. Śrīdevī and Garuḍa

Pl. 47. Vishṇu's *gadā* with Brahmā-Sarasvatī on stela

Pl. 48. Vishṇu's *chakra* with Śiva-Pārvatī on stela

Pl. 49. Architectural piece with Rāma, Balarāma, etc.

Pl. 50. Yoga-Nārāyaṇa on Architrave

Many of the relics noticed by Rodgers are, however, missing now. A pillar 4' 2" long and 12" square seen by him on a well in a sarai in the town[177] is also untraceable now. He had also noticed fragments of large bricks, some 5" thick, and some carved ones, in the walls of some houses. Some of the old large bricks measured 13½" x 9" and 2½".[178]

During the hundred years after Rodgers, though many old relics have disappeared many new ones have come to light. The account presented above is only representative and not comprehensive. Nevertheless it makes it evident that there existed at Pehowa a large number of temples during the medieval times, Pratihāra period in particular, during which the town was at the height of its glory.

SCULPTURES

As a corollary of the abundant architectural remains, we may visualise the existence of numerous reliefs which may have originally adorned the temples at Pehowa. All of them, however, have not come down to us. What has survived and is known is sufficient to provide glimpses of the glory that was Pehowa during the medieval period in particular. We describe below cult-wise some of the important sculptural relics from the site.

Gāṇapatya

Though the antiquity of the earliest depiction of Gaṇapati (Gaṇeśa) is a matter of controversy, yet there is no doubt to the ascendancy of his popularity in the early medieval period.[179] An image of Gaṇeśa, of rare beauty, is now displayed in the Museum of the Department of Archaeology, Haryana, Chandigarh.[180] Made of buff sandstone, it measures 33 x 20 cm and was discovered from the Prāchī Śiva Temple complex. It shows the deity seated on a cushion in *lalitāsana* holding a full-blown lotus and an axe in the rear pair of hands and a *mūlaka* and the bowl of sweet-balls in the proper right and left hands (Pl. 43). The god wears a tiara adorned with pearl strings and jewels, necklace, snake thread, beaded wristlets and anklets. The left tusk is broken and the trunk takes a turn to the left and twirls to pick up a sweet-ball. The mount of the god, mouse, is also shown near the right foot. There is a plain gloriole with beaded rim behind the head and the top corners show garland bearing *vidyādharas*. A *tilaka* mark simulating a vertical third eye adorns the forehead. The god is slightly pot-bellied. A pleasing composition, sparse ornamentation and exquisite chisel work add grace to the image which may have originally adorned a mature Pratihāra shrine.

Amongst other images of Gaṇeśa from Pehowa, mention may be made of small icons of red sandstone measuring 14 x 7.5 cm in the Dasanāmī Akhārā and 8 x 5 cm in the Bālā Sundarī Temple. Another representation, 21.5 x 14 cm, depicting the deity with two female attendants is preserved on the Sarasvatī ghat in a small shrine. All these images may be assigned to the Pratihāra period. It is notable that Gaṇapati *Utsava* is still celebrated at Pehowa on the fourth day of the bright half of Bhādra and the fourth day of the dark fortnight of Māgha.[181]

Vaishṇava

We have seen above that both the Pratihāra inscriptions of Pehowa refer to Vaishṇava temples. Unfortunately they have not survived. Sculptural relics from the site, however, furnish corroborative evidence to their existence. That there existed many other shrines dedicated to Vishṇu at Pehowa in the post-Gupta and early medieval periods is also evidenced by the sculptures and their fragments recovered from the site.

Fragmentary Reliefs

The lower part of a Vishṇu image from Pehowa is now preserved in the Archaeological Museum of the Kurukshetra University, Kurukshetra.[181] On the central offset of the *saptaratha* pedestal, [182] the extant part of the legs below the knees, indicates that the god must have stood in *samapādasthānaka-mudrā*, on a lotus *pīṭha* flanked by Śaṅkhapurusha, Śrī and Balarāma[183] on his right and Chakara-purusha, Sarasvatī and Garuḍa on the left, on the receding *rathas*. The head of Śaṅkhapurusha is mutilated. A substantial part of the *vaijayantī-mālā* has, however, survived. Shukla dates this image to *c.* tenth-eleventh century A.D.

Much more beautiful, however, is a part of a Vishṇu image measuring 83 x 18 cm, which shows Chakrapurusha, Bhūdevī, Garuḍa and a garland bearing female figure on the receding projections of the proper left hand side part of the pedestal. Just above the last figure on the back slab is *gaja-śārdūla* and a *makara-mukha* surmounted by a female standing cross-legged. Her head is broken. Above Bhūdevī in the middle of the slab is a devotee seated in profile supporting perhaps a musical instrument. He is seated on a lotus. The stela above shows four-armed Śiva in *lalitāsana* on a lotus seat, holding a trident in the upper right hand and a snake in the upper left, while the front right is dispensed in *abhaya* and the normal left holds a *kapittha* or *mātuluṅga*. Projecting forward from near the right leg of Śiva is the disc of Vishṇu with a tassel issuing from its hub. A part of the halo with half-diamond decorations may also be seen. All the accessory figures have been carved very beautifully. They wear usual dress and ornaments of pearls.[184] Its counterpart showing four attendant figures on the pedestal is preserved with Shri H.K. Murari, a former B.D.O. of Gharaunda.[185] The complete image must have been a magnificent Pratihāra masterpiece.

That Prāchī Śiva Temple complex was the site of a late Gupta temple is indicated by a fragment of a buff sandstone piece[186] measuring 20 x 11 cm showing Chakrapurusha slightly turned to his left (Pl. 44). He bears a heavy curled coiffure, *kuṇḍalas, ekāvalī, keyūras, valayas* and a *dhotī* reaching only up to the knees. A part of Vishṇu's *vanamālā* is preserved on his left.[187]

A very elegantly carved panel of buff sandstone measuring 46 x 20 cm in its extant form, found from the Prāchī complex at Pehowa[188] depicts Garuḍa, following Bhūdevī, bearing beautifully combed hair with two tiers of frizzled curls at the crown of the head, tied with a twisted band and adorned with a *chūḍāmaṇi* (Pl. 45). The fleshy cheeks, quasi-closed fish-shaped eyes with bow-like eyebrows, smiling face, triple fold of the neck, serpentine earrings, necklace and sacred thread, *dhotī* secured by a simple waistband, jewelled armlets and wings behind the shoulders of Garuḍa are the notable features. His right hand raised above is broken and the left one akimbo seems to have held a snake also. Equally graceful is the figure of Bhūdevī though her head and right arm are lost. Both these figures are broken below the knees. The round shoulder, rotund breast, slightly accentuated middle portion with a heavy ball-like pendent falling from between the breasts, the *pralamba* left hand stylistically holding the dangling end of the *uttarīya* and the exquisitely carved ornaments add an uncanny grace to her figure. The image of Vishṇu, whose part this panel is, must have been a gigantic and very elegant icon belonging probably to one of the temples mentioned in the Pratihāra inscriptions.

Another Vishṇu image in black stone at the same place is evidenced by a panel, very much multilated, showing Śrīdevī and Garuḍa (Pl. 46). This panel was dug out from the Prāchī complex some years back and is now fixed in one of its walls. Garuḍa is shown in *añjali-mudrā* and wears a long garland besides the usual dress and ornaments. The elongation of the female figure, however, indicates a slightly later date.

We have already referred to the part of the socle of a Vishṇu temple showing Garuḍa (Pl. 28) now fixed in the newly built shrine of Prāchī Śiva Temple. It is, however, difficult to correlate it with the Vaishṇava sculptures found from the complex; but it does indicate the Prāchī site to have been an important pilgrimage centre where stood some elegant shrine(s) dedicated to Vishṇu, besides, of course, other deities.

During our first visit to Pehowa in 1964, we had collected from the Dasanāmī Akhārā two fragments of a beautiful Vishṇu icon and deposited them with Dr. Buddha Prakash who was at that time the Director of the Institute of Indic Studies, Kurukshetra University, Kurukshetra.[189] One fragment showed Vishṇu's *gadā* and a stela depicting Brahmā-Sarasvatī (Pl. 47) while the other showed *chakra* and Śiva-Pārvatī on a stela (Pl. 48). The stylistic similarity of the two pieces leaves little doubt that they belonged to the same image. Both show rectangular stele with identically seated divine couples. Tricephalous Brahmā with central bearded face and juvenile side faces in profile sits on the lotus seat in *lalitāsana* with Sarasvatī on his left lap. He holds a lotus (with rosary?) near the chest in his front right hand and touches the left breast of his spouse with the corresponding left which comes winding from behind her. The rear right and left hands support ladle and book. Below the stela is carved an ornamental *makara-mukha* having a foliated tail and a long elephantine snout which holds a lotus flower over which is carved a female figure with a *vīṇā*. The uppermost register shows the divine musicians and garland bearers. Śiva on the other stela holds trident and snake in his rear pair of hands and sits on his vehicle, the bull. A part of the nimbus with *ardha-ratna* decorations on the fringe is also visible here.[190] To judge from the extant fragments, the original image must have been a cult icon and an exquisite Pratihāra specimen.

Another fragment of buff sandstone from the Dasanāmī Akhārā, too, seems to have been a part of a Vishṇu image, of the same period, as it shows Rāma with a bow in left hand accompanied by another male figure holding a lotus. Above Rāma is a conch-blowing male while on the extreme right is carved an outward leaping *gaja-vyāla* (Pl. 49). The fragment measures 17 x 13 cm.

Garuḍāsana, Yogāsana and Incantatory Forms

We have already discussed the Garuḍavāhī Vishṇu figure (Pl. 26) on the lintel of a doorway now fixed in the Prāchī complex and an architrave with Yoga-Nārāyaṇa (Pl. 50) in the same complex. Yoga-Nārāyaṇa has been shown in the centre of a *parikara* (Pl. 51) also. A small pedimented niche in a small modern fane near the Prāchī Śiva Temple shows Kalki[191] on horseback holding a sword in his right hand held above the head (Pl. 52) indicating further that it must have formed part of a Daśāvatāra Vishṇu image during the late ninth-early tenth century A.D.

An elegantly carved buff sandstone fragment of a pedestal, 22 x 15 cm, showing Chakrapurusha and Bhūdevī[192] and a Vishṇu head,[193] 15.5 x 17.5 cm from Pehowa, too, deserve mention. A window screen with a Boar in a medallion now housed in the Kurukshetra University Museum,[194] too, seems to have belonged to a Vishṇu temple. A small fragment of

20 x 10 cm in buff sandstone from Prāchī complex represents the torso of a Nṛi-Varāha. It is, however, badly mutilated. The dagger tucked up in the belt is clear in spite of the mutilation.[195] Another fragment from the same complex, made of buff sandstone and measuring 30 x 12 cm represents the pedestal of a Nṛi-Varāha icon showing in the extant piece the Nāga couple supporting a lotus on which is placed the left foot of the god and the right foot is splayed out on the left projection of the *triratha* pedestal.[196] Stylistically, these pieces belong to the Pratihāra period. Their discovery from the Prāchī site indicates the existence here of a Varāha temple, probably the Yajña-Varāha Temple mentioned in the Garībnāth Temple inscription of Bhoja.

Garuḍa

Prāchī has also yielded two images of Garuḍa. Both are in buff sandstone. One of these, 46 x 26 cm is a part of a pedestal of a Vishṇu image[197] but the other one is iconographically interesting. It is an independent relief and we do not know of any other independent image of this type of Garuḍa from Haryana. It measures 39 x 26 cm. The head and right hand are broken (Pl. 53). The anthropomorphic mount is shown sitting to left in the posture of a warrior (*vīrāsana*). Wings rising at the back are partially visible. Garuḍa holds a snake in his left hand and also wears serpentine necklace, sacred thread and waistband. Garuḍa's association with and antagonism to the snakes are too well known to need any elaboration. The hood of the snake held in the left hand is damaged but can still be made out unmistakably. *Valayas* and *nūpuras* are also clear. Garuḍa wears an *uttarīya* and a *dhotī* also. The folds of the latter have been indicated by double incised parallel wavy lines on the thighs.

The medium of buff sandstone has provided the artist an opportunity to mould his ideas in a solid form. The poise, the posture, the flow of lines and the delicacy of the chisel work bestow a distinctive character to this relief which so far remains unique and is one of the loveliest reliefs of Haryana created during the Pratihāra period.

Śeshaśāyī

In the Mahādeva Mandira near the Sarasvatī *ghat* is fixed a small figure of Śeshaśāyī Vishṇu, measuring 16 x 11 cm, depicting the god lying on the coils of the great serpent with his head to left and right foot lifted and being washed by Lakshmī. Brahmā is seated on the lotus issuing from Vishṇu's navel. The god holds a lotus in his normal right hand near the chest and supports his head with the back right hand, with a mace lying behind. The front left hand holding a conch is placed on the left knee while the extra left hand supports the disc. This miniature relief may be assigned to *circa* tenth century A.D. on stylistic grounds.

Harihara

A fragmentary head of Harihara of nearly the same period is also known from the Prāchī area at Pehowa. Measuring 12 x 11 cm in its extant form, it is broken below the tip of the nose. The long eyes with drooping eyelids and arched eyebrows, ears with long lobes, backward combed hair and the exquisite decorations of the coiffure, however, acquaint us of the care with which the artist carved this figure. The vertical division of the coiffure, the right hand side showing matted locks with a crescent and the left hand side showing an exquisite bejewelled cylindrical crown, however, leave no doubt to the head being that of Harihara. It, too, may be dated to the Pratihāra period.[199]

Vaikuṇṭha

The most exquisite Vaishṇava icon from Pehowa, however, is that of Vaikuṇṭha (Pl. 54)[200] showing the tricephalous octomanous deity standing gracefully in a double-flexion pose wearing a high crown, ear ornaments, necklace, sacred thread, armlets, bracelets, anklets and a lower garment secured by a waistband. A beautiful *vanamālā* hangs down from behind the back of the god very gracefully. On the proper right of the placid human face which bears beatitudinous expression and a *tilaka* mark on the forehead is the lion face and on the other side the boar face, in profile. The fourth face at the back may only be presumed. The front right hand is held is protection and the others hold a discus, a sword and an arrow respectively. The proper *pralamba* left hand holds a conch, the second hand is placed on the thicker end of the *gadā*, the third supports a scutum and the fourth one seems to have held a bow, now missing. This arrangement of the attributes is unique and is not found in any known iconographical text. As such it seems to have been the innovation effected by the artist at Pehowa. Near the feet of the deity stand in symmetrical postures the personified weapons accompanied by female fanners or the Lord's consorts, Śrīdevī and Bhūdevī. Above in the corners are shown garland bearing *vidyādharas*. Measuring 52 x 29 cm this buff-coloured sandstone sculpture found from the Prāchī complex is a veritable masterpiece of the Pratihāra art of Haryana.[201]

Saura

Sūrya

A spotted red sandstone fragmentary relief measuring 34 x 32 cm from Prāchī shows the feet of Sūrya wearing high boots and the typical long *cholaka* with sharp edges in the centre accompanied by the acolyte Daṇḍa on the proper left and Piṅgala on the right (Pl. 55).[202] Daṇḍa has churbish looks and Piṅgala, badly mutilated, may have been bearded. Both stand slightly turned to their master, resting their outer hands on their respective thighs. The other hands may have held their respective attributes, the *daṇḍa* and the manuscript or leaf. The feet of Sūrya in *sama* pose indicate that he stood in the *samapādasthānaka-mudrā*. A scarf which may have been held by him in simulation of the *vanamālā* can be seen partially above the feet. On stylistic grounds the figure may be attributed to the late Gupta period.

A greenish black sandstone relief measuring 27.5 x 24.5 cm in its extant form represents Sūrya seated in *utkuṭikāsana* on a chariot drawn by seven horses (Pl. 56).[203] The relief is so fragmentary and in such an indifferent state of preservation that it is difficult to make out all the charasteristics and details of the figure but the *avyaṅga* on Sūrya's chest, *vamamālā*-like scarf on his arms, lotuses in his two hands, bearded Piṅgala seated near his right leg and three of the seven horses of the chariot may still be seen. The image may have been a cult icon which seems to have adorned some Pratihāra fane.

Ranbir Singh Sangra of Pehowa had collected an image of Sūrya, 15 x 10 cm, showing the dwarfish deity standing on a lotus seat in contraposto, wearing squatty cylindrical crown, ear ornaments, pearl necklace, sacred thread, bracelets, lower garment, boots, etc. with a scarf simulating long garland. He holds in his two hands lotuses by their stalks. The top right hand side corner is broken but the other corner is bedecked with an acanthus leaf decoration.

Interesting, however, are the seated figures of Piṅgala and Daṇḍa near his feet. They sit in *sukhāsana*. The faces of both of them are mutilated. They hold their respective emblems. Stylistically, it may be assigned to *circa* eighth-ninth century A.D.[204]

An almost coeval small figure (Pl. 57) of Sūrya is still worshipped by the people in the Pṛithvīśvara Mahādeva Temple and two others, one seated and one standing, are fixed in the outer wall of Bhaironjī kā Mandira (Pl. 40).

Revanta

In 1974, we had brought to light a broken image of Sun's son, Revanta, wearing a crown, large earrings, beaded necklace, armlets, wristlets, *ardhoruk* and long boots, riding on a caparisoned horse, canopied by an umbrella held by a male attendant, holding a wine-cup in his right hand (Pl. 58).[205] A female figure holding a pot of wine has also been shown behind the head of the horse. A diminutive trumpeter also helped him in his hunting spree as is indicated by pigs being crushed under the hoofs of his horse. Revanta is led by Piṅgala, also on horseback but retrorse, wearing usual dress and also the *avyaṅga*, holding pen in his right hand and leaf in the left. His right foot, too, is shown as crushing a pig. This Tomara-Pratihāra panel was broken at the other end. The missing part representing the equestrian Daṇḍa, another acolyte of Sūrya, holding a long spear in his hands, was also located by us subsequently and published.[206]

Śaiva

Many places of pilgrimage of Pehowa, as we have seen above, are connected with Śiva. It is however, strange that images of the god are very scarce. May be that he was worshipped in his *liṅga* form. The *liṅgas* in many of the present shrines—the Pṛithvīśvara Mahādeva, the Prāchī Śiva Temple, etc. —are said to be very old. Since these shrines have been renovated and rebuilt many a time, it is difficult to vouch for their antiquity.

Umā-Maheśvara

The most beautiful Śaiva image from Pehowa is the Umā-Maheśvara image (Pl. 59) recovered some years back while digging the mound in front of the *Guphā* in the Prāchī complex. Made of buff sandstone and measuring 57.5 x 45 cm, it is now fixed in the outer wall of the Prāchī complex. Śiva is seated in *lalitāsana* on Nandī with Umā on his left lap. He bears an elaborate *jaṭā-mukuṭa*, bedecked with front jewels, large ear ornaments, *hāra, yajñopavīta, aṅgadas, valayas, nūpuras*, a long garland, *adhovastra* and a *yoga-paṭṭa* wound around his right knee and left thigh. A ring in the thumb of his normal right hand can also be made out. In his normal right hand, he holds a fruit-like object (*bījapuraka?*). The rear right hand, broken below the wrist, may have held the trident which, too, is broken, but can be visualized from the lower part of its shaft placed on the right thigh of the god vertically. The extra left hand holds a triple-hooded snake and with the normal left hand, the god embraces his spouse.

Umā also embraces the god with her right hand. His left hand is broken. She is seated somewhat awkwardly with legs moving outwards and bust turned towards the god. Her left foot is placed on the head of Nandī. A dwarfish *gaṇa* stands with a bowl of sweet-balls to feed the bull. His head is broken. Bhṛiṅgī may have been carved in the centre as can be made out

Pl. 51. Yoga-Nārāyaṇa on *Parikara*

Pl. 52. Kalki

Pl. 53. Garuḍa

Pl. 54. Vaikuṇṭha

Pl. 55. Lower part of a Sūrya image

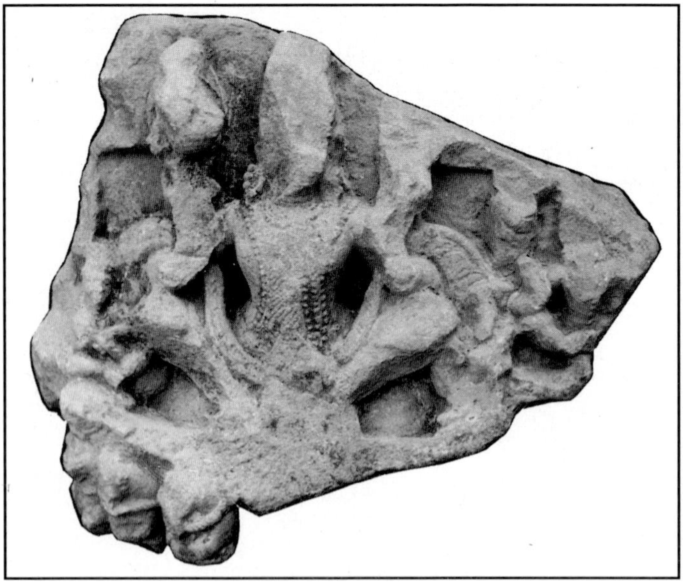

Pl. 56. Fragmentary Sūrya

Pl. 57. Sūrya, Pṛithvīśvara Temple

Pl. 58. Revanta

Pl. 59. Umā-Maheśvara

Pl. 60. Bhairava

Pl. 61. Chaturmukha-*liṅga*

Pl. 62. Mahishāsuramardinī

Pl. 63. Nārasiṁhī

Pl. 65. Fragment of a Pārvatī (?) image

Pl. 64. Fragment of a Chāmuṇḍā image

Pl. 66. Pedestal of a Kshemaṅkarī image

Pl. 67. Fragment of a Mātṛikā image

Pl. 68. Brahmā

Pl. 69. Brahmā on a stela, Prāchī Śiva Temple

Pl. 70. Brahmā on a stela

Pl. 71. Yama

Pl. 72. *Chāmarikā*

Pl. 73. Wall painting, *maṇḍapa,* Paśupatinātha Temple

from the traces of the broken figure. Śiva has placed his right foot on a footrest posited on a lotus flower. Gaṇeśa is seated in *sukhāsana* near Śiva's right foot and Kārttikeya near his left foot is seated similarly on his mount peacock, holding *śakti* in his left hand and right disposed in fear allaying posture. Standing behind Gaṇeśa is a male figure, with head broken, holding a trident in his left hand and the corresponding figure behind Kārttikeya holds a wine-cup in his right hand. It is a beautiful relief assignable to the end of the ninth or the beginning of the tenth century A.D.

Bhairava

The image of Bhairava in the Bhaironjī kā Mandira (Pl. 60) is made of black stone and is a late one. The god is shown standing to front, cross-legged on the mount dog carved to left in profile. The nude god holds a skull (?) in his normal right hand and a sword in the upper right. One of the left hands holds a cup and the object in the other is not clear. This image may have been installed in the shrine in the eighteenth century.

Another late image of Bhairava is set up in an outer niche of the Prāchī Śiva Temple.

Chaturmukha-liṅga (Pl. 61)

Paśupatinātha Temple has in its sanctum now a huge Chaturmukha-*liṅga* of touchstone, the equivalent to which is pointed out to be there in the Paśupatinātha Temple of Kathmandu in Nepal.[207] It may be dated to the Maratha period.

Śākta

Śakti has been conceived in various forms—as the inherent energy of different deities and as the primaeval, supreme, universal energy herself. As such, she has been represented in various manifestations. We describe below some of her important manifestations as encountered at Pehowa.

Mahishāsuramardinī

Mahishāsuramardinī is the most popular manifestation of Śakti. A superb example of the Gurjara-Pratihāra art was found from a field and is now enshrined (and unfortunately badly painted also) in the Satya-Nārāyaṇa Temple. This sandstone relief of 54 x 49 cm depicts the deity standing in *pratyālīḍha* pose, pressing the back of the buffalo demon with her right foot and thrusting a trident in its back. The principal right hand holds a sword horizontally behind the head (Pl. 62). She has severed the neck of the buffalo with the sword and grabs by the neck the anthropomorphic demon which comes out of the decapitated head of the animal with her normal left hand. The three additional right hands hold trident, bows and a disc while the corresponding left hands support a bell, a bow and a shield. The lion mount of the goddess attacks the buffalo from behind and an attendant holding a sword is shown near her left foot. The goddess bears a very high *dhamilla* coiffure adorned with jewels and beaded strings. She wears a large circular ring in her right ear and a *nakra-kuṇḍala* in the left, beaded necklet, *keyūras, valayas, nūpuras* and *sārī.* The top corners show garland bearing *vidyādharas* and the semicircular part between them is carved with lotus-petal design to serve as the nimbus behind the head of the goddess. Shukla has aptly remarked that "The swiftness and violence of the Devī's action have been faithfully conveyed through diagonal representation of the whole composition".[208] Exquisite ornamentation, globular breasts, rounded arms, attenuated waist and deep navel bestow the figure with an ideal feminine beauty.[209]

Another image of Mahishāsuramardinī was found in the Garibnath Temple.[210] Made of red sandstone, it measured 60 x 45 cm. The relief was broken above the waist of the deity and showed the goddess in *ālīḍha* pose with her right foot placed firmly on a lotus *pīṭha* and the left one pressing the back of the buffalo. A human figure was carved as touching the right leg of the goddess. A disc was shown as piercing into the back of the buffalo. Its head was severed by the goddess with her trident and the anthropomorphic demon coming out of the decapitated head wore earrings, necklet and a *sarpa-hāra,* bracelets, *ardhoruk,* etc. and held a sword. The goddess twisted his face with her right hand. The lion was shown as attacking the demon from behind.

Still another very much mutilated image of Mahishāsuramardinī in buff sandstone betraying refined execution shows another figure of a buffalo at the back of the main figure.[211] Fragmentary hands with a bell found from Prāchī Śiva Temple at Pehowa[212] probably represent the upper left hand of Mahishāsuramardinī. All these pieces belong to the Pratihāra period.

Nārasiṁhī

Rodgers had noted amongst others an interesting fragmentary relief in the wall of the Garibnath Temple: "It is that of a seated female feeding a child, but both child and mother have the head of a dog or a monkey".[213] This relief may still be seen fixed up high in a wall of the said temple (Pl. 63). Shukla thinks that it is a 'boar-headed goddess seated on a lion'.[214] The goddess sits on her vehicle lion in *sukhāsana* with right foot placed on the ground. On the folded left leg is seated a child fondling with the left breast of the goddess. The upper left and the lower right arms of the goddess are irretrievably lost. The upper right arm is folded and raised. The wrist touches the right breast but the hand is broken. The face of the goddess and the child, too, have suffered mutilation. The goddess wears a beaded necklace whose pendent string falls to the left of her navel from between her breasts, *valayas, dhotī* and a long garland. There is a beautiful round lotiform gloriole behind her head. On the top corners are the divine garland bearing *vidyādharas*. Behind the lion is a small female figure with *pralamba* right hand touching the thigh and holding some indistinct object in her upraised left hand. The middle portion of the back slab above her shows a stylized *makara-mukha* decoration. We have examined this relief very carefully and feel convinced that it is not 'Boar-headed Siṁhavāhinī' but Nārasiṁhī as can be made out from the braided manes falling on her shoulders, her lion mount and the *vanamālā* 'which is usually associated with Vaishṇavite deity (sic)' as aptly remarked by Shukla.[215] The relief may be dated to *circa* ninth century A.D.

Chāmuṇḍā

Quite a few years back we had seen and photographed a fragment obtained from Pehowa with a friend which shows the left hands of a deity holding a *kapāla*, a drinking bowl and a snake (Pl. 64). As such, it may have been a part of a Chāmuṇḍā figure of the medieval period. It was found from Prāchī Śiva Temple.[216]

Pārvatī?

Some years back, a fragment showing the proper left hand side of the pedestal of an image (Pl. 65) was dug up from the Prāchī complex and is now fixed in one of its walls. It shows a garland bearing female attendant figure followed by another female figure holding a lotus in her right hand and a fly-whisk in the left. Just before the first attendant is an animal with head broken. To us it seems to have been a deer and the main deity may have been Pārvatī in penance. The fragmentary nature of the relief, however, does not allow a very specific identification. The execution clearly indicates it to be a work of late ninth century A.D.

Kshemaṅkarī

Prāchī has yielded the lower portion of another image (Pl. 66) which shows the main deity seated on a lotus seat in *lalitāsana,* resting the right foot also on a lotus *pīṭha*. The deity may be recognised as Kshemaṅkarī from the two lions carved under the lotus seat and the female attendants. This, too, may have belonged to the mature Pratihāra phase.

Fragmentary Relief of a Mātṛikā

A fragmentary relief representing the pedestal and side figures (Pl. 67) was also recovered from Prāchī.[217] On the central facet of the *triratha* pedestal are depicted in profile seven female animal-faced figures. The recessed projections on the sides also show animal-headed female figures seated in meditation. The second figure above the one on the proper left of the pedestal is lion-faced female in *dhyāna-mudrā*. The main deity, thus, may have been some form of a Mātṛikā, datable again to the same period.

OTHER IMPORTANT DEITIES

Brahmā

Pehowa has yielded an interesting image of standing Brahmā (Pl. 68). Though badly damaged, yet the image shows the deity standing to front accompanied by an acolyte on either side of the feet. The normal right hand holds a rosary in *abhaya-mudrā* and the extra one supports a ladle. The left hands are damaged but it may be guessed that the hanging proper left hand may have held a nectar flask and the rear one the manuscript. Ear ornaments, necklace, armlets, bracelets, triple-stringed sacred thread and the lower garment may be made out on the diety. What is, however, most interesting is the placement of the three heads of the god frontally in a single row. All the faces are juvenile. The matted locks on the heads are adorned with jewels and pearl strings. The figure may be assigned to the eighth century A.D. on stylistic grounds.

A small figure of Brahmā, 19 cm in height, is lying fixed in a corner of the Prāchī Temple. It shows the god seated in *sukhāsana* on a lotus seat with front right hand in *abhaya* and others carrying *sruvā,* book and water-pot. The central face is bearded and the side faces in profile are juvenile (Pl. 69). Another almost similar small figure but with all the juvenile faces (Pl. 70) is now displayed in HARDAM which possesses many other stelae of a similar form.[218] Most of these stelae, if not all, probably belong to Vishṇu images. As usual, all these pieces belong to the Pratihāra period.

Yama

A beautiful pedimented *rathikā* in the Dasanāmī Akhārā shows Yama seated in *sukhāsana* on his vehicle buffalo, carved to its left in profile (Pl. 71). The god wears a bejewelled *kirīṭa-mukuṭa,* ear ornaments, *ekāvalī,* long garland, *valayas* and an *adhovastra.* His right hand, raised to the level of the shoulder, is slightly damaged; it may have been held in *abhayamudrā.* The left hand holds a *Khaṭvaṅga.* The top corners show acanthus leaf decorations. It is a beautiful image assignable to the ninth century A.D.

Miscellaneous Figures

Pehowa has yielded numerous other images and fragments which include Kārttikeya,[219] an exquisite fly-whisker (Pl. 72),[220] *Kinnaras,*[221] *vyālas,*[222] lions,[223] elephant,[224] *Kīrtimukhas,*[225] etc.

PAINTINGS

Most of the old *havelīs* in Pehowa contain beautiful murals depicting mythological, mythical, secular scenes and floral decorations. The oldest of these may be dated to the Maratha period and may still be seen in the Paśupatinātha Temple *maṇḍapa* (Pl. 73), Prāchī Śiva Temple,[226] Siddhagīra's *samādhi,* old royal rest-houses and temples. Special efforts should be made to document and preserve these murals which are vanishing every year when these buildings are renovated and/or whitewashed.

NOTES AND REFERENCES

1. B.B Lal, "Excavations at Hastinapura and Other Explorations in the Upper Gaṅgā and Sutlej Basins 1950-52", *Ancient India,* (Bulletin of ASI), 1954-55, New Delhi, pp. 5-151.
2. *Ibid.,* pp. 23 and 150-51. Different views regarding the association of PGW with the later Vedic Aryans and dating it to later centuries have been given in Chapter I above.
3. Lal had explored Pehowa in or around 1950 (*ibid.,* pp. 6-7).
4. Rodgers, *Report,* List of Coins, p. 3, Nos. 47, 35 and 31 respectively.
5. Rodgers calls it a woman attendant.
6. John Allan, *Catalogue of Coins of Ancient India,* 1936, London, pp. ci-ciii; K.K. Dasgupta, *A Tribal History of Ancient India—A Numismatic Approach,* Calcutta, 1974, pp. 103-04.
7. Pehowa being a holy place, the coin may have been brought here by a pilgrim also.
8. Rodgers (*Report,* p. 3, No. 31) assigns this coin to *Probus* and gives the Greek legend as AVPII POBOCCEB.
9. *CASR,* XIV, p. 102, Pl. XXVII.
10. *Ibid.*
11. R.C. Agrawala, "Two Interesting Terracottas from the Region of Kurukṣetra, East-Panjab", *Artibus Asiae,* Vol. XX, No. 2-3, 1957, p. 164.

12. Cf. V.S. Agrawala, *Studies in Indian Art*, Varanasi, 1965.
13. R.C. Agrawala (1957), *op. cit.*
14. Acc. No. 75.445.
15. S.P. Shukla ["Relics of Ancient Art from Pehowa", *Panjab University Research Bulletin (Arts)*, Chandigarh, Vol. XI, Nos. 1-2, April-Oct. 1980, pp. 71-72, Pl. 2 and *Sculptures and Terracottas in the Archaeological Museum Kurukshetra University*, Kurukshetra, 1983, pp. 72-73, LVIII.1] thinks that it was an embroidered design.
16. *Ibid.*
17. Rodgers, *Report*, p. 15.
18. Personal information from Dr. Phadke.
19. *CASR*, XIV, p. 101.
20. For details, see G. Bühler, "The Pehova Inscription from the Temple of Garibnath", *Epigraphia Indica*, Vol. I, Calcutta, 1892, pp. 184-90. We have, however, added our own observations also here and there in this account.
21. *Ibid.*, p. 185.
22. From Fig. 16 and Bühler, *EI*, I, pp. 186-88.
23. Represented by a symbol. Bühler read it as त्र्रो and amended it as त्र्रों in the footnote.
24. Bühler prefers to amend it to संवत्सर.
25. Bühler favours संवत् in stead of सम्वत्.
26. Bühler: संवत्सर.
27. The first letter *sa* is slightly damaged.
28. *Sa* of the word *suta* seems to have been wrongly engraved like *me.*
29. Bühler reads माङ्गक. The form of the conjunct *ṅga* in खङ्ग and शारङ्ग in line 5 is different from the form of this syllable here. So we refer to read it as *hu.*
30. Bühler rightly corrects it to चिण्हसुत and points out that the original may have been ॰मुत.
31. Bühler: चोणराक.
32. Bühler: सेलवण.
33. This is what Bühler reads. We are doubtful about it but are unable to suggest alternative reading.
34. The first letter is slightly damaged and looks like *mu.*
35. Bühler: होद्ध.
36. It seems that *ta* of *suta* was left out inadvertently and when the mistake was detected, it was indicated by a sign and engraved below the line between *su* and *vi* of the next word.
37. Read खड्ग. It is interesting to note that even now some people pronounce and write खङ्ग for खड्ग. The mistake persists from Bhoja's time. Bühler reads खङ्गक but there is no *ka* after *Khaṅga.*
38. *Va* is slightly damaged but can still be made out clearly.
39. Bühler reads शारङ्गदिकेत्य.
40. Bühler reads लोहट in the text and suggests लाहट in the footnote.

41. Bühler: सीहरुदुक्ककेत्य, possibly सीहरुद्धक्ककेत्य.
42. Bühler wrongly reads *Ullaka*.
43. Suta is the restored word and is hardly visible. Probably the engraver made a mistake and tried to rectify it later by carving the last letter above the line.
44. Bühler: प्रगद.
45. Bühler: त्रैघाटकीय.
46. Bühler: [ए] क [ग]ोरक.
47. Bühler reads the first two syllables as दव्वु and then after three or four letters कशिलि. The conjunct after *da,* however, differed in form from *vva* as seen at the end of lines 2 and 6. So we don't think that it can be read as *vvu*. The syllable after it cannot be read as it is damaged. It may have been *ka*. Traces of the following two letters indicate the word to have been तथा.
48. The letter *kha* is not clear.
49. Bühler: उहोवकेत्य.
50. Bühler reads भटा standing possibly for भेटा or हय. He sees the possibility of the next letter being *ta* or *na* or even *da*. For व्युवहरक he suggests that it should be read as व्यवहारक.
51. Bühler suggests देशी or वेशी. The first syllable, however, cannot be read as *de*. We have checked it up even from the original and have, therefore, preferred वेशी.
52. पत्त्रं according to Bühler.
53. Slightly damaged. Bühler suggests that the reading may have been ०सन्ने.
54. The engraver seems to have engraved inadvertently a vertical stroke for the next letter but left it after realizing his mistake.
55. The first letter is not clear.
56. The name is inscribed as Treghāṭaka in line 6 above and here also the stroke for *ai* has been cut thrice.
57. Bühler puts ति धर्म्म हेतो in brackets. *To*, however, is quite clear.
58. Bühler reads तच्चतुर्व्विन्शतिभिर्भागै: For चतुर्व्विन्शति read चतुर्व्विंशति.
59. But for the first consonant, all the syllables put in the brackets are blurred but recognisable.
60. The space between *ka* and *ri* admits of more space than the simple vertical stroke for *ā*. It seems that the engraver carved some other letter inadvertently and then tried to rectify his mistake as a result of which the part of the stone got damaged and thus he carved *ri* after that.
61. Bühler reads भागैकस्तत्पूजकाय. There is no space is after ज which too is not quite clear. The fact that Bühler puts a य in the beginning of the next line also indicates that this line ended with का.
62. Bühler has aptly observed that though the letters put in the brackets are slightly blurred yet they are recognisable.

63. Bühler wrongly reads it as पृथूकस्थानात्. य is quite clear and cannot be confused with त. Even from the grammatical viewpoint पृथूदकस्थानाय is the correct declensional form.
64. The engraver was probably going to engrave घोटिका but soon corrected himself.
65. Read यज्ञवराहाय.
66. Bühler put it as [भा]गा:. *Bhā*, however, is quite clear.
67. The stone is damaged here and Bühler made the restoration by calculating the assigned parts. *Ta* may, however, be made out from the extant engravings.
68. The bracketed letters have been concealed by a thick coat of whitewash now.
69. Though घोटक can be made out, the earlier part is hardly recognisable now.
70. There is a vertical stroke for the full stop here but Bühler has wrongly read it as a *mātrā*.
71. Though blurred, the letters may be recognised.
72. Bühler points out to its superfluousness.
73. The bracketed letters, read clearly by Bühler, are now concealed somewhat by whitewash.
74. The bracketed letters are concealed by whitewash but may be recognised.
75. Denoted by a symbol.
76. Bühler has translated the titles of Bhoja as the supreme sovereign, superior king of great kings and supreme lord.
77. The word *yātrā* literally means a journey, march, pilgrimage, festival, fair, etc. See V.S. Apte, *The Student's Sanskrit-English Dictionary*, Delhi, 1959, p. 457.
78. Bühler observed that "*Paiśāchīchaturdaśī*, literally the 'fourteenth (lunar day) of the female goblin', probably was the name of the fourteenth lunar day of the dark half of Vaiśākha or of Chaitra. For it must have fallen somewhat earlier than the bright half of Vaiśākha and may have belonged to that month or to Chaitra accordingly as the reckoning was *amānta* or *pūrṇimānta*". It may, however, be pointed out that a huge fair is still held at Pehowa on the fourteenth day of the dark fortnight of Chaitra every year. Thousands of people from far and near come to Pehowa to bathe in the Sarasvatī and the holy ponds to earn merit and money.

    The fourteenth of the dark fortnight is sacred to Śiva's worship and is significant astronomically—

तेजोभागाः सूर्यबिम्बं चतुर्दशतिथौ क्रमात् ।
प्रविशन्तिक्षयस्त्वेवं कृष्णपक्षे विधोर्भवेत् ।।
कला षोडश चन्द्रस्य तत्रैका शंभुमूर्धनि ।
तिष्ठत्यद्यावधि पराः क्षयं यान्ति क्षयं विना ।।

कालिका पुराण

Pṛithūdaka being an important Śaiva pilgrimage was popular with the devotees who would visit it and take bath here. It is popularly believed that a person who takes bath at Pṛithūdaka near Śiva's place, i.e., Pṛithvīśvara Mahādeva

Temple, and gives an oblation of rice-balls, does not become a goblin—

चैत्रकृष्णचतुर्दश्यां यः स्नायात् शिवसन्निधौ ।
न प्रेतत्वामाप्नोति पिण्डदानात्पृथूदके ।। *PM*, p.100.

Even if rice-balls are given in oblation keeping someone in mind on this day at Prithūdaka, he also gets emancipation from goblin-hood—

चैत्रकृष्णचतुर्दश्यां यमुद्दिश्य पृथूदके ।
पिण्डं हि दीयते सो वै प्रेतभावाद्विमुच्यते ।। *ibid.*

Chaitra-krishṇā-chaturdaśī is, therefore, known as Paiśāchī-chaturdaśī also.

79. Since the date of the record falls about a week later than the Chaitra-krishṇā-chaturdaśī, it may be presumed that the horse-fair may have continued at least for a week. The worthy persons mentioned in the inscription, may have met during or at the conclusion of the horse-fair and decided about the tithes to be levied and dispensed. They may be presumed to have contributed something initially from the sale-proceeds of their horses and mares.
80. *Māṅgaka* according to Bühler.
81. Bühler reads it as *Choṇarāka*.
82. Bühler connects the word *Chikkari* with Selavaṇa-pura but the word तथा between *Seṇarāka* (Bühler's *Choṇarāka*) and *Chikkari* indicates that they were the sons of Chiṇha- चिण्हसुतो से (चो according to Bühler) णराक तथा चिक्करि . The comparable expressions in the inscription to mention only a few, are—
भट्टवीरुक सुत वन्द तथा राज्यव(ब)ल तथा वल्लुक, रज्जुकसुत
चिण्ह तथा रङ्गक, नारसुत लोहट तथा शङ्कर
etc. The absence of तथा before other place-names like व(ब)लदेवपुर, घंघक°, etc. also indicates that Chikkari is not a part of the place-name.

Chikkari-selavaṇapura sounds strange even otherwise. We think that Chikkari is the name of Chiṇha's son and Salavaṇapura is the name of a place. The *VP* (*SM* XII. 4-5) mentions the following seven forests in Kurukshetra—

काम्यकं च वनं पुण्यं तथादितिवनं महत् ।
व्यासस्य च वनं पुण्यं फलकीवनमेव च ।।
तथा सूर्यवनं स्थानं तथा मधुवनं महत् ।
पुण्यं शीतवनं नाम सर्वकल्मषनाशनम् ।।

Cunningham (*CASR*, XIV, p. 91) adds Prithu-ban and Solanban. Some of these forests had place-names based on them or the forests may have been known after these places, e.g. Kamoda (Kāmyaka-vana), Prithūdaka (Prithu-vana), Mohana (Madhu-vana), Basthali (Vyāsa-vana), Sivan (Śītavana). Salavanapura seems to have been connected with Solan-ban mentioned by Cunningham. It lay in the Kurukshetra region and may be equated with Salwan, located about 13 km north of Safidon. Salwan is an archaeological site and has yielded sculptural relics also.

83. Bühler reads this name as Hoddha.
84. Bühler wrongly read the name as Khaṅgaka. There is no *ka* at the end. The mistake of writing खड्ग as खङ्ग as indicated above, seems to have persisted from the medieval times.
85. *Śāraṅkadika* according to Bühler.
86. Bühler reads it as *Ullaka.*
87. Bühler reads it as *Pragada.*
88. *Sīharudukkaka* according to Bühler.
89. *Ekagoraka* according to Bühler.
90. Bühler reads *Traighāṭaka.*
91. Bühler reads *Davvu.*
92. Bühler takes this word along with the following to read Kaśilimāṇa as one word.
93. Bühler considers it to be a part of the following word.
94. Bühler reads it as *Uhovaka* and together with the preceding word regards Aśvala-Uhovaka as the place-name.
95. Since the temples mentioned subsequently to share the grant are dedicated to Vishṇu and his incarnatory forms, this temple, too, may have been dedicated to the same god.
96. Probably a Vishṇu temple
97. *Bhaṭṭa* is the title generally used with the names of learned *Brāhmaṇas* and the literal meaning of *Nāgara* is town-born, town-bred. Bühler observes that "Nāgara is either the name of the subdivision of the Brāhmaṇas to which Prabhākara belonged, or an honorific title indicating that he was the chief Bhaṭṭa of the town of Kanauj".
98. For Yajña-Varāha form of Vishṇu, see *Tait. Ār.*, X; *Narasiṁha Purāṇa*, 39.10-13; *Vāyu P.* 23.103-08. Also see *Purāṇa*, Vol. V, No. 2 (July 1963) and V. Raghavan, "Yajñavarāha—Some More Material", *ibid.*, Vol. VI, No. 1 (Jan.1964), pp. 202-03.
99. Bühler has taken *rūpa* to mean 'an animal' and we have followed his interpretation.
100. Bühler reads it as *Traighāṭaka.*
101. *Dharma* may have been the popular coin-denomination (<Darma <Drachma, Cf. present-day rupee) of Bhoja's time or may have been a kind of a self-imposed tax for religious and charitable purposes. *Dharma* funds are still a living tradition in some of the business communities. Bühler has observed that "The exact amount cannot be ascertained. It no doubt was regulated by custom, and so well known that its specification seemed unnecessary".
102. *Akshaya-nīvi.* For its connotation, see D.C. Sircar, *Indian Epigraphical Glossary*, Delhi, 1966, p. 15.
103. Goshṭhikās were the members of the committee who used to manage the affairs of the temples. For details see *ibid.*
104. *EI*, I, p. 242.
105. Rajendralal Mitra published his reading of ll.1-8 of the horse-dealers' grant in *JASB*, Vol. XXII, pp. 673-74ff. and the facsimile of these eight lines in *ibid.*, Vol. XXXII, p. 96. Mahendrapāla's *Praśāsti* also appeared in Vol. XXII, pp. 675ff.

106. *CASR* II, p. 225; XIV, pp. 101-02.
107. *Report*, p. 17.
108. *Ibid.*, The inscription is published with detailed description, facsimile, text and translation in *EI*, I, pp. 242-50.
109. *Ibid.*, p. 242.
110. Bharadwaj (1986), *op. cit.*, p. 176. There is, however, the possibility of Yakshapālaka being the modern Jakhal, on the bank of the Ghaggar, on the Bathinda-Delhi section of the Northern Railway.
111. *EI*, IX, pp. 4ff.
112. Sadhu Ram, "Pehowa Praśasti of Mahendrapāla", *Journal of Haryana Studies*, Vol. I, No. 1 (Jan.1969), pp. 16-25 dates it to A.D. 895.
113. From Figs. 17 and 18. We have drawn help from Bühler (*EI*, I, pp. 244-48) and Sadhu Ram (*op. cit.*, pp. 17-20) where the damaged portions of the inscription have been read and restored by these scholars.
114. Denoted by a symbol.
115. Bühler has put भव in paranthesis. The word, however, is quite clear in the photograph of the inscription.
116. The *visargas* are quite clear. Even *Cha* can be made out adequately though the preceding syllable is only a guess.
117. Faint traces of the bracketed letters are visible. Bühler has put the following *ma* also in the brackets but it is quite clear in the photograph.
118. Restoration after Sadhu Ram.
119. The syllable before *ata* seems to have been a conjunct.
120. Restoration after Sadhu Ram.
121. Bühler suggests the restoration as मनुग्रहीतु.
122. Sadhu Ram wrongly transcribes it as मृद्धया.
123. The *na* of मानसं has an ornamental tail, turned to the right, to which two small hooked flourishes are attached.
124. Sadhu Ram wrongly transcribes it as रञ्जित.
125. Bühler wrongly transcribes it as तत्संतानं. The conjunct *nta* is very clear. Sadhu Ram does not seem to have cared to examine the facsimile and has therefore followed Bühler.
126. Sadhu Ram is certainly wrong in reading प्रख्याताजनि यस्स्व.
127. The vertical stroke for the stop is very clear but Bühler has put it in the brackets. Sadhu Ram has put the additional star mark to the brackets.
128. There is no stop mark but both Bühler and Sadhu Ram have put it in the text.
129. The stone above *ta* is slightly damaged to give the impression of an *anusvāra*.
130. Bühler:अ[सू]त [च वि-]. All the letters, however, are quite clear though there is a slight damage immediately after the last letter.
131. Bühler has put the *upadhamānīya* in the text but we fail to see it clearly.
132. At the end of the metre we usually have the double *daṇḍa* mark but here only one *daṇḍa* has been used.
133. Bühler has read विणो and suggested विष्णो for it. विष्णो, however, is quite distinct.

134. Bühler wrongly transcribes it as पूर्णराजेन. Sadhu Ram has read it correctly.
135. Here again only one *daṇḍa* has been used at the end of the verse.
136. After Sadhu Ram.
137. The poet invokes Vishṇu, the Supreme Being, to protect the people at the time of the destruction of the whole universe at the end of a *kalpa*.
138. शरण्य: is an epithet of Śiva also. So here, there may be a veīled allusion to Mahendrapāla's comparison with Śiva.
139. Bühler translates it as: "The wives of his foes, covering their lips, (red) like young shoots, with their hands, and straightening their rich curls, moistened their hollow cheeks, that possessed little splendour, with the water of their tears". We, however, feel that the poet wants to convey that the enemy-women moistened with their tears not only their cheeks but also their unkempt locks of hair which they had not combed in grief.
140. Bühler renders it as '...may this temple be resplendent as a mansion of Śrī'. He, however, suggests in the footnote that Śrī may be taken to mean the original splendour.
141. Dhanvantari, in Indian mythology, is an incarnation of Vishṇu and the divine doctor.
142. Bharadwaj has identified it with Jakhepal in district Sangrur (Bharadwaj 1986, *op. cit.*, p. 176). There is no definite evidence to corroborate this identification. It may be identified with Jakhal also.
143. Identified with Ghaggar in district Patiala by Bharadwaj (*ibid.*).
144. Patran according to Bharadwaj (*ibid.*).
145. I.e., for the temple-service.
146. G.B. Sharma has informed us that many years ago he had seen a very large stone slab, which was used for washing clothes bearing traces of some letters, in a *havelī* in the town. Nothing is known about this slab now.
147. *CASR*, XIV, p. 103.
148. Rodgers, *Report*, p. 17.
149. *Ibid.*
150. *Ibid.*
151. Rodgers (*ibid.*) has confused this doorway with another fitted in the *Guphā*. His measurements of the doorway, however, are correct. Unfortunately, the elevation of this beautiful doorway illustrated by him in Plate XXVII is not published along with his report.
152. *Ibid.*
153. *Ibid.*, p. 16.
154. Rodgers wrongly described both the upper hands as holding flowers.
155. Cf. *Chaturvarga-Chintāmaṇi* (Bibliotheca Indica Series, Calcutta, 1878) II.114; Kalpana Desai, *op. cit.*, pp. 58-59, Fig. 52.
156. Percy Brown, *Indian Architecture* (*Buddhist and Hindu Periods*), Bombay, 1959, p. 48, Pl. XLIII, Fig. 2.
157. Rodgers could not identify the figures properly and has wrongly described this panel as having "one male figure, six seated female figures, one with a horse's

head, one other male and one of Ganesh, in all nine figures" (*Report*, p. 16).

158. Rodgers, however, had rightly observed that "At the bottom of the innermost band of sculpture on each jamb is a *Nāga* figure".

159. The Śilpa texts suggest *lalāṭa-bimba* as the representative of the enshrined deity. This rule was not observed invariably, however, in the medieval north Indian temples.

160. *Report*, p. 16.

161. *Ibid.*, p. 15. Rodgers, however, seems to have confused it with the door-frame recovered from Viśvāmitra kā Ṭīlā as the ensuing description belongs to the latter.

162. Rodgers had recognised lotus flowers in the upper two hands of the figure on the doorway found from Viśvāmitra kā Ṭīlā. As such, the deity may be identified with Yogāsana-Sūrya or Sūrya-Nārāyaṇa.

163. Devendra Handa, "A Pratihāra Doorway from Pehowa", *Panjab University Research Bulletin* (*Arts*) Vol. XVII, No. 2 (October 1986), pp. 151-55, Fig. 2.

164. S.P. Shukla (1980), *op. cit.*, p. 77.

165. Preserved in the Department of Archaeology and Museums, Haryana, Panchkula (henceforth HARDAM). Accession No. 1/355. The fragment measures 27 x 11.5 cm.

166. HARDAM, Acc. No. 1/396. It measures 21 x 14 cm.

167. HARDAM, Acc. Nos. 1/426-27. They measure 68.5 x 17 and 68 x 17, 68 x 16 cm respectively.

168. Many of these fragments are preserved in HARDAM now.

169. HARDAM, Acc. No. 1/425.

170. We had studied and photographed them on the site when they were dug out.

171. *Report*, p. 16.

172. *Ibid.*, pp. 16-17.

173. *Ibid.*, p. 17.

174. We used to see these remains and fragments of an image of Revanta in this temple but found them missing when we visited the temple on 18 December, 1989. On enquiry, we were told that an I.A.S. Officer of Haryana had acquired these relics.

175. *Report*, p. 17.

176. *Ibid.*

177. *Ibid.*, pp. 16-17.

178. *Ibid.*

179. A.K. Narain, "Ganesa On Hermaeus' Coin", *Numismatic Digest*, Vol. VI, pp. 26-29; "On the Earliest Ganesa" in *Senart Paranavitana Commemoration Volume*, Eds. Prematileke, Indrapala and Lohuizen de-Leeuw, Leiden, 1978, pp. 142-44; "Some Brahmanical Divinities on the Indo-Greek Coinage Revisited", paper presented at the Inaugural Seminar on Numismatics & History, Indian Institute of Research in Numismatic Studies, Anjaneri (Nasik, Maharashtra), Jan.8-10, 1984 (cyclostyled copy, pp. 9-14); Joe Gibb, "The Earliest Ganesa: A Case of Mistaken Identity", *Numismatic Digest*, Vol. VI, pp. 30ff; J.N. Banerjea, *The Development of Hindu Iconography*, Calcutta, 1956, pp. 354ff.

180. Acc. No. 1/354.
181. U.S. Chakrapāṇi, *Pṛithūdaka (Pihovā) Tīrtha Mahātmya* (Hindi), Pehowa, no date, p. 50.
182. Shukla (1983), *op. cit.*, p. 50, Pl. XLIII, 3. However, Shukla wrongly describes it as *pañcharatha.*
183. For the identification of the male figures holding the shaft of an attribute with Balarāma see our paper "Balarāma as an Attendant of Vishṇu", in *Gleanings of Indian Archaeology History & Culture, (Prof. R.N. Mehta Felicitation Volume),* Eds. Prof. K.D. Bajpai *et al.*, Vol. II, Jaipur, 2000, pp. 87-91, Pls. XLI-XLIV, Figs. 1-9.
184. We had examined this piece in the collection of Dr. Ranbir Singh Sangra (Sangra Nursing Home, Ambala Road, Pehowa) on 10 November, 1985. In a recent visit to Pehowa, we learnt that he has donated this and other sculptures of his collection to HARDAM.
185. We had examined this piece when Murari was posted at Gharaunda. Lately, he has retired and settled at Panchkula.
186. HARDAM, Acc. No. 1/357.
187. Devendra Handa, "Vaishṇava Icons from Haryana", *Punjab University Research Bulletin (Arts)*, Chandigarh, Vol. XVI, No. 2 (October 1985), p. 129, Fig. 3.
188. *Ibid.*, pp. 144-45. HARDAM, Acc. No. 1/549.
189. I worked under Dr.Buddha Prakash in the Institute at that time.
190. These fragments were first published by us in our popular-type article "Pehowa-An Ancient Holy Place", *Advance*, Chandigarh, Vol. XIII, No. 1 (Jan-March 1966), pp. 26-29 and Handa (1967), *op. cit.*, p. 306. A detailed account of these fragments was published by our friend K.K. Saxena ("A Study of Two Sculptures of Pehowa", *Journal of Orient Institute*, Baroda, Vol. XVI, No. 2 (December, 1966, pp. 161-63). Later, these fragments have been illustrated by Buddha Prakash, Muztar, Shukla, Phadke, etc. from the earlier negatives. Probably Dr. Buddha Prakash took away these sculptures to his place at Saharanpur, U.P.
191. Another architectural piece with Kalki, measuring 15.5 x 10 cm, found from Prāchī Śiva Temple, is housed in HARDAM, Acc. No. 1/408.
192. HARDAM, Acc. No. 1/358.
193. Handa (1988), *op. cit.*, p. 141.
194. Shukla (1980), *op. cit.*, p. 75, Fig. 9; (1983), *op. cit.*, p. 50, Pl. XLIII, 1.
195. Devendra Handa, "Varāha Image from Haryana", *Researches in Indian History, Archaeology, Art And Religion* (Prof. Upendra Thakur Felicitation Volume), Edited by G. Kuppuram and K. Kumudamani, Vol. I, Delhi, 1990, p. 84, Pl. 47.
196. *Ibid.*, p. 84, Pl. 46.
197. It was transferred to HARDAM in early 1985 from the collection of the Registering Officer, Karnal, along with another independent relief of Garuḍa and some other fragments.
198. Handa (1985), pp. 132-33, Fig. 5.
199. Devendra Handa, "Harihara Images from Haryana", in *Studies in Indian History and Culture* (Kanaklal Barua Commemoration Volume), edited by R.D. Choudhury and Bhagwan Singh, Delhi, 1990, p. 102, Fig. 2.
200. HARDAM, Acc. No. 1/353.

201. For details, see Devendra Handa, "An Interesting Vaikuṇṭha-Mūrti from Pehoa", in *Svasti Śrī* (Dr. B.Ch. Chhabra Felicitation Volume), edited by Dr. K.V. Ramesh *et al.*, Delhi, 1984, pp. 297-302; "Vaikuntha Images from Haryana", *Journal of the Indian Society of Oriental Art*, New Series, Calcutta, Vol. XIV (1984-85), pp. 54-58, Fig. 3; (1985), *op. cit.*, pp. 130-31, Fig. 3, etc.
202. It was transferred from the office of the Registering Officer, Karnal to HARDAM in early 1985. See also Handa (1985), p. 133, Fig. 8.
203. HARDAM, Acc. No. 1/286.
204. Dr. Sangra has lately donated this and other relics from Pehowa to HARDAM.
205. Devendra Handa, "Hariyānā men Revanta Pūjā", *Journal of Haryana Studies*, Kurukshetra. Vol. VI (1974), pp. 16-18. See also B.N. Sharma, *Iconography of Revanta*, New Delhi, 1975, pp. 48-49, Fig. 21.
206. Handa (1985), *op. cit.*, p. 130, Figs. 2 & 2A. In a visit (March, 1991) to Pehowa, we learnt from the priest of the Paśupatinātha Temple that this panel had been acquired by an I.A.S. Officer of Haryana.
207. U.S. Chakrapāṇi, *Pehowa (Pṛithūdaka) Tīrtha*, Pehowa, 1989, p. 4.
208. Shukla (1980), *op. cit.*, p. 73, Fig. 4.
209. *Ibid.*
210. Its present location is not known.
211. Devendra Handa, "Some Medieval Images of Mahishāsuramardinī from Haryana", *Punjab University Research Bulletin (Arts)*, Chandigarh, Vol. XXII, No. 1 (April 1991).
212. There are two such examples, one measuring 15 x 10 cm and the other 11 x 7 cm. Both are now housed in HARDAM and bear respectively Acc. Nos. 1/407 and 1/422.
213. *Report*, p. 16.
214. Shukla (1980), *op. cit.*, p. 73, Fig. 5.
215. *Ibid.*
216. It is now preserved in the collection of a senior I.A.S. official of Haryana.
217. It has now been shifted to HARDAM.
218. E.g. Brahmā in a miniature *rathikā*, buff sandstone, 24 x 16 cm, from Viśvāmitra kā Ṭīlā (Acc. No. 1/244); Brahmā on a stela with *makara-mukha* below, buff sandstone, 21 x 12.5 cm (Acc. No. 1/253); Brahmā on stela, buff sandstone, 12 x 10 cm, Prāchī Śiva Temple (Acc. No. 1/356), etc.
219. HARDAM, Acc. No. 1/418, buff sandstone, 12 x 8 cm, Prāchī Śiva Temple.
220. HARDAM, Acc. No. 1/111. It measures 45.5 x 11 cm.
221. Shukla (1983), *op. cit.*, p. 50, Pl. XLIII.1.
222. HARDAM, Acc. No. 1/398, 17 x 15.5 cm and 1/421, 9.5 x 4 cm.
223. *Ibid.*, Acc. No. 1/406, 10 x 5.5 cm and 1/411, 7.5 x 4.5 cm.
224. *Ibid.*, Acc. No. 1/403, 12.0 x 11.5 cm, Prāchī.
225. *Ibid.*, Acc. Nos. 1/419-20, 9.5 x 8.0 cm and 16 x 8.5 cm, both from Prāchī.
226. Unfortunately whitewashed very recently.

5

RESUMÉ

A retrospective review of the foregoing pages would make it clear that situated in the holy land of Kurukshetra, Pehowa is one of the oldest and most sacred *tīrthas,* located on the banks of the Sarasvatī which may herself be called the holiest of the holy rivers of India. The present name has come down to us from the original Sanskrit name Pṛithūdaka which is met with not only in the two Pratihāra inscriptions found from here but also in the *Mahābhārata,* various Purāṇas and other texts. The name Pṛithūdaka may be explained variously, but two explanations, viz., (1) having abundant waters, and (2) Pṛithu's water or pool, are more reasonable and appealing. The former is the logical literary explanation and the latter based on tradition. Both have their parallels in the place names Bahūdaka (*Bahu* + *udaka,* i.e. having abundant waters) and Agrodaka (Agra + *udaka,* i.e. Agra's pool). Agrodaka is identified with modern Agroha in Hissar district and connected with the eponymous king Agra, the progenitor of the Agrawal *banias.* Since the region of Kurukshetra was inhabited by the early Aryans where their princes and sages lit the sacrificial fires, the association of some of the places with their names is a natural consequence. Hence the possibility of the association of Pṛithūdaka with king Pṛithu seems to carry heavier weight than the mere literal explanation of the word. There are hundreds and thousands of other places in India which are connected with the names of kings, heroes, sages, tribes, gods, etc.

King Pṛithu was the son of Vena who is mentioned in the *Ṛigveda, Atharvaveda, Kāṭhaka Saṁhitā* and *Pañchaviṁśa, Śatapatha, Taittirīya* and *Jaiminīya Upanishad Brāhmaṇas.* The fact that the *Ṛigveda* describes him as one of the richest persons (X.93, 14) as well as the seer (X.148) indicates him to be an enlightened and accomplished person. The *Atharvaveda* describes him, in an allegory, as the milker, Manu Vaivasvata, the calf, and the earth, the cow, which yielded the milk of agriculture and crops. Pṛithu is also known as the first consecrated king, Lord of both the worlds of men and animals, and the innovator of agriculture.

Haryana is known as the cradle of civilization. Even geologically, the flat alluvial flood plain of the Satluj-Yamunā divide including the clayey loam of the Sarasvatī in which Pehowa is located, consists of the siltation of the streams flowing through it, belongs to the Pleistocene period. It will not be surprising, therefore, if the Atharvavedic imagery alludes to the inception of agricultural activity in this region, the first innovator being king Pṛithu. Later, this activity was extended in a larger area by king Kuru after whom it came to be known as the Land (literally 'Field') of Kuru, i.e. Kurukshetra.

Pehowa's association with king Pṛithu may obviously claim a hoary antiquity which is supported by the extensive mound on which is located the present town. This mound has yielded Painted Grey Ware dated to *circa* 1100-800 B.C. by archaeologists, but may yield still earlier remains when excavated systematically.

A place connected with the first consecrated king and the innovator of agriculture was naturally to be considered important. Its location on the banks of the most divine and the best of the rivers, Sarasvatī, created by Brahmā (the Creator) himself, added to its significance and it came to be known 'in all the three worlds', as possessing merit, remover of sins, auspicious, sacred, meritorious, deliverer and the holiest of the holy. Gods and mortals and sages and celestials vied with each other to live here and take a bath in the Sarasvatī, considered to be one of the most sacred rivers. The tradition that Pṛithu had performed the funerary rites of his father here elevated its position to Gayā, Kāśī, Prayāga, Kurukshetra and even more and made it the foremost *tīrtha* for such rituals. Various gods, heroes and kings were advised to have a dip in the Sarasvatī to get rid of their sins and perform the funerary rites for the deliverance of their forefathers. Yudhishṭhira is said to have performed here the obsequies of all those killed in the Great War. Of course, Pehowa has been famous for the performance of obsequies throughout and the most recent instance is the immersion of the ashes of the late Prime Minister Rajiv Gandhi in the Sarasvatī at Pehowa on May 28, 1991.

Since the early Aryans are known to have settled in the valleys of the Sarasvatī, the Dṛishadvatī and the Āpayā rivers which flowed in the Kurukshetra region in ancient times, the Purus and the Bharatas, two illustrious peoples of those times, may have played a dominant role in the development of the region. The descendants of the Purus whose kings Durgaha, Girikshit, Trasadasyu, etc. are known through the Vedic literature, may have held sway here. Later they merged with the Bharatas and came to known as the Kurus who excelled not only in military pursuits but also had the best and purest speech. These Kurus extended the ideas of civilization towards the east. Kuru continued to be one of the sixteen *mahājanapadas* up to the time of Buddha (*c.* sixth century B.C.).

With the development and extension of the kingdom of Magadha, Pehowa and the region around seem to have passed into the hands of the Nandas, and subsequently the Mauryas. Pushyamitra Śuṅga may have been able to retain his hold over this land but it seems to have slipped off from the hands of his descendants. The Indo-Greek invasions and occupation ultimately led to the rise of the republican peoples like the Yaudheyas, the Kuṇindas and the Agras and the monarchical Mitras in the region around Pehowa. Scythians and Parthians, too, seem to have held sway here for sometime but it ultimately came to be occupied by the Kushāṇas. In about the middle of the third century A.D., if not earlier, the Kushāṇas left India and some small principalities may have sprung up in Haryana. Kings Yajñajita and Baladatta are known from their coins found at Rohtak and Theh Polar. Soon, however, the Yaudheyas seem to have filled the vacum. They were defeated by Samudragupta whose overlordship they accepted and agreed to pay taxes and tributes. They probably suffered a fatal blow at the hands of the Hūṇas in the fifth century A.D. whereafter the Pushyabhūtis or the Vardhanas got ascendancy. When, however, Harsha vardhana shifted his capital from Thanesar to Kanauj, Thanesar-Pehowa region lost its importance considerably. Important flashes of light on the subsequent history of the region are thrown by some literary and epigraphic references, but much of the history remains clouded by darkness till a floodlight is thrown over it by Pratihāra inscriptions. From about eighth to early eleventh centuries A.D. Pehowa was perhaps at the height of its glory and numerous temples seem to have been built here. It was an outpost of Uttarāpatha and lay on the trade route which connected the Gangetic valley with the north-west. As such, it flourished as a trade-centre also. This is well evidenced by the Horse Dealers' Grant or the Garibnath Temple inscription. The Tomaras of the line of Jāula were the feudatories of the Pratihāras at that time whose princes Gogga, Pūrṇarāja and Devarāja also built a Vaishṇava temple at Pehowa.

In the early eleventh century A.D., Pehowa seems to have been destroyed by Mahmud Ghaznavi during his raid of Thanesar. Thereafter, Pehowa could perhaps never regain its old glory. At the decline of the Pratihāra power, the Tomaras may have declared independence but were soon subjugated by the Chauhans. With the defeat of Pṛithvīrāja Chauhan, the whole northern region passed into the hands of the Muslims. Pehowa seems to have been reduced to an insignificant place as nothing is heard of it during the Sultanate and even the Mughal period. That it continued to exist, however, is indicated by Guru Nanak's visit to the place which was commemorated by the establishment of a gurudwara. Nadir Shah

Abdali is said to have destroyed the Pṛithvīśvara Mahādeva Temple at Pehowa in A.D. 1739 during his raid of Thanesar and other places. Nadir Shah's invasion weakened the Mughal authority and gave rise to local chiefs. Pehowa probably came to Najbat Khan's share. When the tottering Mughal power sought the help of the Marathas, Pehowa was put under Hingne brothers in A.D. 1754 and many *ghats* and temples were built at Pehowa. Falling under the Sirhind *sarkar*, Pehowa came to be governed by Faujdar Zain Khan when the Marathas were defeated in the third battle of Panipat in A.D. 1761. In 1763, however, it was seized by the Bhais of Kaithal who were taken under British protection in 1809. They confiscated Kaithal in 1834, Ladwa in 1843, Ladwa in 1845 and Thanesar in 1850. The place built by the Bhais of Kaithal at Pehowa was used by the British as rest-house.

The importance of Pehowa waned further and its population fell from 3, 408 in 1881 to 2, 048 in 1901. It, however, continued to survive somehow and became a part of India in 1947 when the country became free. Now its population is growing again.

Pehowa has a large number of holy *ghats*, spots, fanes and hermitages connected with Agni, Ārshṭisheṇa, Āśvins, Auśanasa (Śukra), Bhṛigu, Bṛihaspati, Devāpi, Kubera, Maṅkaṇaka, Paraśurāma, Pṛithu, Rushaṅgu, Sindhudvīpa, Soma, Śukra, Trita, Uttaṅka, Varāha, Vasishṭha, Viśvāmitra, Yayāti, etc. It is said to be the spot where Brahmā started the work of creation. It was here that Kārttikeya was consecrated as the commander-in-chief of the divine forces. It is the permanent abode of not only of Kārttikeya but also of Śiva. It is a pilgrimage which delivers one of all the sins, even of killing the kins and the *brāhmaṇas*. A *śrāddha* performed here delivers the forefathers. It was here that the Sarasvatī took eastward turn. It was here again that the sacred river flowed into seven streams. It is the holiest of the holy places.

This ancient *tīrtha* has yielded some important archaeological remains. Besides the main mound which is almost covered by the present town, there is a mound known as Viśvāmitra kā Ṭīlā and another near the Prāchī Śiva Temple, the latter one having been levelled substantially recently. The main mound has yielded Painted Grey Ware. Viśvāmitra kā Ṭīlā perhaps represents the site of a Gupta and a Pratihāra temple. Similar temples may have stood in the Prāchī area also. The site of the confluence of the Aruṇā and the Sarasvatī is marked by Saṅgameśvara Mahādeva Temple near the village Aruṇāya which too is located on an ancient mound and yields the Painted Grey Ware, the Early Historic and Medieval pottery and other relics, indicating that the place is as old as Pehowa.

During 1888-89, Rodgers had recovered from Pehowa copper coins of the Kuṇinda ruler Amoghabhūti and the Kushāṇa emperors Kanishka and Huvishka. The literary evidence of the *Mahābhārata* and the Purāṇas regarding the continued existence of Pehowa is corroborated by two terracotta figurines of a royal personage and perhaps an ostiary, obtained from the northern parts of the town near Viśvāmitra kā Ṭīlā and probably Prāchī complex, both belonging to the Gupta period. Carved bricks may still be picked up from Viśvāmitra kā Ṭīlā. Rodgers, too, had seen such bricks at Pehowa. These carved bricks and the two terracottas furnish evidence of the existence of Gupta temples at the site. The curled locks of both the figures indicate that people at Pehowa adopted the hairstyles of the other parts of the Gupta empire. The attire of the royal personage betrays the popularity of sewn garments, in the upper strata of society at least. Sewn garments had come into vogue during the Kushāṇa period. That a temple existed at Pehowa during the late Gupta period also is evidenced by some sculptured fragments. A part of the pedestal of a Vishṇu image showing Chakrapurusha wearing an *ardhoruk* is worth noticing in this connection.

As noted above, a floodlight on the history and life of the people of Pehowa is thrown by the two inscriptions and a large number of relics of art belonging to the Pratihāra period. One of the inscriptions is still studded in a wall of the Garibnath Temple. Dated *Saṁvat* 276 (of the Harsha era = A.D. 882). it refers to Bhojadeva, son of Rāmabhadra, as the ruling king. The inscription records that a large number of pious horse-dealers, hailing from different countries, met here and agreed to impose upon themselves and upon their customers, certain voluntary taxes or tithes, the proceeds of which were to be distributed amongst the following donees: (1) the temple built by the illustrious Guhāditya at Kanauj, (2) the temple built by Kadambāditya at Go-*tīrtha* in Kanauj, (3) the temple of Garuḍāsana Vishṇu built by *brāhmaṇa* Bhūvaka at Bhojapura near Kanauj, (4) the temple of Yajña-Varāha built by Bhūvaka at Prāchī-Sarasvatī in Pṛithūdaka, (5) the *Pūjaka* of the preceding shrine, and (6) the sanctuary of Pṛithūdaka. The collected tax served as the *akshaya-nīvi*, the perpetual endowment for the donees and the share of each was fixed. The collection and distribution of the charity was entrusted to the *Goshṭhikas*. The inscription is an important document of the social, cultural, economic and religious history and reveals that Pehowa was an important commercial and religious centre. People from far off countries, perhaps even from distant north-west, came here to sell their horses and other animals. Horses for the royal cavalry, too, seem to have been acquired at the horse-fair at Pehowa. Sūrya's son Revanta, whose worship was quite popular with traders and at places connected with horses, was worshipped at Pṛithūdaka also.

The second inscription belongs to the time of Bhoja's successor Mahendrapāla. It is, however, not dated specifically. It was recovered from Siddhagir's *havelī* and is now preserved in the Lahore Museum. Beautifully engraved and written in very good Sanskrit and metrical throughout, it records the construction of a triple temple of Vishṇu by Gogga, Pūrṇarāja and Devarāja, the three sons of Jajjuka, himself son of Vajraṭa and a scion of Jāula of the Tomara clan. Three villages, viz., Yakshapālaka, Gejjara and Pāṭala, were assigned for the *bhoga* of the three deities in the triple shrine. The epigraph gives the name of the architect as Achyuta, son of Rāma, a native of Kamboja. This again tells us of the movement of people from one part to another of this country and the social mobility of the period. The poet was the son of Bhaṭṭa Rāma, the *sūtradhāra* was Durlabhāditya and the engraver (Bā)lāditya.

A fragmentary inscription carved on an *uttaraṅga* of a Sun Temple is now fixed in an *almirah* of the Garibnath Temple but nothing can be made of it. There may have existed some other inscriptions also but they are lost now.

Pehowa has yielded two beautiful door-frames now fitted in the Sarasvatī Temple and the *Guphā*. The former certainly and the latter probably were recovered from the Viśvāmitra kā Ṭīlā. The former belongs to a main shrine and the latter to some sub-shrine. The full-size doorway may have belonged to the Yajña-Varāha Temple built by Bhūvaka near the Prāchī-Sarasvatī. The smaller door-frame now fitted in the *Guphā* in the Prāchī complex shows the *nava-grahas* and the eight *Vasus* on the sur-lintel, a feature not met with anywhere else. Another incomplete doorway with Garuḍavāhī Vishṇu as the *lalāṭa-bimba*, recovered again from the Viśvāmitra kā Ṭīlā, is also fitted in the Prāchī complex. It is important as it indicates that Pehowa itself was the centre of art. Many other door-frames, smaller in size and betraying cruder workmanship furnish evidence that there existed at Pehowa numerous Hindu temples during the Pratihāra period.

Pehowa has yielded a large number of sculptures also, mostly fragmentary but a few complete ones also, mostly belonging to the Pratihāra period. The deities represented are Gaṇeśa, Vishṇu, Śiva, Sūrya and Śakti. Vishṇu was generally represented along with his personified weapons, spouses and vehicle. Garuḍāsana Vishṇu has already been referred to above. His Yoga-Nārāyaṇa, Nṛi-Varāha, Śeshaśāyī and Vaikuṇṭha forms, too, have been met with. The Vaikuṇṭha-*mūrti* from Prāchī Śiva Temple is a veritable masterpiece of the Pratihāra art of Pehowa as also is an independent headless image of Garuḍa. A Harihara head, too, has been found.

A late Gupta broken image of standing Sūrya, some small Pratihāra figures of the god in the same posture and one sitting in *utkuṭikāsana* in a chariot drawn by seven horses are the important representations of Sūrya. His son Revanta, accompanied by equestrian Daṇḍa and Piṅgala, is also known.

Śiva was popularly worshipped in his *liṅga* form. However, a beautiful Umā-Maheśvara image now fixed on a wall of the Prāchī complex betrays the elegance of the style which had developed during the Pratihāra period at Pehowa. A late medieval Bhairava in touchstone and a gigantic Chaturmukha-*liṅga* in the same material belonging to the Maratha period and enshrined in the Paśupatinātha Temple are the other notable Śaiva representations.

Mahishamardinī image recovered while ploughing a field and now enshrined in the Satya-Nārāyaṇa Temple is another Pratihāra masterpiece. Some fragmentary reliefs of the deity have also been recovered. Nārasiṁhī, Chāmuṇḍā, Kshemaṅkarī and Mātṛikā were the other forms in which Śakti was represented at Pehowa.

Images of Brahmā, Yama, Kārttikeya, *kinnaras, vidyādharas,* fly-whiskers, etc. too have been found.

The dresses and ornaments of all the images present an interesting study which requires detailed treatment.

In the late medieval period, most of the important buildings at Pehowa were decorated with beautiful murals. Many of these have disappeared and it is unfortunate that every year we lose some very important murals when these buildings are renovated and whitewashed. Modernization of the temples, like those of Pṛithvīśvara Mahādeva, Prāchī Śiva, etc., is also playing its apathetic part by removing the old features and relics. It is high time to save those important buildings and their murals.

The government of Haryana should set up Pehowa Vikas Board on the lines of Kurukshetra Development Board to retrieve its old glory and develop it as a tourist centre. The Tourism Department should provide the modern amenities of stay and catering and the Department of Archaeology and Museums, Haryana should set up a local museum.

BIBLIOGRAPHY

ORIGINAL SOURCES

Aitareya Brāhmaṇa, Ānandāśrama Series, Poona, 1931.

Aṅguttara Nikāya, Pali Text Society, London, 1885-1990.

Ashṭādhyāyī of Pāṇini, edited with Eng. tr. and notes by S.C. Vasu, Reprint, Delhi, 1977.

Āśvalāyana Śrauta Sūtra, Ānandāśrama Series, Poona, 1917.

Atharvaveda Saṁhitā, edited by S.D. Satavalekar, Aundh, 1943.

Baudhāyana Śrauta Sūtra, edited by W. Caland, Calcutta, 1904.

Bhāgavata Purāṇa, Veṅkaṭeśvara Press edn., Bombay, 1908; Gītā Press edn., 1971; ed. J.L. Shastri, Delhi, 1983.

Bhagavatī Sūtra, ed. G.C. Bhatia, Shailan, 1966.

Brahma Purāṇa, More edn., Calcutta.

Brahmāṇḍa Purāṇa, Veṅkaṭeśvara Press, Bombay; Baṅgavāsī Office, Calcutta.

Bṛihadāraṇyaka Upanishad, Nirṇayasāgara edn., Bombay, 1930.

Bṛihannāradīya Purāṇa, Veṅkaṭeśvara Press, Bombay.

Chandravṛitti on Chāndravyākaraṇa, ed. B. Leibich, Leipzig, 1923.

Chaturvargachintāmaṇi, Bibliotheca Indica Series, Calcutta, 1878.

Devī-Bhāgavata Purāṇa, More edn.

Dīgha Nikāya, PTS, 1890-1911; ed. Jagdish Kashyap, Nalanda, 1958.

Dvayāśrayakāvya, ed. A.V. Kathvate, Bombay, 1915.

Garuḍa Purāṇa, Jīvānanda Vidyāsāgara, Calcutta.

Gauḍavaho of Vākpatirāja, ed. S.P. Pandit, Bombay, 1887.

Harivaṁśa, Gītā Press edn.

Harshacharita of Bāṇa, ed. K.S. Parab, Bombay, 1892.

Kāśikā of Vāmana and Jayāditya, ed. S.C. Chakravartti, Rajshahi, 1913-25.

Kātyāyana Śrauta Sūtra, ed. A. Weber, Chowkhamba, Banaras, Reprint, 1972.

Kāvyamīmāṁsā of Rājaśekhara, ed. C.D. Dalal and R.A. Sastry, GOS, Baroda, 1934.

Kharataragachchhabṛihadgurvāvali, ed. Muni Jina Vijaya, Bombay, 1959.

Kūrma Purāṇa, Veṅk. Pr. Edn., Bombay; ed. A.S. Gupta, Varanasi. 1971.

Lāṭyāyana Śrauta Sūtra, ed. Ānand Chandra, Calcutta, 1870.

Mahābhārata, Critical edn., Poona, 1971-74.

Mahāvastu, ed. E. Senart, Paris, 1882-97.

Majjhima Nikāya, PTS, 1889-89; ed. Jagdish Kashyap, Nalanda, 1952; ed. Rahul Sankrityayana, Sarnath, 1933.

Manu Smṛiti, ed. (with Hindi com.) Haragovinda Śāstrī, Varanasi, 1970.

Matsya Purāṇa, More edn., Calcutta.

Narasiṁha Purāṇa
Nirukta of Yāska, ed. V.K. Rajvade, Poona, 1921-26.
Padma Purāṇa, More edn., Calcutta; ASS, Poona, 1893-94; Veṅk. Pr., Bombay, 1927.
Pañchaviṁśa Brāhmaṇa, ed. W. Caland (with Eng. tr.), 1931; ed. A. Vedāntavāgīśa, Calcutta, 1869-74.
Rājataraṅgiṇī, (Eng. tr.) by R.S. Pandit, New Delhi, 1977.
Rāmāyaṇa, Lahore edn., Veṅk. Pr. edn.; Gītā Press edn.
Ṛigveda Saṁhitā, Vaidika Saṁśodhana Maṇḍala, Poona, 1933; ed. S.D. Satavalekar, Pardi, 1957.
Śāṅkhāyana Śrauta Sūtra, ed. A. Hillebrandt, Calcutta, 1886.
Śatapatha Brāhmaṇa, ed. A. Weber, Reprint, Leipzig, 1924; Veṅk. Pr. ed., Bombay, 1940.
Śiva Mahāpurāṇa, Veṅk. Pr. edn., Calcutta; ed. Pushpendra Kumar, Delhi, 1981.
Skanda Mahāpurāṇa, More edn., Nag Publishers, 1982.
Taittirīya Āraṇyaka, ASS, Poona, 1898 (Reprint 1969).
Taittirīya Saṁhitā, ed. S.D. Satavalekar, Pardi, 1957.
Theragāthā, PTS, 1883.
Vaijayantī Kosha of Yādavaprakāśa, ed. G. Oppert, Madras, 1893.
Vāmana Purāṇa, Veṅk. Pr. edn., Calcutta; ed. A.S. Gupta, Varanasi, 1967; Gītā Press edn.
Varāha Purāṇa, ed. A.S. Gupta, Varanasi, 1981.
Vāyu Purāṇa, ASS, Poona, 1905; Veṅk. Pr., Bombay.
Vishṇu Purāṇa, Veṅk. Pr., Bombay, 1904; Gītā Press edn., V.S. 2024.

SECONDARY SOURCES

Agrawal, G.C. (1979), *Age of the Bharata War* (Edited), Delhi.
Agrawala, R.C. (1955), "Kurukshetra in Early Sanskrit Literature", *Journal of Indian History*, Vol. XXXIII (i), No. 97, pp. 85-90.
—— (1957), "Two Interesting Terracottas from the Region of Kurukṣetra, East-Punjab", *Artibus Asiae*, Ascona, Switzerland, Vol. XX.No. 2-3, pp. 163-64.
Agrawala, V.S. (1963), *India as Known to Pāṇini*, 2nd ed., Varanasi.
—— (1964), *Vāmana Purāṇa—A Study*, Varanasi.
—— (1965), *Studies in Indian Art*, Varanasi.
—— (V.S. 2016), *Mahābhārata kī Nānānukramaṇikā* (Hindi), Gorakhpur.
Ahir, D.C. (1971) *Buddhism in the Punjab, Haryana and Himachal Pradesh*, New Delhi.
Airi, Raghunath (1977), *Concept of Sarasvati*, Rohtak.
Allan, John (1936), *Catalogue of the Coins of Ancient India*, London.
Apte, V.S. (1959), *The Student's Sanskrit-English Dictionary*, Delhi.
Asthana, Shashi (1981-83), "The Dynamics of Pre-Harappan Culture", *Purātattva*, New Delhi, Nos. 13-14. pp. 45-50.
Bhan, Suraj (1971-72), "Siswal: A Pre-Harappan Site in Drishadvati Valley", *Purātattva*, No. 5, pp. 44-46.
—— (1972), *Pre-historical Archaeology of Sarasvatī and Dṛṣadvatī Valleys*, Ph. D. Dissertation (Ms), M.S. University, Baroda.
—— (1975), *Excavations at Mitathal (1968) and Other Explorations in the Sutlej-Yamuna Divide*, Kurukshetra.

Bhan, Suraj and Jim J. Shaffer (1978), "New Discoveries in Northern Haryana", *Man and Environment*, Vol. II, pp. 59-68.

Banerjea, J.N. (1956), *The Development of Hindu Iconography*, Calcutta.

Bharadwaj, O.P. (1986), *Studies in the Historical Geography of Ancient India*, Delhi.

—— (1991), *Ancient Kurukṣetra: Studies in Historical & Cultural Geography*, New Delhi.

Bhargava, M.L. (1964), *The Geography of Ṛgvedic India*, Lucknow.

Bhargava, P.L. (1956), *India in the Vedic Age*, Lucknow.

Briggs, John (1966), *The Rise of the Muhammadan Power in India*, Reprint, Calcutta.

Brown, Percy (1959) *Indian Architecture (Buddhist and Hindu Periods)*, Bombay.

Bühler, George (1892), "The Peheva Inscription from the Temple of Garibnath", *Epigraphia Indica*, Vol. I, Calcutta, pp. 184-90.

Bühler, George (1892), "An Undated Praśasti from the Reign of Mahendrapāla of Kanauj", *ibid.*, pp. 242-50.

Chakrapani, Pt. Upendra Sarma (1989), *Pehowa (Pṛithūdaka) Tīrtha*, Pehowa

—— (-), *Pṛithūdaka (Pihovā) Tīrtha: Mahātmya*, Pihovā.

Chandra, Satish (1978), *Prāchīna Pṛithūdaka* (Hindi), M.Phil. Dissertation, K.U., Kurukshetra.

Chattopadhyaya, Sudhakar (1958), *Early History of North India.*

Chaudhuri, B.N. (1969), *Buddhist Centres in Ancient India*, Calcutta.

Cowell, E.B. and Rouse (1877-97), *The Jātaka* (Eng. tr.), Cambridge.

Cowell, E.B. and E. Thomas (1971), *Deeds of Harsha* (Eng. tr.), Reprint, Delhi.

Cribb, Joe (1982), "The Earliest Ganesa: A Case of Mistaken Identity", *Numismatic Digest*, Bombay, Vol. VI, pp. 30ff.

Cunningham, Alexander (1963), *The Ancient Geography of India*, Reprint, Varanasi.

—— (1970) *Archaeological Survey Report*, Vol. XIV, Reprint, Varanasi.

Cunningham, J.D. (1972), *A History of the Sikhs*, Reprint, New Delhi.

Das, A.C. (1971), *Ṛgvedic India*, 3rd ed., Delhi.

Dasgupta, K.K. (1974), *Tribal History of Ancient India—A Numismatic Approach*, Calcutta.

Desai, Kalpana (1973), *Iconography of Vishṇu*, New Delhi.

Deshpande, M.N. (1975), *Indian Archaeology 1971-72: A Review (Edited)*.

Devahuti, D. (1970), *Harsha: A Political Study*, Oxford.

Dey, N.L. (1971), *Geographical Dictionary of Ancient & Medieval India*, 3rd ed., Delhi.

Dvivedi, H.N. (1973), *Dillī ke Tomara* (Hindi), Gwalior.

Fleet, J.F. (1888), "Inscriptions of the Early Gupta Kings & Their Successors", *Corpus Inscriptionum Indicarum*, Vol. III, Calcutta.

Gupta, Hari Ram (1961), *Marathas and Panipat*, Chandigarh.

—— (1982), *History of the Sikhs*, Vol. IV, Delhi.

—— (1975), *Panjab on the Eve of the First Sikh War*, 2nd ed., Chandigarh.

Gupta, P.L.(1981), "Chronology of the Post-Kushāṇa Rulers and the Allied Tribes", in *K.P. Jayaswal Commemoration Volume* (Ed. J.S. Jha), Patna, pp. 291-99.

Gupta, S.P. and K.S. Ramachandran (1976), *Mahabharata: Myth and Reality* (Edited), Delhi.

Habib, Mohammad and K.A. Nizami (1970), *A Comprehensive History of India*, Vol. V, Delhi.

Haig, Woolseley (1958), *Cambridge History of India*, Reprint, Delhi.

Handa, Devendra (Jan. March 1966), "Pehowa—An Ancient Holy Place", *Advance*, Chandigarh, Vol. XIII, No. 1, pp. 26-29.

—— (July 1967), "Pehoa—The Ancient Pṛthūdaka", *Purāṇa*, Vol. IX, No. 2, pp. 297-306.

—— (July 1968) "Kapāla-mocana: An Ancient Holy Place", *Purāṇa*, Vol. X, No. 2, pp. 148-53.

—— (1974), "Haryānā Meṅ Revanta Pūjā", *Journal of Haryana Studies*, Kurukshetra, Vol. VI, pp. 15-18.

—— (1981-81), "A New Agacha Coin", *The Journal of the Academy of Indian Numismatics & Sigillography*, Indore, Vol. IV, pp. 7-8, Pl. I.2.

—— (1984), "An Interesting Vaikuntha-Murti from Pehoa", in *Svasti-Śrī* (Dr. B.Ch. Chhabra Felicitation Volume), eds. Dr. K. Ramesh *et al.*, Delhi, pp. 297-302.

—— (1984-85), "Vaikuntha Image from Haryana", *Journal of the Indian Society of Oriental Art*, New Series, Calcutta, Vol. XIV, pp. 54-58.

—— (1985), *Studies in Indian Coins and Seals*, Delhi.

—— (Oct. 1985), "Vaishṇava Icons from Haryana", *Panjab University Research Bulletin (Arts)*, Chandigarh, Vol. XVI, No. 2, pp. 125-57, Figs. 40.

—— (1986), "An Inscribed Image of Chakrasvami and New Light on the Tomaras of Delhi", in *Rupanjali (in memory of O.C. Gangoly)*, edited by K.K. Ganguli and S.S. Biswas, Delhi, pp. 103-05.

—— (Oct. 1986), "A Pratihāra Doorway from Pehowa", *Panjab University Research Bulletin* (*Arts*), Chandigarh, Vol. XVII, No. 2, pp. 151-55, Fig. 2.

—— (1987), "Arṇorāja's Expedition to the Sindhu and the Sarasvatī", Haryana Sahitya Academy, *Journal of Indological Studies*, Chandigarh, Vol. II, pp. 188-91.

—— (1988), "An Interesting Yaudheya Seal from Naurangabad", "*Journal of the Epigraphical Society of India*, Mysore, Vol. XV, pp. 81-85.

—— (1989), *Buddhist Remains*, Heritage of Haryana Series, Chandigarh.

—— (1989), "Kuninda Coins in Relation to Trade and Economy", *Coinage, Trade & Economy*, The 3rd International Colloquium, Anjaneri, pp. 33-35.

—— (1990), "Varaha Images from Haryana", *Researches in Indian History, Archaeology, Art and Religion* (Prof. Upendra Thakur Felicitation Volume), eds. G. Kuppuram and K. Kumudamani, Vol. I, Delhi, pp. 81-91.

—— (1990), "Harihara Images from Haryana", *Studies in Indian History and Culture* (Kanaklal Barua Commemoration Volume), edited by R.D. Choudhury and S.B. Singh, Delhi, pp. 100-10.

—— (1991), "The Yaudheyas and Their Coins", *Numismatic Studies*, Vol. I, New Delhi, pp. 63-77.

—— (April 1991), "Some Medieval Image of Mahishāsuramardinī from Haryana", *Punjab University Research Bulletin(Arts)*, Chandigarh, Vol. XXII, No. 1.

—— (2000), "Balarama as an Attendant of Vishṇu", in *Gleanings of Indian Archaeology History & Culture, (Prof. R.N. Mehta Felicitation Volume)*, Eds. Prof. K.D. Bajpai *et al.*, Vol. II, Jaipur, 2000, pp. 87-91, Pls. XLI-XLIV, Figs. 1-9.

Husain, Agha Mahdi (1938), *Futuh-us-Salatin* (ed.), Agra.

—— (1953), *The Rehla of Ibn-Batuta* (Eng. tr.), Baroda.

Irvine, William (1971), *Later Mughals* (Edited by J.N. Sarkar), Vol. II, Reprint, New Delhi.

Jagannath (Dec. 1944), "Further Light on the Identification of the River Devika", *Journal of the U.P. Historical Society*, Lucknow, Vol. 17, Part 2.

Jayaswal, K.P. (1955), *Hindu Polity*, Part I, 3rd ed., Bangalore City.

Joshi, J.P. (1975-76), "A Note on the Excavations at Bhagwanpura", *Purātattva*, No. 8, pp. 178-80.

Kane, P.V. (1953), *History of Dharmaśāstra*, Vol. IV, Poona.

Keith, A.B. and A.A. Macdonell (1967), *Vedic Index of Names and Subjects*, Reprint, Delhi.

Khan, Mohd. Israel (1978), *Sarasvati in Sanskrit Literature*, Ghaziabad.

Khazanchi, T.N. (1976), "Pit-dwellers of Burzahom", *The Illustrated Weekly of India*, Sept. 5.

Kramrisch, Stella (1988), *The Presence of Siva*, Ist Indian ed., Delhi.

Krishnan, M.S. (1956), *Geology of India and Burma*, Madras.

Kumar, Manmohan (1978), *Archaeology of Ambala and Kurukshetra Districts (Haryana)*, Ph. D. Dissertation (Ms), K.U., Kurukshetra.

Kutasthananda, Swami (V.S. 2024), *Śrī-Sarasvati-Mahānadī Nirṇayaḥ*, Hoshiarpur.

Lal, B.B. (1954 & 1955), "Excavations at Hastināpura and Other Explorations in the Upper Gaṅgā and Sutlej Basins 1950-52", *Ancient India* (Bulletin of the Archaeological Survey of India), New Delhi, pp. 5-151.

Lal, B.B., S.P. Gupta and Shashi Asthana (Eds.) (1984), *Frontiers of the Indus Civilization*, New Delhi.

Majumdar, R.C. and A.S. Altekar (1964), *The Vākāṭaka-Gupta Age* (Edited), Banaras.

Majumdar, R.C. and A.D. Pusalkar (1951), *The Vedic Age*, (Edited), Bombay.

—— (1955), *The Struggle for Empire* (Edited), Bombay.

McCrindle, J.W. (1896), *The Invasion of India by Alexander the Great as Described by Arrian, Curtius, Diodorus, Plutarch and Justin*, Westminster.

Mohapatra, G.C. (1966), "Preliminary Report of the Explorations and Excavations of Stone Age Sites in Eastern Panjab", *Bulletin of the Deccan College Research Institute*, Poona, pp. 1-17.

Mohapatra, G.C. and Mukesh Singh (1979), "Stratified Occurrence of Lithic Artifacts in the Siwalik Frontal Range of Western Sub-Himalaya", *PURBA*, Vol. X, pp. 65-77.

Muztar, B.K. (1978) *Kurukshetra: Political and Cultural History*, Delhi.

Narain, A.K. (1978), "On the Earliest Ganesa", in *Senart Pranavitana Commemoration Volume*, eds. Prematileka, Indrapala and Lohuizen-de-Leeuw, Leiden, pp. 142-44.

—— (1982), "Ganesa on Hermaeus' Coin", *Numismatic Digest*, Bombay, Vol. VI, pp. 26-29.

—— (1984) "Some Brahmanical Divinities on the Indo-Greek Coinage Revisited", *Inaugural Seminar: Numismatics & History*, Indian Institute of Research in Numismatic Studies, Anjaneri (Nasik, Maharashtra), Jan. 8-10, Cyclostyled copy, pp. 9-14.

Pargiter, F.E. (1913), *Purāṇa Text of the Dynasties of the Kali Age*, Oxford University Press.

—— (1972), *Ancient Indian Historical Tradition*, Reprint, Delhi.

Phadke, H.A. (1967), "Haryana and the Gurjara-Pratiharas", *Haryana Research Journal*, Vol. I, No. 3, pp. 5-10.

—— (1976), "Buddhism in Kurudeśa", *Proceedings of the International Seminar on Buddhism and Jainism*, Cuttack.

—— (1990), *Haryana: Ancient and Medieval*, New Delhi.

Pingree, David (1976), "Brahmagupta, Balabhadra, Pṛithūdaka and Al-Bīrūnī", *Proceedings of the First International Sanskrit Conference*, Vol. II, Pt. II (Ed. V. Raghavan), New Delhi, pp. 166-80.

Prakash, Buddha (1970), "Kashmir and Haryana in Eleventh Century", *Journal of Haryana Studies*, Kurukshetra, Vol. II, pp. 13-17.

Prinsep, James (1858), *Essays on Indian Antiquities* (Edited by E. Thomas), London.

Przyluski, J. (1960), *Ancient Peoples of the Punjab: The Udumbaras and Salvas*, Reprint, Calcutta.

Puri, B.N. (1967), *History of the Gurjara-Pratiharas*, Bombay.

Puri, Mahanta Bamsi (1989), *Samkshipta Śrī Pṛithūdaka Tīrtha: Pihovā: Mahātmya evaṁ Kurukshetra Parichaya*, Pehowa.

Raghavan, V. (Jan. 1964), "Yajñavarāha—Some More Material", *Purāṇa*, Vol. VI, pp. 202-03.

Ray, H.C. (1973), *Dynastic History of Northern India*, Reprint, Delhi.

Raychaudhuri, Hemachandra (1958) *Studies in Indian Antiquities*, Calcutta.

—— (1953), *Political History of India*, 6th ed., Calcutta.

Reynold, James (1858), *Kitab-i-Yamini* (Eng. tr.), London.

Rizvi, S.A.A. (1956), *Tughlag Kālīna Bhārata*. Vol. I, Aligarh.

Rodgers, C.J. (1888-89), *Report of the Panjab Circle of the Archaeological Survey for 1888-89*, Calcutta.

—— (1891), *Revised List of Objects of Archaeological Interest in the Panjab*, Lahore.

Rose, H.A. (1904), "A Note on Kurukshetra", *Indian Antiquary*, Vol. XXXIII, pp. 298-300.

Roy, S.B. (1976), *Date of the Mahabharata Battle*, Gurgaon.

Sadhu, Ram (Jan.1969), "Pehowa Praśasti of Mahendrapāla", *Journal of Haryana Studies*, Vol. I, No. 1, pp. 16-25.

Sachau, Edward (1989), *Al-Berumi's India* (Ed.),

Saksena, K.K. (1966), "A Study of Two Sculptures of Pehowa", *Journal of the Oriental Institute*, Baroda, Vol. XVI, No. 1, December, pp. 163-65.

Sarasvati, Swami Omanand (V.S. 2036), *Ancient Mints of Haryana*, Jhajjar.

Sarkar, J.N. (1971), *Fall of the Mughal Empire*, Vol. I, Reprint, Calcutta.

Sarma, Gajanana (V.S. 1980), *Pṛithūdaka (Pihovā) Mahātmyam* (Hindi), Pehowa.

Sharma, B.N. (1975), *Iconography of Revanta*, New Delhi.

Sircar, D.C. (1960), *Studies in the Geography of Ancient and Medieval India*, Delhi.

—— (1966), *Indian Epigraphical Glossary*, Delhi.

Sharma, Dasharatha (1966), *Rajasthan Through the Ages*, Vol. I, Bikaner.

—— (1975), *Early Chauhan Dynasties*, 2nd revised ed., Delhi.

Sharma, G.B. and Manmohan Kumar (1979), "Mitra Coins from Ghuram (Patiala)", *Numismatic Digest*, Bombay, Vol. III, Part II, pp. 4-16.

Sharma, R.S. (1975-76), "The Later Vedic Phase and the Painted Grey Ware Culture", *Purātattva*, No. 8, pp. 63-67.

—— (1987), *Urban Decay in India*, New Delhi.

Shukla, S.P. (1980), "Relics of Ancient Art from Pehowa", *PURBA*, Chandigarh, Vol. XI, pp. 69-79, Fig. 13.

—— (1983), *Sculptures and Terracottas in the Archaeological Museum Kurukshetra University*, Kurukshetra.

Silak Ram (1972), *Archaeology of Rohtak and Hissar Districts (Haryana)*, Ph. D. Dissertation (Ms), K.U., Kurukshetra.

Singh, M.R. (1972), *Geographical Data in the Early Puranas—A Critical Study*, Calcutta.

Singh, U.V. (1979), "Sources of the History of Ancient Haryana" in *Sources of the History of India*, ed. S.P. Sen, Vol. II, Calcutta.

Smith, R. Morton (1973), *Dates and Dynasties in Earliest India*, Delhi.

Smith, V.A. (1897), *Journal of the Royal Asiatic Society.*

Sorensen, S. (1978), *An Index to the Names in the Mahābhārata*, Reprint, Delhi.

Spate, O.H.K., *India, Pakistan and Ceylon: The Regions*, 3rd ed., London.

Terra, H. De and T.T. Paterson (1939), *Studies on the Ice Age in India and Associated Human Cultures*, Washington.

Tod, James (1971), *Annals and Antiquities of Rajasthan*, Reprint, Delhi.

Tuteja, K.L. (1974), "Timur's Invasion of Haryana and People's Opposition", *Journal of Haryana Studies*, Kurukshetra, Vol. VI, pp. 26-34.

Vaidya, C.V. (1921-26), *History of Medieval Hindu India*, Vols. I-III, Pune.

Wadia, D.N. (1957), *Geology of India*, London.

Watters, Thomas (1961), *On Yuang Chwang's Travels in India* (Edited), Reprint, Delhi.

Yadav, K.C. (1971), "Political History of Haryana 1750 to 1805", *Journal of Haryana Studies*, Kurukshetra, Vol. III (1), Jan., pp. 20-32.

—— (1972), "British Rule in Haryana: 1809-56", *ibid.*, Vol. IV.

—— (1981), *Haryana kā Itihāsa*, New Delhi.

GAZETTEERS AND CENSUS REPORT

Imperial Gazetteer of India, New Series, XX, Oxford, 1908.

Karnal District Gazetteer, 1890.

Punjab District Gazetteers: Ambala District, Lahore, 1925.

Census of India 1981, Series-6, Haryana, Part XIII-A&B, Kurukshetra District.

INDEX

[The following abbreviations have been used here: a- author, b- book or text, c- chief, d- deity, dyn- dynasty, i- image, k- king, p- place, q- queen, r- river, s- sage, t-tīrtha, T- temple, v- village. Words occurring in the Notes have been indicated by n after the page number.]